Affirmative Development

Affirmative Development

CULTIVATING ACADEMIC ABILITY

Edited by
Edmund W. Gordon
And Beatrice L. Bridglall

ROWMAN & LITTLEFIELD PUBLISHERS, INC.
Lanham • Boulder • New York • Toronto • Plymouth, UK

ROWMAN & LITTLEFIELD PUBLISHERS, INC.

Published in the United States of America
by Rowman & Littlefield Publishers, Inc.
A wholly owned subsidary of The Rowman & Littlefield Publishing Group, Inc.
4501 Forbes Boulevard, Suite 200, Lanham, Maryland 20706
www.rowmanlittlefield.com

Estover Road
Plymouth PL6 7PY
United Kingdom

British Library Cataloguing in Publication Information Available

Library of Congress Cataloging-in-Publication Data

Affirmative development : cultivating academic ability / edited by Edmund W. Gordon and Beatrice L. Bridglall.
    p. cm.
Includes bibliographical references and index.
ISBN-13: 978-0-7425-1658-8 (cloth : alk. paper)
ISBN-10: 0-7425-1658-X (cloth : alk. paper)
ISBN-13: 978-0-7425-1659-5 (pbk. : alk. paper)
ISBN-10: 0-7425-1659-8 (pbk. : alk. paper)
1. Compensatory education—United States. 2. Children with social disabilities—Education—United States. 3. Academic achievement—United States. 4. Educational equalization—United States. I. Gordon, Edmund W. II. Bridglall, Beatrice L.

LC213.2.A44 2007
370.111—dc22   2006019287

Printed in the United States of America

♾™ The paper used in this publication meets the minimum requirements of American National Standard for Information Sciences—Permanence of Paper for Printed Library Materials, ANSI/NISO Z39.48-1992.

For my crew
EWG

For V., D., and M.
With love and gratitude, always
BLB

Contents

Part II: Affirmative Development of Academic Ability

Foreword

Michael E. Martinez
University of California, Irvine

The Affirmative Development of Academic Ability articulates an alternative vision for education and human development. At its conceptual center is an imperative: To promote the optimal development of *intellective competence* in every person. The editors define intellective competence as the *effective* orchestration of cognitive, affective, and situative mental processes in the service of sense making and problem solving. This definition extends beyond literacy, numeracy, and the mastery of subject matter knowledge. Broader still than intelligence, it is more accurately the learned ability and propensity to think well in the service of individual and collective good.

Intellective competence is a developed human capacity rather than a fixed inborn trait. Like the learned proficiency in subject-matter knowledge and skills stressed in schools, intellective competence emerges from positive, pro-educative experience. Intellective competence originates in part from school experiences; it emerges also from experiences outside of schools, including interactions with family, peers, and community. Intellective competence has many different sources. Gordon and Bridglall suggest that the emergence of intellective competence is significantly associated with exposure to wealthier, academically relevant, subcultures that actively promote the ideas, skills, and attitudes that schools reward. Moreover, such a subculture reproduces itself from generation to generation.

Through immersion into a matrix of thinking and value patterns, and through the effective exploitation of social capital, some children, but not all, are groomed for readiness to engage academe and the broader world successfully. Children born into and raised in academically privileged situations are advantaged to succeed in schools and are primed for admissions to elite universities and to prestigious careers. Children not exposed to such subcultures often have difficulty in school and less frequently attain high levels of academic and professional success. This book's imperative is that intellectual competence, a potent form of wealth diffused through diverse societal channels, must be distributed more liberally, more deliberately, and more equitably. But how? What can be done to develop intellective competence more strategically in children who are not born into conditions that predispose them to develop high levels of academic ability and subsequent success? The contributors to this volume suggest that the project of developing intellective competence should include all children and adults; not just the privileged nor the disadvantaged exclusively. In decades past, this vision would have been less feasible, and perhaps less necessary. The allocation of educational resources was more arguably restricted as a limited resource. Resource scarcity implied that the development of human capability in some meant that others must receive less. In the present era, zero-sum conceptualizations and strategies are no longer useful. Rather, they are positively harmful. We must now conceive of a responsible and wise society as supporting optimal intellective development of all its members. Toward what end? Here, also, the editors take a position: Intellective character is not an end in itself, but rather is instrumental to what students must become—"compassionate and thinking interdependent members of humane human communities" (Gordon, chapter 1, this volume).

We are presented, in this volume, with a collection of essays that cast *intellective competence* as the universal currency of societies in advanced stages of technological development. Intellective competence and related character traits are perceived as powerful meta-products of experiences gained from schools and other institutions, including the family. The cultivation of intellect through varied educational experience leads not simply to the development of academic knowledge and skills, but more significantly to facility with verbal and numeric symbol systems, the capacity to employ such higher-order cognitive processes as problem-solving and design, as well as the ability to engage such quotidian tasks as consumer and political decision making. Intellective competence includes an evolving ability to bring order to the potential chaos of an information welter: the capacity to hypothesize and confirm relationships between the disparate phenomena, the cognitive skills needed to reason by analogy and metaphor, and the broad disposition to *use* these intellectual tools to make sense of one's experience and to think and act intelligently in a complex world.

The essays in this volume articulate *why* the intellectively competent person is a product of definable kinds of socialization experiences. The essays show *how* the deliberate orchestration of such experiences is logically consistent with—indeed, absolutely vital for—advancing a democratic conception of justice. Affirmative development as a societal commitment entails a realization that the total life experience is relevant to academic and professional success. We need this fresh vision of what education does for human learners, and we need to take hold of the challenge posed by such a broad vision of education. Then, action is required.

The Affirmative Development of Academic Ability engages the most pressing goal of education—to advance social equity in the service of values embraced by a free society. The collective research of the past fifty years is very clear: Schools, acting alone, cannot achieve that vaunted and worthy end. Pro-development forces of many sectors of society have roles to play, schools being one vital but nonexclusive source of educative experience. The essays in this volume expose a broad vista of possibilities. From that vantage, we can see tracks that lead toward our most cherished hopes for a good society, hopes that in the past seemed within reach, yet until now have remained tantalizingly elusive.

I

AFFIRMATIVE ACTION AND AFFIRMATIVE DEVELOPMENT

1

Intellective Competence

The Universal Currency in Technologically Advanced Societies

Edmund W. Gordon

GLOBALIZATION AND THE COMMON DEMAND FOR SYMBOLIC REPRESENTATION AND PROBLEM SOLVING

In a recent trip to ten of the world's oldest cities, scattered through Africa, Asia, and the Middle East, this volume's senior editor and his wife were struck by the ubiquitous presence of modern, technologically advanced artifacts—evidence of the process of cultural and economic globalization. In a ger (a small tent home) on the steppes of Mongolia, while we were being entertained with a cup of tea by a nomad family, the social exchange was interrupted by a call on the shepherd's cell phone. In the remote hills of Tibet, children stopped their games to practice their English. In Laos, Cambodia, and Uzbekistan, children and adults were beginning to use computers. In none of these remote areas of the world was it impossible to access one's e-mail. Customs, costumes, electric plugs, and languages differed, but electronic and mechanical amplifiers and extensions of human abilities were present. In all of these places, literacy and numeracy were privileged over illiteracy and concrete object-referenced counting. Thanks to radio, television, telephones, and modern transportation, the commodities of the world were seldom unavailable, and the conversations referenced the current events of our twenty-first-century "one world." Nowhere in that world is the ability to use number and word symbols to communicate and solve problems unwelcome. All over the globe, the ability to bring order to the chaos created by information overload or multiple and concurrent sources of stimulation is increasingly in demand. Even in technologically underdeveloped communities, the ability to reason, to uncover relationships among phenomena, to use comparison, context, intent, and values in

3

arriving at judgments are respected and sought after. The capacity to function effectively in these domains is the stuff of intellective competence, and intellective competence, increasingly, is the universal currency in modern, technologically advanced societies.

Intellective competence is increasingly the universal currency in a modern, technologically advanced society. We use the term *currency* in a metaphorical sense and refer to the fact that the functional medium of exchange worldwide is the capacity to handle, interpret, and bring order to large masses of information in order to function effectively in the twenty-first century and beyond. Increasingly, across the world the ability to use words and numbers to convey, understand, and interpret information is in great demand. In a world dominated by technology that operates on the basis of complex abstract concepts and numeric relationships, basic literacy, while important, is simply not sufficient. Calfee and Drum (1979) and others have suggested that survival in modern societies requires both *critical* literacy and orality. Although both literacy and orality have been defined quite narrowly—as the capacity to decode and read written language and the capacity to communicate through speech, respectively—more frequently, the terms are being used interrelatedly to refer to a much broader range of competencies in highly specialized domains of human cognition.

Literacy, for example, increasingly refers to the capacity to exercise oral competence through the use of graphic symbols. Similarly, orality is more broadly defined as the capacity to receive, generate, and express feelings, signals, descriptors, ideas, and concepts through language. Listening, as both a cognitive and a sensory phenomenon, is also an important aspect of orality, especially discriminative and selective listening for comprehension and understanding. Other features of orality include mastery of verbal and symbolic descriptors, concept development, and ideational exchange. Orality thus enables and facilitates social exchange and complex communication, both of which are made easier by the use of symbols.

Literacy is probably the quintessential condition for the application of intellect to academic advancement, comparative canon interpretation and mastery, and abstract cultural transmission. The concern with the extension or development of intellect raises problems with respect to the way basic literacy is generally viewed and the requirements of advanced intellectual development. For example, Gordon (1979) argued that advanced reading is actually symbol-guided thinking. An individual who reads at a high level of proficiency, he claimed, is no longer decoding (making sense of letters and words); instead, the printed material is a stimulus for thought. At lower levels of proficiency, or with unfamiliar material, most of a reader's effort is spent on the decoding function. Overemphasis on the attainment of primary decoding skills may be dysfunctional to the achievement of higher levels of reading proficiency. Thus, critical literacy cannot be taught without a critical pedagogy with goals of opening the minds of learners and enabling them to engage in struggles relevant to their own interests. Such critical pedagogy focuses on getting students to think critically and to delve deeply into the structure and meaning of textual material and brings relevance to the classroom by grounding the learning experience in problems that are a part of students' lives.

Other competencies of critical literacy and orality include:

1. *Multicultural and multilingual communication*: the capacity to communicate in a variety of contexts using multiple symbols;
2. *Multicultural adaptive competence*: the capacity to function in more than one culture;
3. *Tertiary signal system mastery of alphabetic and numeric formulae*: the capacity to use symbols to represent symbols (in terms of literacy, this involves the more complex capacity to use symbols to represent symbols that represent still more symbols to the extent that an individual can generate alphabetic or numeric formulae, use metaphors, and use abstract phenomena to represent other abstract phenomena);
4. *Scientific and technological literacy*: the capacity to read and understand scientific and technological material;
5. *Political economic literacy*: the capacity to understand the interlocutory, systemic alignments that sustain and reinforce race, class, and gender biases within the larger society;
6. *Social and interpersonal literacy*: the capacity to understand human relationships and perspectives;
7. *Numeracy and quantitative literacy*: the capacity to manipulate and interpret quantitative data;
8. *Cultural literacy*: An individual's command of the information, problem-solving strategies, symbol systems, and currency (instruments of exchange) of the cultures that form the contexts of his or her life.

The composite mastery of the domains listed above is increasingly referred to as *critical literacy*. In each of these domains, the implied competencies include the capacity to analyze and utilize knowledge structures, differential contexts, and hypothetical relationships; to think about and interpret text; to solve problems; and to identify the interests served by and the implications of information mediated through literacy.

The phenomena of the world, for example, can be represented by digits and by numbers (Hawkins, 1988). Hawkins argues that if we can digitally represent phenomena, everything can be understood through the relationships among those digits. The people who are most advanced in dealing with modern physics, modern chemistry, or almost any body of knowledge, for example, are not dealing with the reality of these things anymore but are dealing with the numeric representation of their components. Under these conditions, the people who cannot think numerically and/or handle numerical relationships are handicapped because the problems of the world are both presented and solved in that context and modality.

Although we tend to think of the latter half of the twentieth century and beginnings of the twenty-first as the age of technology, technology is not a new phenomenon in human societies. The use of fire, stone tools, the plough, the hammer, the combustion engine, and the telephone are instances of the use of technology. Instruments and machines that amplify and extend human abilities and senses are technological. The current period is more appropriately referred to as *the age of advanced technological development*, and it denotes the progression from the mechanical technologies to the chemical, electric, and electronic devices that can amplify, speed, and facilitate human capabilities. We can now use electronic devices to extend hearing, sight, touch, and reach. These devices add speed, accuracy, and reliability to human functions. They change dramatically the size of the stimulus field and the magnitude of data points on which the human mind can focus. But what further complicates this world of advanced electronic technologies is that they not only change the ways humans do things and what we can do, they also have the potential to change the way we perceive and think about the world and our experiences in the world. With such powerful technologies, unless we would cede the place of humans to our machines, the quality of human intellect—intellective competence—must continue to advance. Not only must the capabilities of humans increase, but these gains will have to be achieved almost universally.

INTELLECTIVE COMPETENCE AS THE CURRENCY OF CHOICE IN A TECHNOLOGICALLY ADVANCED WORLD

We take the position that the competencies of critical literacy and orality, referenced above, enable the achievement of intellective competence, which we define as developed abilities and dispositions to perceive critically, to explore widely, to bring rational order to chaos, to bring knowledge and technique to bear on the solution of problems, to test ideas against explicit and considered moral values and against empirical data, and to recognize and create real and abstract relationships between concrete and imaginary phenomena. In other words, intellective competence essentially reflects the effective orchestration of affective, cognitive, and situative mental processes in the service of sense making and problem solving. These achievements are less focused on what we want learners to know and know how to do, and are more sharply focused on what it is that we want learners to become and be, that is, compassionate and thinking interdependent members of humane human communities.

We use *intellective* to distinguish our concerns—the variety of cognitive, affective, situative, and emotional processes that are integral to daily functioning and problem solving—from both *intelligent* and *intellectual* behavior. We worry that the term *intelligent* is too closely associated with *intelligence*, which is too often thought of as that which is measured by IQ tests. Intellectual behavior seems too easily confused with the work or habits of intellectuals and professional scholars. How, then, can we begin to frame the construct *intellective competence*? We can start by defining pedagogy as the "art and science of teaching." This definition is not incorrect, but it is narrower than the conception we choose to advance. We prefer to think of pedagogy (inclusive of teaching, learning, and assessment) as dialectical and transactive components of a maieutic process that enables the development of intellective competence.

From our perspective, "to teach" is to enable and empower through directed learning experiences, guided exploration, structured problem and question posing, mediated problem solving, and explicated modeling of examples. In contrast to earlier notions of teaching as primarily involving the transfer of knowledge, skills, and values, our perspective casts the teacher as guide, as coach, as model, and as resource person who respects the fact that learning is something that one does for oneself and cannot be done for the student by someone else. Our reference to learning is bifocal, and references the assimilation and accommodation of that which is old, and the active construction and integration of that which is new. While not rejecting the traditional emphasis on such processes as attending to, associating, memorizing, and retrieving other people's data, our vision of human learning privileges situative social processes that require constructive, hermeneutic, and transformative engagement, by learning persons, with data that are or become one's own—no matter the source.

In our vision of teaching, learning, and assessment, outcome standards are central, but the explication of what we want learners to know about specific disciplines and to be able to do must be considered *as* instrumental to what we want learners to become. There is no question about the importance of what students learn and are taught. Most of us would agree that teaching and learning independent of content (subject matter) is problematic. However, just as teaching and learning without subject matter are vacuous, learning and teaching should not be so constrained by content that the purpose of engagement with these pedagogical endeavors is precluded. We are more and more persuaded that the purpose of learning, and the teaching by which it is enabled, is to acquire knowledge and technique in the service of the development of adaptive human intellect. Thus, we perceive teaching, learning, and the development of an adaptable intellect as being at the core of intellective competence.

The old "scholastic aptitudes," for instance, may not have been so far from the mark. In efforts to achieve some distance from the actual material covered in the nation's diverse curricula, the scholastic aptitudes were seen as more generic capacities to handle academic tasks. Those scholastic aptitudes should be thought of as generalized developed abilities that not only reflect the capacity to handle academic work, but more importantly, reflect the meta manifestations of intellective abilities that result from particular kinds of education and socialization. Instead of scholastic aptitudes, it may be more appropriate to think of developed intellective abilities or intellective competencies as the meta-expressions of a wide range of human learning achievements that are related to what happens in schools.

These developed abilities are not so much reflected in the specific, discipline-based knowledge a student may have, but in the ability and disposition to use knowledge, technique, values, and intellect to adaptively and efficiently engage and solve both commonplace and novel problems. The assessment component of our conception of pedagogy must then be directed at the measurement of these developed abilities. Assessment so conceived is best thought of as diagnostic, formative, and summative. We envision such assessment to be so embedded in the teaching and learning processes as to be indistinguishable. Its data, however, should be extractable for purposes of diagnostic planning, admission and placement appraisal, progress determination, and accountability evaluation.

James Greeno (2001) suggests that what I call intellective competence is really "intellective character." What is intellective competence? We have come to use the term to refer to a characteristic way of adapting to, appreciating, and knowing and understanding the phenomena of human experience. We also use the construct to reference the quality with which these mental processes come to be applied to one's engagement with quotidian, novel, and specialized problems. Intellective competence reflects one's habits of mind, but it also reflects the quality or goodness of the products of mental functioning. Like social competence, which we feel is one manifestation of intellective competence, it reflects "goodness of fit" or the effectiveness of the application of one's affective, cognitive, and situative processes to the solving of the problems of living.

Fifteen years ago, Gordon used the term *intelligence* or *intelligent behavior* to capture a characteristic or quality of one's mental capacity or performance. In 2001, we are concerned with more. We are trying to capture aspects of human capacity, developed ability, and the disposition to utilize both in addition to fostering an appreciation of the use of human adaptive processes in the service of intentional behavior. Thus Greeno's (2001) suggestion of the mutuality of intellective competence and intellective character meshes quite well with our framework.

INTELLIGENCE AND HUMAN SOCIAL DIVISIONS

Whether we consider intellective competence to be an aspect of character or not, there are explicit and implicit problems associated with the fact that high levels of intellective competence are not universally achieved in and across the social divisions into which humans are grouped. Since the assignment of persons to ethnic and racial groups has been based upon inexact social designations, very little is known concerning intelligence in reliably identified biological subgroups. However, there is considerable evidence that higher intellect, as measured by traditional intelligence tests, favors persons and groups holding higher status in the society (Kamin, 1974; Ogbu, 1983). Some of the most sophisticated analyses of the extant statistical data concern comparisons of test scores in high-status and low-status persons. It is legitimate to ask whether it is the natural intelligence of the group members or the status of the group that contributes to the quality of intelligence demonstrated. Clearly, assumptions concerning the gene pool origins (races) of the groups studied are imposed upon these data, are reflected in the results of these traditional analyses, and favor a hypothesis of heritability as the determining factor in the association between the social divisions by which humans are grouped and the quality of developed intellectual function. Quite apart from the validity of some of these assumptions, it is useful to examine some of the issues concerning the construct of *intelligence* and the character of extant measures of intelligence.

Guralnik (1980, 732) defined intelligence as the "ability to learn or understand from experiences, the ability to acquire and retain knowledge, mental ability . . . the ability to respond quickly and successfully to a new situation, [and] the use of faculty of reason in solving problems." When Cole et al. (1971) concluded that all groups of human beings appear to represent in their developed abilities a wide range of intellectual competencies, they were, no doubt, thinking of intelligence as the capacity to adapt to one's environment, and to use past adaptation experiences in response to similar as well as novel environmental encounters. The origins of the word *intelligence,* however, speak to a narrow and more fixed idea of intelligence than that used by Cole et al. The word *intelligence* comes from the Latin *inteligere,* which means to select (and particularly to select the good grain from the bad). This definition is evident in standardized intelligence tests, which give preference to the subject's ability to select or distill, a practice that resulted in the establishment of a hierarchy for behavioral adaptabilities that gives an advantage to these abilities. What is also interesting is that the Latin derivation is also reflected in the use of the tests for the selection and prediction of successful individuals. Since selection and prediction are favored in many advanced technological enterprises, these same features have been reinforced and rarified, as if they were the sole or most important aspects of intellectual function. Anastasi (1980), Brown and Burton (1975), Gardner (1993), Glaser (1977), Resnick (1987), Sternberg (1986), and others, however, have advocated much broader conceptions of intelligence and contributed to a growing awareness of (a) the importance of context for the expression of intelligence, and (b) the restrictive and overly selective nature of extant standardized tests of intelligence.

Attention to possible differences in the potentials of persons and contexts for revealing quality of intellect distinguishes the "splitters'" conceptions of intelligence from the "lumpers'" (Mayr, 1982). Weinberg (1989) refers to Mayr's (1982) "lumpers and splitters" and attributes the notion of intelligence as a "general unified capacity for acquiring knowledge, reasoning, and solving problems that is demonstrated in different ways (navigating a course without a compass, memorizing the Koran, or programming a computer)" to the lumpers. Although Weinberg introduces some possible lumperian recognition of the diversity in expressions of intelligence in his reference to "different ways," the lumpers' approach to intelligence is basically a narrow one in its reference to an overall summative ability. This summative ability is manifested in universalist conceptions of intellectual function, that is, those aspects of intellectual function that are privileged in advanced technological cultures and are assumed to apply universally. Abstract reasoning and decontextualized recall are examples. The "splitters," in contrast, seek to isolate (at least for the purpose of study) different types of intellectual ability. Gardner (1993), for example, has called attention to linguistic, bodily kinesthetic, and other specific intelligences, some of which would benefit from different contexts for their optimal expression and assessment. The lumpers' general conception of intelligence privileges communicentric or common indicators of ability, and the splitters' view favors more heterogeneous indicators. Thus the tenuous and protean character of the intelligence construct contributes to some of the confusion concerning usage when it is studied in people whose life experiences differ.

Modern psychological theories of learning and cognition bring us closer to understanding intelligence as a complex phenomenon that is a composite of developing aptitudes, abilities, dispositions, and achievements (Anastasi, 1980). Intelligence is referred to as a complex phenomenon that results from a combination of factors (Glaser, 1977); that is multicomponential (Sternberg, 1994); that develops in response to stimulation from experiential encounters (Birch, 1968; Hunt, 1961); and that is modifiable (Bruner, 1966; Hunt, 1961; Sternberg, 1986). These complex developed abilities are expressed through behaviors that are defined socially and culturally, and often are weighted subjectively to reflect the hegemonic culture (Hernnstein, 1971).

How intelligent behavior is perceived and specific potentials for adaptations are valued vary from individual to individual and in different contexts (McGuire, 1983; Sternberg, 1994; Gardner, 1993). An individual may display intelligence in a way that is congruent with or different from the way that is traditionally honored in his or her culture. When the display is incongruent with the hegemonic culture, it is assumed generally and often faultily that this is indicative of intellectual deficit, since the individual appears not to have learned in the same way as others. Recent work in behavioral individuality indicates that such assumptions are erroneous in making judgments concerning individuals and groups (Bronfenbrenner, 1979; Messick, 1976; Shipman and Shipman, 1988; Thomas, 1980). When these same assumptions are applied to diverse groups, the error is even more obvious because it is unreasonable to assume that groups whose life experiences differ should be expected to have had similar learning opportunities or to have responded in similar ways. Further, it is a mistake to assume that the absence of a specific pattern of developed ability called for by the test reflects an inability to make other adaptations. Even in the presence of undeveloped abilities, there is evidence that the quality of intellective behavior can be altered through the combined force of environmental change and the plasticity of developing human intellect (Bloom, 1964; Hunt, 1961; Scarr and Weinberg, 1976; Sternberg, 1986).

INTELLIGENCE AND EXPERIENCE

As an educational psychologist concerned with understanding the mechanisms by which patterned behaviors emerge, are directed, and may be modified, Gordon (1968) found that the construct *race* has little or no utility. Gordon (1968) was not arguing that race as a construct had no validity; rather, he was readily acknowledging the existence of differences in structure and behavior potentials that may be functions of reasonably stable genetic patterning and that these differences can and do emerge as dominant in or characteristic of a particular animal strain, stock, or race. Thus, the question is not whether groups with common characteristics exist or whether there are differences between groups classified according to certain common characteristics, but rather: What is the relevance of such classification to understanding the mechanisms of behavioral development? And more significantly, what is the relevance of specific characteristics or behavior potentials to the emergence, guided development, and modification of patterned behavioral development and learning?

Historically, human societies have not had the privilege of being concerned with the universal optimal development of their members. Governed largely by economic scarcity, greater attention was given to selecting those members most likely to succeed or those whose station in life "entitled" them to the opportunity. Under such a system, the rather static concern with identification and classification was appropriate to the limitations inherent in those stages of societal development. Given such circumstances, the construct *race* and the distortions in its use are at least understandable; it may even be said that for such outdated social systems, the construct *race* had some utility. For example, through its use one could quickly identify those members from whom little would be expected and for whom little would be done.

As more and more societies have reached a point in development where material resources are sufficient to move from favoring those most likely to succeed toward ensuring that all will have adequate opportunity to succeed, and as these societies reach the stage of technological development where it is essential that all members reach optimal levels of intellective competence, the major focus in assessment can no longer be on prediction and selection. Prime attention must be given to directed behavioral development and modification. In fulfilling the important task of advancing behavior development in today's complex societies, race studies serve little useful purpose, but behavior and genetic analyses directed at understanding and guiding the development of the intellective behavior of individuals and groups are of crucial importance.

A principle function of education is to guide the development of such behavior; yet education has been dominated by views that behavioral development is predetermined and greatly limited by heredity and that behavior potentials are at least significantly influenced by race and sometimes class. The impact of these views on education is reflected in the following conditions, which are found frequently in the educational enterprise:

1. A laissez-faire or neglectful attitude toward the training and development of intelligence;
2. A monitoring as opposed to a stimulating approach to academic and social readiness and development;
3. An exaggerated emphasis on the predictive value of classification and quantification of psychological appraisal data, and a neglect of qualitative appraisal data as a basis for planning and intervention;
4. Distortion of aspiration and expectation levels based upon unjustified ceilings on potentials for human development and adaptation;
5. Placement of the burden of proof (a) on the examinee rather than on the appraiser or appraisal method; (b) on the learner rather than on the teacher or teaching method; and (c) on the counselee rather than on the counselor or counseling method;
6. Emphasis on adjustment or acceptance of assumed realities rather than on modification of the environment and the individual's interaction with it;

7. Overemphasis on selection and placement (educational and vocational) and underemphasis on the nurturing of interests and aptitudes and the development and training of capacities and skills; and
8. An eclectic and empirical approach to research in directed learning with little application of the scientific method in exploration, experimentation, and investigation.

In no aspect of the educational enterprise are these influences more deleterious than in our current efforts at improving education for disadvantaged populations by utilizing a narrow range of traditional educational practices. In a nationwide review of special programs and practices designed for such persons, one is impressed by the magnitude of this effort. However, it is distressing to note that few of these endeavors have made significant changes in the instructional behavior of teachers or the functioning of the students toward whom they are directed. One could argue that there is little payoff in these programs because the students are of limited potential. An alternative argument is that the programs do not constitute an appropriate match between learner characteristics, learning tasks, and learning experiences. Consequently, they do not result in significant improvements in student performance. We do not have the empirically derived data to give definitive support to either of these positions; however, they are the kinds of questions that grow out of the controversial issues underlying the growing academic achievement gap between majority and some ethnic minority groups. We can argue these issues forever, but their solution will come only from better-conceptualized research. It is hopeful that we are at least asking questions rather than advancing positions polemically.

The fact that education has, to date, failed in bringing all of our students to optimal levels of achievement does not mean that the goal is not achievable. We have raised the possibility of a mismatch between the learning needs of some of our students and the range of options generally made available through education. In this book we raise the possibility that certain prior conditions predispose toward the development of academic ability, and that when these conditions are absent, effective education is harder to achieve. We conclude our volume by elaborating on some of the best bets for making education more effective. However, these speculations are based on the assumption that the quality of intellective function can be improved upon and that the ability to effectively handle academic work can be developed.

J. McVickor Hunt (1966, 363) closed his provocative book *Intelligence and Experience* with the assertion that "The problem for the management of child development is to find out how to govern the encounters that children have with their environments to foster both an optimally rapid rate of intellectual development and a satisfying life." The debate continues as to whether Professor Hunt overstated the implications of the data available to him. Some argue that the malleability of intellect is far more limited than is suggested by Hunt's observations. Others are more optimistic. Hunt argued that the enrichment of learning experiences, especially early in the life of the developing person, could have the effect of greatly improving the quality of human intellect. He did not think that experiential enrichment would eliminate differences in intelligence, but he was convinced that the quality of intellect could be improved, if the "problem of the match" (Hunt 1966, 267–88) was solved appropriately. For Hunt, the secret to high-quality intellective development rests with our ability to match learning experiences with the learning characteristics of learners, where it is the function of the learning experiences to elaborate and build upon the schemata with which the learner has begun.

Hunt's perspective experienced a short period of popularity before traditional views of fixed intellect reclaimed center stage. However, the notions that learning is somehow related to human activity (experience); that effective learning is a function of the goodness of fit between learner and learning experience; and that knowledge and competence are more likely to be self-constructed than transferred to one by another, continue to have a ubiquitous presence in pedagogical thought. The field is fortunate that these ideas have such resilience. The increasingly universal demand for intellective competence requires the development of the capacity to orchestrate a wide variety of abilities and resources in the service of problem solving. Appropriate to this task are the ideas that:

- Human abilities can be developed through appropriate activity (experience);
- The meta-products of effective academic learning are reasoning ability; problem solving ability; perspective, and judgment;
- Learner engagement with the discovery, construction, and validation of knowledge appears to be associated with learner ownership of the product.

REFERENCES

Anastasi, A. 1980. Abilities and the measurement of achievement. In W. B. Schroder (Ed.), *Measuring achievement: Progress over a decade. New directions for testing and measurement* (pp.1–10). San Francisco: Jossey-Bass.

Birch, H. 1968. Boldness and judgement in behavior genetics. In M. Mead, T. Dobzhansky, E. Tobach, and R. E. Light (Eds.), *Science and the concept of race.* New York: Columbia University Press.

Bloom, B. S. 1964. *Stability and change in human characteristics.* New York: Wiley and Sons.

Bronfenbrenner, U. 1979. *The ecology of human development.* Cambridge: Harvard University Press.

Brown, J. S., and Burton, R. R. 1975. Multiple representations of knowledge for tutorial reasoning. In D. G. Bobraw and A. Collins (Eds.), *Representation and understanding.* New York: Academic Press, p. 311–49.

Bruner, J. 1966. *Toward a theory of instruction.* Cambridge, Mass.: Belknap Press of Harvard University.

Calfee, R. C., and Drum, P. A. (Eds.). 1979. *Teaching reading in compensatory classes.* Newark, Del.: International Reading Association.

Cole, M., Gay, J., Glick, G., and Sharp, D. 1971. *Cultural context of learning and thinking.* New York: Basic Books.

Gardner, H. 1993. *Frames of mind: The theory of multiple intelligences.* New York: Basic Books.

Glaser, R. 1977. *Adaptive education: Individual diversity and learning.* New York: Holt, Rinehart and Winston.

Gordon, E. W. 1968. Education for socially disadvantaged children. In Stella Chess and Alexander Thomas (Eds.), *Annual progress in child psychiatry and child development.* New York: Brunner/Mazel Publications.

———. 1979. Implications for compensatory education drawn from reflections of teaching and learning of reading. In Lauren Resnick and Phyllis Weaver (Eds.), *Theory and practice of early reading,* vol. 2. Potomac, Md.: Erlbaum Associates.

Greeno, J. 2001. Students with competencies, authority, and accountability: Affording intellective identity in classrooms. Unpublished paper.

Guralnik, D. B., Ed. 1980. *Webster's new dictionary.* Cleveland, Ohio: Williams Collins Publishers, Inc.

Hawkins, Stephen. 1988. *A brief history of time.* New York: Bantam.

Hernstein, R. 1971. I.Q. *The Atlantic Monthly.* September, 43–58, 63–64.

Hunt, J. McVickor. 1961. *Intelligence and experience.* New York: Ronald Press Co.

Kamin, L. J. 1974. *The science of politics of I.Q.* Potomac, Md.: L. Erlbaum Associates; distributed by Halsted Press, New York.

Mayr, E. 1982. *The growth of biological thought: Diversity, evolution, and inheritance.* Cambridge: Harvard University Press.

McGuire, W. J. 1983. A contextualist theory of knowledge: its implications for innovations and reform in psychological research. In L. Berkowitz (Ed.), *Advances in experimental social psychology.* New York: Academic Press.

Messick, S. 1976. *Individuality and learning.* San Francisco: Jossey-Bass.

Ogbu, J. U. 1983. Minority status and schooling in plural societies. *Comparative Education Review,* 27(2), 168–90.

Resnick, L. B. 1987. Learning in and out of school. *Educational Researcher,* 16 (9), 13–20.

Scarr, S., Weinberg, R. A., and Levine, A. 1986. *Understanding development.* San Diego, CA: Harcourt Brace Jovanovich.

Shipman, S., and Shipman, V. 1983. Cognitive styles: Some conceptual, methodological and applied issues. In E. Gordon (Ed.), *Human diversity and pedagogy.* Westport, Conn.: Mediax.

Sternberg, R. J. 1986. *Intelligence applied.* San Diego, CA: Harcourt Brace Jovanovich.

Sternberg, R. (Ed.). 1994. *The encyclopedia of human intelligence.* New York: Macmillan.

Thomas, A., and Chess, S. 1980. *The dynamics of psychological development.* New York: Brunner/Mazel.

Weinberg, R. 1989. Intelligence and IQ: Landmark issues and great debates. *American Psychologist,* 44(2), 98–104.

2

Toward the Development of Intellective Character

James G. Greeno

In this chapter, I explore a concept, which I call *intellective identities*, that is closely related to Edmund Gordon's (2000) concept of *intellective competence*. I begin with a brief discussion of the idea of intellective identities, as I mean to use the term, including its relation to the concept of intellective competence. In section 2, I discuss some empirical analyses of classroom activities that I interpret in terms of intellective identities. In section 3 I sketch a theoretical progression in the research that I, along with several colleagues and students, have conducted over the past ten years, and I offer a suggestion that the concept of intellective identities can contribute to an integration of theories of individual and social aspects of learning. Finally, in section 4, I discuss a question raised by the idea for educational practice and policy.

INTELLECTIVE IDENTITIES

Gordon (2000) has defined the concept of *intellective competence* as follows:

> the developed abilities and dispositions to perceive critically, to explore widely, to bring rational order to chaos, to bring knowledge and technique to bear on the solution of problems, to test ideas against explicit and considered moral values, as well as, against empirical data, and to recognize and create real and abstract relationships between concrete and imaginary phenomena. Intellective competence reflects the effective orchestration of affective, cognitive and situative mental processes in the service of sense making and problem solving. (2000: 1)

Gordon also noted that "these achievements are less focused on what we want learners to know and know how to do, and more sharply focused on what it is that we want learners to become and be, i.e., compassionate and thinking interdependent members of humane human communities" (2000, 1). It is this focus, on the contributions that school learning can make to the kinds of persons that students can become, that I want to emphasize by using the term *intellective identities*.

In adopting this focus, I follow Lave and Wenger (1991), who proposed that "learning involves the construction of identities" and that "one way to think of learning is as the historical production, transformation, and change of persons" (1991: 51–52). The concept of *identities* that I use here is in the tradition of Mead (1934), Goffman (1959), and many others who have conceptualized an individual's identity as being co-constructed by that person and the other people he or she interacts with in socially organized activity. In this view, it makes sense to distinguish between the identities an individual has in the different communities of practice in which he or she participates. In this chapter, I concentrate on the construction of identities in classrooms, following Packer and Goicoechea's (2000) proposal to consider "school as a site for the production of persons" (2000: 235).

Identities in Participation

I frame this discussion with a concept, *positional identity*, developed by Holland et al. (1998). I consider schools and, more specifically, classrooms, as *figured social worlds*, Holland et al.'s term for systems of social practice, including patterns of interaction, cultural understandings, assumptions, beliefs, values, attitudes, and norms that organize activity.[1] An analysis that focuses on positional identities in a classroom includes an account of the kinds of participation that are afforded in the classroom practice and identifies ways that different individuals come to participate in those practices differently.

The importance of identities in classrooms was emphasized by Lampert (1990; 2001), whose understanding of the aims of teaching includes "influencing students to be the kinds of persons who are academic resources for themselves and for one another" (2001: 266). Lampert discussed a fundamental challenge of teaching, inherent in the effort to support students' learning.

> At the same time the teacher is getting to know students and respecting who they are, she is trying to change them. She must accept and support each individual in order to build trust, and at the same time, make that individual over into one more inclined to study, to initiate the investigation of ideas, and to be identified as someone who will and can do what needs to be done to learn in school. For the student, taking on the "new" self that the teacher imagines is risky, and feelings toward the teacher for encouraging such risk taking may not be wholly positive. (2001: 267–68)

To support this transformative learning, Lampert proposed that the adoption of *intellectual virtues* is a necessary aim of teaching and learning. Following Polya (1954) she identified, as essential virtues, intellectual courage, intellectual honesty, and wise restraint, terms that designate readiness to revise beliefs when there are good reasons, conditioned on serious examination. Lampert's teaching practice included maintaining these virtues in classroom discourse, thereby supporting positional identities of students as responsible and contributing members of the classroom community, rather than only as students who could display what they had learned.

For analytic purposes, I distinguish between two general aspects of classroom identities and the classroom practices that shape them, involving (a) *conceptual* relations of individuals and groups to the subject-matter domain of the class, and (b) *interpersonal* relations of the students and teacher with each other.

Focusing on interpersonal relations involves attention to ways that individuals are entitled, expected, and obligated to act with and toward each other. For example, is it appropriate in a class for students to present questions or opinions that challenge information or interpretations by the teacher or by other students, are questions and ideas presented by students taken up as topics by the class, and do students attend and respond to each others' contributions, rather than only attending and responding to the teacher? Interpersonal aspects of practice and identity also involve ways that students and the teacher maintain relationships involving respect, courtesy, friendship, dominance, antipathy, or antagonism in their interactions. One pattern of classroom discourse that shapes interpersonal identities is the often-prevalent Initiate-Respond-Evaluate pattern of interaction, identified by Mehan (1979), in which students are limited to addressing questions initiated by the teacher. In a different kind of pattern, identified and called *revoicing* by O'Connor and Michaels (1996), the teacher invites a statement by a student, but instead of just giving feedback to that statement and then initiating another sequence, the teacher invites other students to respond to the statement. The teacher's move in revoicing can relate the student's statement to a general issue or question, thereby appropriating the student's comment to some aspect of the teacher's pedagogical agenda. As O'Connor and Michaels pointed out, revoicing sets up a pattern of interpersonal interaction in which students participate in joint constructions of information and meaning with each other, rather than just receiving and accepting information and interpretations provided by the teacher.

Focusing on conceptual relations involves attention to ways that individuals, the class, and groups within the class are entitled, expected, and obligated to act in and toward the subject-matter content of the class. I understand knowing in a subject-matter domain as being analogous to knowing in an environment such as a neighborhood (Greeno, 1991) or a workshop or kitchen (Schoenfeld, 1998), which includes knowing what resources the environment has, how to find them, and how to use them in activities. In this view, knowing in a subject-matter domain includes knowing its conceptual and representational resources, how they are related to each other, and how to use them in constructing meanings, making inferences, and solving problems.

Extending this idea to intellective practices and identities involves considering issues of entitlement, expectation, and obligation in making claims and assertions, applying and adapting concepts and methods in activities, and adding to or modifying concepts and methods in the domain. In classroom discourse, students may be limited to animating information and ideas for which they are not the source, or they may be positioned as authors and principals of their contributions (Goffman, 1959; 1981).

The analyses I discuss in this chapter attend to three issues of participation by students in classroom practices, among others. These issues, on which I focus this discussion, are competence, authority, and accountability.

Competence Constructed in Interaction

In this discussion, I consider intellective competence as an aspect of participation in activities in a setting. A community's practices include shaping ways in which an individual's participation counts as being competent or incompetent. "What it means to be a competent learner" is different in different learning environments. Consider different classrooms. In some classrooms, competent students ask questions to indicate that they are unclear about a meaning or uncertain about whether a procedure should be used, and these questions are construed as furthering the collective effort toward understanding. In other classrooms, asking questions is construed as a sign of incompetence, because students are expected to know or figure out how to solve the problems that are set. In such classrooms, a student's question indicates that he or she is unable to do what is expected, and it is a diversion from the class's progress. In some situations, a student's silence indicates that he or she cannot or declines to contribute to the learning process, at least at that moment. In other situations, a student's silence is taken to signal that he or she is making satisfactory progress on the assigned task and does not need help.

A characterization of competence depends on the frame of reference that is used in viewing the activity. A competence frame selects some aspect or aspects of activity to attend to in considering competence. Attention may be focused on interpersonal or on subject-matter aspects of activity. The analyst may focus on interpersonal aspects of a student's participation in discourse, whether he or she honors the social norms of the classroom involving turn-taking, and attends and responds to others' presentations.

Within a subject-matter focus, the analyst may focus on whether an individual is competent in the use of disciplinary methods of mathematics, such as computational accuracy, correct and appropriate use of representational systems, and valid methods of reasoning. As another alternative, the analyst may focus a student's adherence to what Yackel and Cobb (1996) call *sociomathematical norms*, the practices in the classroom involving forms and contents of explanation and argumentation, ways of using systems of symbols in justifying conclusions, and other aspects of classroom practice that involve both interpersonal and subject-matter aspects of interaction.

Authority and Accountability

Along with constructing the nature of competence, classroom practices also construct the nature of authority and accountability in the participants' contributions. In some classrooms, authority rests entirely in the teacher, in her or his role as an agent of the subject-matter discipline. There is a presumed authority of correct information, action, and interpretation of concepts in the domain, to which the teacher has access, partly through the medium of a textbook and other sources and partly through her or his own knowledge. The teacher is accountable to the authority of disciplinary knowledge for the information and interpretations that he or she conveys to the students. They are accountable to the teacher for their answers to questions and solutions to problems, and the teacher judges the students as successful or not, according to whether their answers and solutions correspond to those that are authorized in the discipline.

In other classrooms, the teacher and students have more authority and accountability for the knowledge and understanding that they construct, and it is distributed differently, with more authority vested in students for reaching conclusions and more accountability for contributing to each others' understanding and learning. Questions and problems are often presented as occasions for students to offer candidate answers and solutions, for which multiple contributions are expected. Students explain assumptions underlying their own and each others' ideas and methods. Indeed, students often generate questions and problems that become topics for the class. The authority of disciplinary knowledge is not erased, but it is not sufficient. The information, interpretations, and methods of the discipline are understood to be legitimate and valuable resources for the class's learning, but the central aim of the class's activity is to construct understanding and knowledge as products of its collective and individual experience and reasoning.

A discussion by Pickering (1995) clarifies an important aspect of authority and accountability in intellective practices. Pickering distinguished between *conceptual agency* and *disciplinary agency*. He drew this distinction in mathematical practice, but it is important in any domain of intellective inquiry. Conceptual agency involves activities of formulating problems and definitions, choosing approaches to problems, and otherwise carrying out what he called *free moves* in mathematical inquiry, "free" because the mathematician(s) choose what to do. Disciplinary agency involves use of accepted methods sufficiently so that discretion does not enter into their outcome. Once a mathematical problem is fully formulated and a method is applied, the result is out of the human mathematician's hands, assuming that he or she performs the method correctly. In other words, in carrying out the method, the mathematician makes only *forced moves,* so the mathematician's agency is limited to performing a sequence of actions correctly according to accepted practice.

A related discussion, by Stein, Grover, and Henningsen (1996; also see Stein et al., 2000) about mathematics classroom activity draws a distinction similar to Pickering's. Stein et al. characterized mathematical tasks in terms of their cognitive demands. In some tasks, students need to remember a fact, definition, or something else that has been presented. In other tasks, students need to apply a procedure correctly, with no requirement of explaining the procedure or why it is appropriate to use it. Still other tasks require students to explain how a procedure works or why it is useful, relating the procedure to general mathematical concepts or principles. And still other tasks involve "doing mathematics," which involves inquiry into mathematical meanings or alternative approaches to a problem. Stein et al.'s classification of mathematical classroom tasks involving *doing mathematics* and *procedures with connection* corresponds to Pickering's *conceptual agency,* and their categories of *remembering* and *procedures without connection* correspond to Pickering's *disciplinary agency.*

Distinctions analogous to these in mathematical inquiry and learning can be drawn in any subject-matter domain. In science, for example, if questions are answered and problems solved entirely on the basis of procedures and information acquired from authoritative sources, students are limited to exercising disciplinary agency. If they explore questions and problems meaningfully, formulating alternative hypotheses and obtaining and evaluating evidence, they exercise conceptual agency as well. Di Sessa (1985) illustrated this distinction with two case studies involving students in a project-oriented college physics class. One of the students, who called himself a "results man," was impatient with Di Sessa's efforts to explore theoretical explanations of procedures for solving problems. Another student was dissatisfied unless he felt he had grasped the conceptual principles behind the procedures for solving problems. As Pickering (1995) explained, scientific inquiry also includes *material agency* in the conduct of experiments or naturalistic observations. Outcomes of experiments depend on the behavior of material systems (pieces of apparatus), and are not controlled by the experimenter. Rosebery, Warren, and Conant (1992) studied school activities in which students participated in formulating questions for empirical inquiry and in the interpretations of findings. In the Itakura method of elementary science instruction studied by Hatano and Inagaki (1991), students engage in extensive discussion of alternative possible outcomes of experiments and arrive at conclusions about alternative hypotheses when the experiments are conducted.[2]

Productive Agency

I hypothesize that an important aspect of identities in school learning is an aspect of participation that Schwartz (1999) called *productive agency.* Any group's activity can be considered as having a product of some sort. In school, the main intended products are increased student knowledge and understanding. As Schwartz pointed out, activities can be organized for students to share in the products of knowledge construction, as recipients, but they also can be organized for students to be agents in the means of producing knowledge and understanding. In the latter case, students have productive agency, that is, they share agency in the means of production. I consider productive agency as an aspect of learning practices, which can be understood as applying to individuals or to students as a group. I hypothesize that classroom practices that afford productive agency can contribute to students' development of positive identities as learners and knowers. And I hypothesize that positioning students with competence, authority, and accountability are important factors in supporting their exercising productive agency in their learning.

A key feature of reorganizing participation in classrooms involves supporting productive agency by redistributing competence, authority, and accountability so that students are active contributors to the shared understanding of subject-matter that the class develops. For example, Lampert (e.g., 1990; 2001) has written extensively about her teaching in which students are expected to explain their and other students' thinking, so they are positioned as coauthors of their and their fellow-students' understanding, for which the virtues of intellectual courage, intellectual honesty, and wise restraint are essential. Ball (1993) has reported her practice of positioning students by identifying them as authors of conjectures and explanations. Yackel and Cobb (1996) have emphasized the importance of social and sociomathematical norms in the classrooms they and their colleagues have organized and studied, involving expectations and obligations of students to provide mathematical explanations for their solutions of problems and to attend to and use others' explanations.

Students do not participate only in the figured social world of school; their current and future participations may include a family, a workplace, a religious practice, a political organization, a gang. The situative view of identities that I adopt here requires that we consider how development of an individual's positional identity in one of her or his social worlds is influenced by the other social worlds that the person has participated and is participating in, and, in turn, how the identity he or she forms there can influence the positional identities of her or his concurrent and future participations.[3] Rosebery, Warren, and Conant (1992) discuss learning in a bilingual program in which projects were developed out of students' questions about water quality, for which students and teachers generated methods of investigation and developed stronger capabilities for scientific inquiry and understanding. Gutiérrez, Baquedano-López, and Tejada (1999) discuss ways in which diverse and initially conflicting discourse practices can be a source of developing a "third space" of discourse that is productive for learning. And Lipka, Mohatt, and the Ciulistet Group (1998) and Moll and Greenberg (1990) discuss uses of diverse cultural resources that can position students as sources of knowledge who enrich classroom learning.

EXAMPLES

To provide examples of classroom interactions that I interpret as contributing to students' intellective identities, I describe activities that we have observed in a few classrooms that were organized by teachers and students to afford collaborative inquiry and construction of understanding. I focus on ways that students are positioned in the participation structures of these classrooms, especially on ways that agency is distributed with regard to competence, authority, and accountability. At a general level, I discuss aspects of the curriculum and classroom practices that can support positional identities that include productive agency. At a more micro-level I discuss hypotheses about features of discourse that can position students with competence, authority, and accountability at specific moments of interaction.

The Algebra Project: Affording Competence

I start by discussing some preliminary findings of an analysis we have begun of mathematics teaching and learning in a middle school that participates in the Algebra Project (Moses and Cobb, 2001). The Algebra Project is motivated by a belief, articulated by Robert Moses, that access to academically oriented mathematics learning in high school should be considered a civil right, especially as the prevalent practices of mathematics teaching and learning function to disentitle many, many students from access to respected institutions of higher education. Moses believes, as do many of us, that the large discrepancies among racial and economic groups in mathematics achievement—the "achievement gap"—results in significant part from the way in which mathematics is usually taught in middle school, which privileges mainstream children, especially mainstream boys, over minority children. Moses has developed principles of teaching and learning, as well as some curriculum materials, that are intended to make success in learning mathematics accessible to a much broader group of students in middle school, especially African-American children.

In collaboration with Frank Davis and Mary Maxwell West, Melissa Sommerfeld, Sarah Lewis, Taylor Martin, and I have begun a study of mathematics teaching and learning in what will eventually be three schools that have participated in the national Algebra Project. Our goal is to identify practices that are productive for students' mathematics learning, especially students of color. During the 2000–2001 school year we observed and videotaped classes and interviewed teachers and videotaped their meetings at one of the schools, and we have begun to examine and analyze some of the classroom videotapes.

Some of the principles of the Algebra Project were stated by Moses and Cobb (2001) as follows:

> Students learn that math is the creation of people—people working together and depending on one another. Interaction, cooperation, and group communication, therefore, are key components of this process. Students also help generate part of the content of instruction as well. Cooperation and participation in group activities, as well as personal responsibility for individual work, become important not only for the successful *functioning* of the learning group, but for the generation of instructional materials and various representations of the data as well. (2001: 120)

A learning environment organized in this way affords very different intellective identities from those afforded by many mathematics classes.

In an early discussion by our research group about possible ways to focus analyses of videotapes from the first phase of our research, Marian Currell, a teacher with whom we work closely, said that it would be valuable if we could become clearer about "what it means to be a mathematically competent learner." We have adopted this as one of the main research questions in our study. Our analyses, which are at an early stage, treat mathematical competence as a version of intellective competence, as I discuss that idea in section 1, above. An individual's mathematical competence, in our analyses, is an aspect of her or his participation in activities that have mathematical content. We consider mathematical competence, like other aspects of identity, as being socially constructed in interaction. This requires that to characterize someone's mathematical competence requires adopting a frame of reference, which is selective regarding the aspect(s) of competence that are focused upon, and also selects a view of what constitutes mathematics for the purpose of that characterization.

One focus of our examinations of classroom videotapes in the Algebra Project has been on the construction and recognition of students' mathematical competence. The basis of this discussion is a set of videotapes from two sixth-grade classrooms engaged in activities of the Transition Curriculum. The sixth-grade book of this curriculum develops the concepts of integers, displacements, and addition and subtraction of integers.

I discuss two levels at which construction of positive student competence was supported in the classrooms that we observed. One of the levels involves the design and conduct of activities in the Algebra Project Transition Curriculum and ways that students were positioned to participate competently in those activities. The other way involves features of specific discourse interactions that the teacher had with students.

Curriculum Activities

The sequence of activities in the Transition Curriculum is designed to afford students' competent participation. In Moses and Cobb's terms,

> We say "transition" because the Algebra Project focuses on a cluster of elementary but elemental concepts that are essential for bridging the gap between arithmetic and algebra so that *all* middle school students are prepared to succeed in the college preparatory mathematics sequence when they reach high school. . . . It's a "floor." Our transition curriculum is rooted in the conviction that intellectual development is, in part, a matter of integrating knowledge. You want the kids to learn how to engage the inquiry process. (2001: 119)

The curriculum design is called the Five Step Curricular Process. The design is guided by Quine's (1981) characterization of mathematical discourse as regimentation of ordinary language. In the five-step process,

> simple events experienced by students lead to observational statements whose symbolic representations may be interpreted and checked for truth. The experiential contents of the 5-step process provide a basis for the extended reflection and discussion that undergird the students' gradually deepening understanding. . . . Mathematical ideas in the AP are embedded in a series of activities that include the following steps:
> 1) Posing of an environmentally familiar physical event with rich potential for the development of mathematical concepts; students experience this event.
> 2) Pictorial representation and other physical modeling of the event; students depict this event.
> 3) Articulation of the event in intuitive or natural language—"people talk"; students discuss this event in a variety of formats, guided by the teacher.
> 4) Articulation of the event in structured, regimented language—"feature talk"; working with each other and the teacher in a variety of activity types, students gradually refine and structure their language about the

event, formalizing and mathematizing their talk and writing about the
event.

5) Symbolic Representation of the event (development of nonstandard symbolic representations, introduction to standard symbols, and discussions of the properties of both); students continue their exploration into the realm of formal symbols, becoming familiar with the conventions and practices involved in mathematical symbolization. (Moses, 2001: 120–22)

A curriculum designed according to this scheme can afford students being positioned to develop positive intellective identities through participation with intellective competence, authority, and accountability. Students can be positioned with competence because at each step, the things they are required to do are based on experience they are known to have had. This design feature is related to the behaviorists' or cognitivists' concern about ensuring that students have prerequisite skills and knowledge, but it differs significantly from that idea. Instead of focusing on prerequisite skills or knowledge, the Five-Step Curriculum design focuses on shared experience that members of the class can draw on in their participation, and their shared experiences progress through discourse in which the concepts and methods of academic mathematics play an increasingly large role.

This curriculum design also can afford students being positioned with authority and accountability for constructing mathematical knowledge in the classroom community and, thereby, with productive agency. The students are expected to represent their shared experience with "people talk," that is, in language they can use authoritatively. As they develop representations in "feature talk," students may use symbols that reflect intuitive, visual, and artistic feelings, which are reflected in their "people talk," and which need to be refined in order to represent unambiguously the features of trips that are needed to support development of the concept of integers. But the process of developing symbols, and the concepts that the symbols represent, is intended to be one in which the ideas are brought through a shared experience and a social history of discourse that mathematizes that experience, to a discourse that continues to extend the experience, with students participating authoritatively and accountable throughout.

In classes we observed, taught by Marian Currell, the physical event was a trip to a local science museum (Step 1).[4] In each working group of four to five members, students drew a mural representing scenes from their trip that they felt were significant (Step 2). Each group wrote a story to go with its mural, and the stories and murals were presented by the groups to the whole class (Step 3). As these presentations were made, the teacher said that students in each of the listening groups should be able to contribute a compliment and a question to the presenting group. The whole class then developed a representation called a "trip line," a set of nine exhibits and landmarks from the trip that the class agreed to include, which were listed in an order that the class agreed they would consider as a sequence of visiting the sites (beginning of Step 4). They then developed the concept of a *trip*, an event with four features: a starting place and an ending place, corresponding to sites on the trip line, the number of stops that would be made in a trip with those starting and ending places, and the direction of the trip (more of Step 4). In the next activity, each student listed ten possible trips, choosing a symbol for each of the trip features that could be interpreted by the other students, including symbols for the nine sites (to represent starting and ending places) and (most significantly for the curriculum) for the numbers of stops and the direction of the trip (beginning of Step 5). The next task was to estimate what the most popular values of the four features were in the class. To do this, each student was to collect a sample of three trips from every student in the class. The students in each group were to decide on a method of representing these data in a way that would enable them to determine which starting place, ending place, number of stops, and direction, were the most popular (more of Step 5).

This is as far as the classes we observed progressed. In the intended continuation (which the teacher was unable to complete because of excessive requirements for testing) the class would have developed concepts of signed integers and operations of adding and subtracting integers, corresponding to combining trips. (This was discussed by Moses and Cobb [2001] in general terms. Godfrey and O'Connor [1995] reported an analysis of discourse in Godfrey's class involving construction of a direction symbol for comparisons between heights, another Algebra Project activity closely related to the one involving trips.)

In this sequence of activities, students were positioned to be competent participants with significant agency in accomplishing tasks that the teacher specified in general terms, but with significant details to be determined by the students' choices. It was not assured that the students would complete their tasks successfully; however, sensible attempts were always within reach of the students.

Initially, they took a trip together, an experience they all could participate in without special academic preparation. In the activity of drawing murals and writing stories about their trips they were positioned with authority for choosing the sites that they remembered with interest and to which they attached significance. In the discussions that accompanied the presentations to the class, individuals were accountable for explaining why they had included what they had, and why they chose the pictorial and narrative representations they used.

Currell directed the students to include the four specified features in their representations of possible trips. Students had to construct symbols for those features. The teacher directed students to choose symbols that would communicate to others. Discussions occurred between the teacher and individual students regarding the need for a legend for symbols for the sites (they could be pictorial or numerical; either way, they related to a diagram that represented the ordered set of sites along a line), the meaning of "number of stops" (should the starting place be included in the count?), and the direction (some consistent symbols needed to be used; for example, compass directions or arrows).

Currell also directed the activity of collecting data, in this case to include three trips that had been represented by each of the students in the class. Each working group of students was responsible for deciding on a method of organizing and representing the data, but there was a discussion in the whole class in which individual students proposed methods. The stated goal of this activity was to determine which values of the features (starting place, ending place, number of stops, and direction) were "most popular." In one of the classes, the teacher needed to correct a misunderstanding when she found that some students were asking others which values they liked most. She explained that finding the "most popular" values could not be done until the data had been collected.

Because it involves a sequence of tasks in which students can participate competently, the Transition Curriculum could be viewed as an example of Vygotsky's (1934/1987) idea of the *zone of proximal development*. It does have the property that tasks are designed to be in reach of the students. However, there also is an important characteristic of the Transition Curriculum involving productive agency. Although none of the tasks in the curriculum was routine for the students, and the students therefore needed some scaffolding to accomplish them, the students were not simply in the position of being helped to find the correct way to accomplish the tasks. Because the tasks were open-ended, with multiple ways for them to be accomplished, the students were positioned so that their actions provided valuable candidates for methods that could be used by themselves and others in the class.

Interactions in Discourse

The curriculum specifies activities in which students *can be* positioned with competence by virtue of their knowledge and experience. However, for them to *be* positioned with competence, authority, and accountability required interpersonal interactions of the students with the teacher and each other that supported their competent participation.

In our preliminary analyses, we have developed a conjecture that *presuppositions of competence* may play an important role in positioning students as competent participants in classroom activity. In examining videotapes of Currell's classrooms, we observe patterns of interaction that we hypothesize establish presuppositions of competent contributions by students. In whole-class discussions, these presuppositions apparently were supported by the open nature of tasks and by the teacher's practice of adopting proposals and questions from individual students as topics for consideration by the class. This supported students' expectations that their own and other students' questions and proposals would be construed as being competent and would function constructively in the class. In interactions with individual students or with groups at their work tables, the teacher almost always asked questions that seem to us as presupposing that students were making progress on their task or, at least, intended to work constructively as soon as they finished what they were doing (which she encouraged them to do quickly). These interactions, then, addressed questions of how the students were progressing or how they would be progressing shortly, without questioning whether they were capable of moving ahead or willing to work toward accomplishing their tasks. We conjecture that presuppositions of competence are a significant aspect of interaction, contributing to the positioning of students as competent mathematical learners.

Students' interactions with Currell also positioned them with authority and accountability, so that they participated in the class with productive agency. She emphasized that the information and symbols in the students' representations were to be authored by the students, and that every student had the responsibility of contributing. Some of the assignments were required to be constructed collaboratively by groups of students sitting at work tables, and these were to be shared with the class through reports given at appropriate times.

Fostering Communities of Learners: A "Big Ol' Argument"

My second example comes from a study of teaching and learning in Brown and Campione's (1994) Fostering Communities of Learners (FCL) project. Brown and Campione's project aimed to develop

> a learning community designed to encourage distributed expertise. . . . In order to foster such a community, we feature students as designers of their own learning: we encourage students to be partially responsible for designing their own curriculum. (1994: 233)

Randi Engle, Muffie Wiebe, Cathy Lachapelle, Gertraud Benke, and I observed and videotaped classrooms and began the analyses. Subsequently, Frederick Erickson and Faith Conant collaborated with us in analyses of videotapes. We collected these data in an urban, racially diverse, public elementary school, in two fifth-grade classes, taught by teachers who had participated in FCL for several years. We observed these classes about three times per week during the time they worked on an FCL unit on endangered species, which extended through about twelve working weeks of the school year.

Curriculum Activities

The learning activities in these classes were organized in several ways to support productive agency, positioning students with authority, accountability, and competence. The classes were divided into research groups, each with four to five students. Each group studied a species and prepared a report about its endangered condition. The main resource for the reports was a large supply of books about the various species to be studied. Each group of students also had a field trip to a site where they could observe the species they studied, and they were encouraged to use other information that they might obtain from television or with questions that they were able to ask biologists who responded to their e-mail messages. The work of each group was divided between the students, with each student responsible for contributing a report section on one or two of the key concepts, called "survival needs," that the teachers and class agreed would be used to organize all of the reports. When the reports were finished, each student had the responsibility of presenting the complete report in a group of students formed as a "jigsaw" including one or two members from all the other groups in the class. Assigning different conceptual topics to the students provided responsibility and authorship for each student; the requirement of every student to present the report provided accountability for all students to understand the material that others in the group contributed, not just their own. A strong presupposition of competence in literacy was in place, as students were expected to use the available books as sources of information to compose their texts.

An event that we have analyzed in some detail was an extended debate about whether killer whales—that is, orcas—should be classified as whales or dolphins. The issue arose about midway through the unit, when the students were constructing bulletin boards to display information they had obtained by that point about their respective species. There were two groups studying whales, one from each class, and they were working on a bulletin board together. Their plan was to present general information about whales, along with more specific information about killer whales and blue whales, and members of the groups had assembled some of the materials, including pictures and text, that they expected to be included in the display.

Each group of students took a field trip sometime during the unit to get information about their species. The whales groups went to Marine World where there was a showing of orcas and dolphins. One of the staff members included in her talk that "killer whales aren't whales, they're dolphins."

The next day, one of the students remarked that the group should not include orcas on the bulletin board, because they had learned that they are not whales. This set off an intense interaction with other students, and especially one student who had been studying features of whales. One of the teachers organized the whales groups to discuss the question, which they did for nearly a half-hour, the event that came to be called "the big ol' argument." The students put forward substantive arguments involving anatomical features and terminology and debated whether outside sources (the Marine World staff person, as well as textbooks) should be taken as authoritative. During the discussion, most, but not all, of these students became persuaded to the view that orcas should be classified as whales. This issue was discussed several more times during the unit. The question of whether to include discussion of orcas in the group's research report was resolved by including these animals, along with an explanation that "scientists will never know for sure."[5]

Engle and Conant (2002: 399–483) used an analysis of this episode to develop and evaluate hypotheses about four factors that can support productive disciplinary engagement:

- positioning students with authority,
- positioning students with accountability,
- practices of problematizing issues, and
- access to resources.

These factors included aspects of general classroom practices and curriculum activities involved in positioning students with authority, accountability, and competence. For example:

- *Positioning with authority.* Students were positioned with authority for their contributions to the products of their groups' work. They were, literally, the authors of sections of the reports that their groups produced. This authorship involved use of information that they found in texts and other sources, and the students made judgments of relevance and significance in deciding to include information and choosing which sections to include it in. Each student's experience in conducting research was taken as endowing her or him with authority to form and defend opinions in the domain. This was shown clearly in the "big ol' argument" debate, in which students contested alternative interpretations and the authoritative status of information from texts and the speaker they heard on their field trip. In setting up this discussion, the teacher authorized the students in the whales groups to resolve the issue.
- *Positioning with accountability.* The division of work in the research groups, with individual students responsible for conceptually defined topics, created accountability for their scholarly work. The group's achievement in completing its assignment depended on each of its members' contribution. The requirement of each student presenting the entire report in the jigsaw created accountability of each student for understanding the results of all of the group members' scholarly work. In the "big ol' argument," the students were accountable to each other for reaching a mutually agreed resolution, with attention to evidence

from their research and recognition of each others' "good points," as characterized by the teachers and students.

The classroom practices and curriculum activities were also arranged to support positioning of the students with competence, discussed here in terms of the other two of Engle and Conant's supporting factors:

- *Practices of problematizing.* In general, the teachers encouraged discussions involving different points of view. Specifically, when the controversy about classifying orcas arose, one of the teachers legitimized its problematic status and organized the students concerned with it to discuss it for a substantial period of time. This presupposed that students were competent to resolve the issue, a presupposition that they acted on energetically.

- *Access to resources.* The classroom had a large supply of books about the species that were subjects of their study, and students' main activity involved research in which they consulted these texts. These texts provided conflicting information, a resource that supported problematizing issues. The students also had e-mail access to outside authorities and had a field trip in which they observed marine mammals. More generally, there was time for discussion, and the students had previous experience in productive argument. The students were expected to consult the sources and interpret their contents independently for the purposes of composing their reports, an expectation that presupposed their competence to understand the information productively. The teachers attended to each group with frequent conversations in which they checked on each student's progress and provided supportive assistance and advice.

Interactions in Discourse

We also have observed aspects of specific discourse interactions that we interpret as supporting students' positioning with authority, accountability, and competence.

- *Authority.* Generally, students were positioned—by other students as well as by the teachers—as the authors of ideas (e.g., as having "good points") or as principal purveyors of information (e.g., "you have important information to include in the report"), rather than as animators of others' ideas (Goffman, 1959; 1981).

- *Accountability.* Students were also positioned with responsibility for contributing to others' thinking.

- *Competence.* Generally the teachers positioned students as being competent—indeed, as being expert—in their activities. For example, in setting up what came to be called the "big ol' argument," the teacher referred to the various students' "good points."

Conceptual Learning in Participation

I propose that a cognitive analysis of the content of people's understandings of concepts should include an account of their participation in its construction. This means that an account of these students' understanding of the concepts "whales," "dolphins," "killer whales," and, more generally, their understanding of biological classification, needs to include the history of their constructing this understanding. In this case, the "big ol' argument" was central.

We have unusually direct evidence that, for these students, their understanding of this issue included their history of discourse and debate. About halfway through the unit, a new student teacher took up her assignment in one of the classes we were studying. Each of the student research groups met with the student teacher and reported the results of their research up to that time. The whales group's report was quite remarkable. Each student took a turn, presenting facts about whales in a matter-of-fact way, while the others waited quite politely. But during the presentation of results about features, the reporter mentioned that "some people believe that killer whales are actually the biggest dolphin, but scientists proved that is not true." As he was making this statement, he made eye contact with the student who was his main antagonist in the debate, who indicated that she was one of those "people," and the other two members of the group became actively involved in communicating their positions in this controversy.

The students' task was to report what they knew. The history of their discourse was an important part of what they reported. We can hardly erase that if we want to give an account of their knowledge and conceptual understanding. But we also believe that if we accept this argument for these students' understanding of orca taxonomy, it implies that the history of participation in constructing understanding should become a part of cognitive analyses generally. During most of their reports, these students followed the convention of erasing their learning activities from their accounts of what they had learned. However, when they reached the dramatic events of the "big ol' argument" they violated that norm and included reports of what they did to learn what they learned, rather than just what they learned.

Their identities as participants in the controversy were an important part of their reports, and therefore, we conclude, of the knowledge and understanding they achieved. It was important, especially to the advocate of the view that eventually prevailed, that several participants changed their minds during the "big ol' argument." It was also important that he had been influential in getting this to happen—a role that was shared by another member of the group who enthusiastically asserted his claim to helping bring about the changes in opinion. It follows that identities—however we can come to understand them—are important ingredients in what students learn. In other words, we cannot relegate our understanding of students' identities as learners to the context of their learning, factoring it away from the processes and outcomes of learning per se. Instead, identities need to be considered as an integral aspect of what is learned and developed, as well as how and why learning occurs successfully or unsuccessfully as it does.

This example also suggests some factors that may be important in shaping the kinds of identities that students can develop in their learning at school. A plausible hypothesis is that students are most likely to learn how to do what they, in fact, do when they are learning. That is, the practices of learning in the environments where students learn are likely to be the kinds of practices in which they are able to become capable, and the ways in which students are positioned in those learning practices are likely to correspond to the kinds of positional identities that the students can most easily develop. By positioning students with authority, accountability, and competence, and by encouraging their engagement with problematic issues in the subject-matter domain, we can at least conjecture that participation in this class afforded them the possibility of developing aspects of their identities as learners to participate authoritatively, accountably, and competently, and to recognize and address problematic issues.

Finally, I suggest that the ways in which students participated in constructing understanding of biological concepts in the "big ol' argument" could be a prime example of Schwartz's (1999) concept of *productive agency*, discussed above. In the process of constructing their understanding of the taxonomy of marine mammals, the students had significant ownership of the means of producing knowledge and understanding, that is, of the forms of argument and the validation and interpretation of information that they used in support of their views.

INTELLECTIVE IDENTITIES IN AN INTEGRATIVE THEORY

In this section I briefly discuss a way that I believe the concept of intellective identities can contribute to an integrative theory of learning and cognition in activity. This discussion relates to an effort to develop a scientific account of learning and cognition that includes both its informational and its interpersonal aspects. Accounts of each of these have been developed impressively during the past forty or so years, but they have developed quite separately. Accounts of information structures in learning and cognition have been developed in cognitive science, and accounts of interpersonal aspects of interaction have been developed in ethnography, interactional sociolinguistics, and related research efforts.

An effort to develop integration between these two lines of research has been under way for about a decade. The general strategy is to observe and analyze activity involving understanding, reasoning, and learning by groups of people in settings such as classrooms or work settings. Different investigators are approaching this in different ways. Some are working "from the inside out," taking cognitive theory as the basis and extending the analyses of cognitive processes by including interactions between individuals. These include studies by investigators such as Dunbar (1995), Okada and Simon (1997), and Schwartz (1995). Other investigators are working "from the outside in," taking interactional theories of activity as the basis and incorporating analyses of information structures in analyses of interaction. I have been working with the second of these approaches, as have many others, such as Goodwin (1995), Hutchins (1995), and Ochs, Jacoby, and Gonzalez (1994).

Some contributions to this effort are sketched in table 2.1. The table presents four levels of accounts of cognition in interaction. The time line in the table goes from the bottom to the top, as each proposed theoretical integration builds on the one below it in the table. The left cell of each row mentions a kind of achievement in interaction that theories of learning and cognition should explain. The middle cell mentions some concepts that have been developed in cognitive science and psychology that provide accounts of those achievements. The entries in the righthand column mention concepts at the level of activity systems and social practices that have been proposed and that I believe are promising candidates for providing explanations that are more inclusive than those that we have been able to achieve with the cognitive analyses.

Level 1

In 1991, Randi Engle and I commenced an effort to study conceptual understanding as an aspect of discourse activity. The idea behind this research was that conceptual understanding occurs in discourse, when people are working to plan, coordinate or evaluate their activities, explain their actions, or reach shared understanding of something. Our strategy was to take the information-processing analysis of reasoning and understanding, developed in cognitive science, and embed it in a theory of conversational interaction, which we adapted from Herbert Clark's (1996) contributions. The information-processing theory (Level 1) explains routine understanding and reasoning as processes of constructing coherent representations that connect various pieces of information according to stored schemata and fill in pieces of information that are missing using stored inference rules (e.g., Just and Carpenter, 1980). In this information-processing theory, the content of understanding depends on schemata that are retrieved from memory. Most understanding that occurs, in this theory, involves assimilation of information to known schemata, guided by comprehension strategies (e.g., Kintsch, 1998). Understanding that goes beyond simple assimilation can occur when a schema is mapped onto information in a domain different from the one in which it is already known, as in analogical reasoning. But that kind of reasoning is quite hard, according to current cognitive accounts.

Table 2.1. Progress in integrating information contents in situative analyses

Achievements to be explained	Analysis from Cognitive Science and Psychology	Situative Analysis
(4) Conceptual growth, commitment to learning goals, sustained, persistent participation in learning practices.	• Cognitive development • Academic self-esteem, general motivational traits. • Ways of knowing.	• Changes in discourse practice; legitimate peripheral participation (Bowers, Cobb & McClain, 1999; Greeno et al., 1998; Hall & Rubin, 1998; Lampert, 2001; Lave & Wenger, 1991; Rosebery, Warren & Conant, 1992; Strom et al., 2001) • General intellective identities, positional identities in school and classrooms with mutual engagement and productive agency in relation to a community's joint enterprise of learning. (Holland et al., 1998; Wenger, 1998)
(3) Adopting tasks, expending effort toward accomplishing goals.	• Understanding task instructions. • Task-level motivation.	• Practices that encourage problematizing and position students in disciplinary discourse with competence, authority, and accountability in participation structures. (Ball, 1993; Ball & Bass, 2000; Brown & Campione, 1994; Engle & Conant, 2002; Hatano & Inagaki, 1991; Lampert, 1990)
(2) Emergent understanding, strategies, methods.	• Generative (e.g., analogical) reasoning, heterogeneous representations. • Flexibility in thinking.	• Negotiating different interpretations for mutual understanding. (Dunbar, 1995; Engle & Greeno, 1994; Okada & Simon, 1997; Schwartz, 1995; Tudge & Rogoff 1989; Rosebery, Warren & Conant, 1992) • Problematizing and positioning in interaction. (Greeno, Sommerfeld & Wiebe, 2000; Stenning et al., 2002)
(1) Routine comprehension, performing procedures, conceptual understanding, reasoning, planning.	• Information-processing operations. • Schemata, strategies.	• Conversational contributions, mutual attention, understanding propositions and reference (Clark & Schaefer, 1989). • Conceptual common ground, patterns of reasoning in practice. (Hanks, 1996) • Shared repertoire of schemata and procedures. (Greeno & Engle, 1995)

Our theoretical move was to hypothesize that these constructive processes occur in conversation through the joint actions of the participants (Level 1). The information structures that are built are the common ground that the participants construct in their interaction. In this view, the information-processing operations of cognitive theory are assumed to occur as joint actions in conversation, in which the units are what Clark and Schaefer (1989) called *contributions to discourse*. Each contribution includes, minimally, a presentation and an acceptance that signals mutual understanding sufficient for the participants' present purposes. A contribution may also include an action that signals uncertainty or confusion or presents a question or a challenge to the initiating presentation in the form of an alternative idea or proposal. In that case, there has to be some negotiation to reach mutual understanding and completion of the contribution, to place new information in the common ground. Much understanding depends on the participants' sharing of a vast amount of common ground (e.g., Hanks, 1996), a more inclusive version of the cognitive idea of schemata. Using these ideas, Engle and I developed an analysis of some examples of conceptual understanding and reasoning in conversation (Greeno and Engle, 1995).

Level 2

Level 2 involves understanding and reasoning that produces nonroutine insights, which are novel for the participants. Accounting for novel insights has traditionally been challenging. In psychology, nonroutine insights require flexible thinking, associated with gestalt analyses such as Duncker's (1935/1945). In more recent work in cognitive science, generative analogical reasoning has been studied and analyzed in detail (e.g., Gentner, Holyoak, and Kokinov, 2001). In situations involving more than one person reasoning collaboratively, novel insights (for the participants) can be produced based on negotiation that occurs when they express differing understandings (Engle and Greeno, 1994). The value of diverse opinions in collaborative reasoning and understanding has been studied by Okada and Simon (1997), Schwartz (1995), Tudge and Rogoff (1989), and Rosebery, Warren, and Conant (1992).

In detailed analyses of some episodes involving generative reasoning, we have focussed on a kind of interaction that we are calling *problematizing*. We have examined some cases in which a group did or did not problematize an issue that they might have, which we have discussed in terms of semantic trajectories in conversation (Greeno, Sommerfeld, and Wiebe, 2000; Stenning et al., 2002). For an issue to be problematized, we hypothesize, alternative trajectories need to be considered. This can occur if the participants recognize alternatives and create a choice point or if one of the participants questions or challenges the group's current trajectory and succeeds in having the group consider whether a different trajectory might be preferable. This raises another issue in our analyses, the *positioning* of individuals in the participation structure of their classroom activity. In any episode of interaction, different individuals participate in different ways. Quite often, someone is initiating segments of activity, functioning as the director. Others are at least monitoring the actions of the director, providing approval or raising questions. Sometimes agency is distributed across two or more of the participants, so that other participants are actively contributing to the progress of discourse. This distribution of agency is important in the opportunities to problematize issues. If one of the participants is positioned so as to present virtually all of the information and ideas, with others positioned mainly as bystanders, it is difficult for anyone except the leading participant to introduce a question or challenge that is taken up by the group. However, if one participant initiates a contribution and another participant is positioned with significant agency for questioning or challenging that participant's presentation, rather than being positioned as a bystander, it is much easier for her or him to get the floor and introduce a question or alternative idea and have that taken up by the group.

Level 3

Issues at the next level involve students' engagement with learning tasks. Cognitive theories account for some aspects of these issues with models of students' understanding of problems and setting goals to solve them (e.g., Hayes and Simon, 1974). More generally, psychological theories of motivation include hypotheses about students' motivation to expend effort in tasks of specific subject-matter domains and tasks that have moderate perceived difficulty (e.g., Stipek, 1998).

In situative studies, students' engagement is considered as an aspect of their participation in classroom practices. Recent research on classroom practices has focussed on structures of participation in which students are entitled, expected, and obligated to propose conjectures, raise questions and problems, and formulate explanations and arguments, rather than only being entitled to answer questions and solve problems given by the teacher (Ball, 1993; Ball and Bass, 2000; Brown and Campione, 1994; Hatano and Inagaki, 1991; Lampert, 1990). Our study of classrooms in the Fostering Communities of Learners project, described above, contributes to this literature and proposes that authority, accountability, problematizing, and access to resources are critical factors in supporting productive engagement by students in activities of disciplinary learning (Engle and Conant, 2002).

Level 4

Issues at this level involve long-term conceptual growth and orientations toward learning practices. Psychological accounts of these factors include the large literature in cognitive development and general motivational orientations, such as achievement values (e.g., Graham and Taylor, 2002), orientation toward learning goals versus performance goals (Dweck and Legett, 1988), and individuals' beliefs about themselves as learners and knowers (Belenky et al., 1986).

Situative studies of conceptual growth have provided analyses of changes in discourse practices, in which participants' conceptual discourse can become more elaborated and integrated, can include representational practices used in conceptual reasoning and understanding, and can include more advanced forms of explanation and argumentation (Bowers, Cobb, and McClain, 1999; Greeno et al., 1998; Hall and Rubin, 1998; Lampert, 2001; Rosebery, Warren, and Conant, 1992; Strom, Lehrer, and Forman, 2001).

I believe that the concept of intellective identities can provide a way of framing research questions and explanations that can support the next level of integration between the social and individual perspectives on learning and cognition. Studies of classroom practices have focussed mainly on patterns that support different kinds of participation by students and the development of more advanced knowing and understanding of subject-matter concepts in the class as a whole. There has been relatively less attention, in these studies, to learning and development by individual students. By understanding identities as developed relationally in interaction, we may be able to understand how identities of students and teachers, and the social practices of classrooms, can be understood as two analytical perspectives, allowing us to understand individuals' learning and knowing both as aspects of their social participation and of their personal intellective growth and development.

A QUESTION FOR PRACTICE AND POLICY

I argue in this chapter that a concept of *intellective identities* provides a plausible and potentially productive way to formulate some significant aspects of learning in school. The importance of identity development in school has been recognized by many researchers and scholars. Ethnographic studies of high schools such as Eckert's (1989), Fine's (1991), Olsen's (1997), Weiler's (2000), and Wexler's (1992) have focussed on students' identities in school. Meier's (1995) discussion of learning, teaching, and the curriculum at Central Park East Secondary School emphasized students working individually and collaboratively with each other, with guidance by teachers, accountable for development of intellectual products for which they had primary individual responsibility. In the classrooms organized according to the Fostering Communities of Learners project (Brown and Campione, 1994), groups of students are responsible for developing academic products collaboratively, with each individual primarily responsible for information in one or two of its sections, and every student is responsible for presenting the whole report in another group.

The evidence and analyses I discuss here are limited to the affordances and development of positional identities in classrooms. The issues raised at the beginning of the chapter are broader than single classrooms. There is some suggestive evidence that the kinds of identities students can develop in mathematics classrooms affect their general identities, at least regarding the subject-matter of mathematics. Boaler (1997) found that students who learned mathematics in an environment involving exploration and inquiry developed what she called a different *form of knowledge* from that developed by students in a didactic learning environment that emphasized learning correct performance of procedures. These students treated mathematics as a resource for understanding and solving problems and reported that they considered the thinking they did in mathematics as being continuous with the kinds of thinking they did in everyday activities. Similarly, in interviews reported by Boaler and Greeno (2000), most students in Advanced Placement calculus courses that included extensive discussions of concepts and methods reported that they considered mathematics a subject that they enjoyed and were engaged in, in contrast to most students whose AP calculus courses positioned them simply as recipients of knowledge. Boaler (2001) has suggested that these findings indicate that differences in the ways that students participate in mathematics classes influence their identities regarding the subject matter domain, and I join her in that suggestion.

If this suggestion is supported in further research and development, it can inform discussions of educational practice and policy by raising a fundamental issue about educational aims. If development of the concepts of intellective competence and intellective identities is theoretically productive, it will become feasible and desirable to consider whether and how these ideas can become part of our explicit agenda for students' growth in their school learning. If the growth of intellective competence and identities were to be adopted and taken seriously as an explicit aim in education, it would have significant implications for the nature of the curriculum, teaching, and assessment. Curriculum resources designed to support students' participation with competence, authority, and accountability would be significantly different from curricula that are designed primarily to cover a list of content topics. Teachers explicitly entitled to and responsible for fostering development of their students' intellective competence and identities would need to function as mentors, as well as transmitters and coaches in their students'

learning. This would significantly affect the ways in which teacher education and professional development occur and would require a different
kind of professional standing for teachers than they now have.

I believe that the research in which the concepts of intellective competence and identity are developing is promising and may well lead to a basis
for reformulating our aims in education. But much remains to be done. I
look forward to the next developments.

ACKNOWLEDGMENTS

The research results discussed in this chapter have been obtained in projects
funded by grants from the Spencer Foundation and the National Science
Foundation. I am grateful to Edmund Gordon for several conversations
about intellective competence and related concepts, which occurred in the
course of my appointment as a visiting scholar to the College Board. I am
also grateful for comments on a draft of this chapter by Jo Boaler, Faith
Conant, Frank Davis, Randi Engle, Sten Ludvigsen, Na'ilah Nasir, and Mary
Maxwell West. Portions of this chapter were presented as an invited address
at the annual meeting of the American Psychological Association in San
Francisco, August 2001.

REFERENCES

Ball, D. L. 1993. With an eye on the mathematical horizon: Dilemmas of teaching
    elementary school mathematics. *Elementary School Journal*, 93, 373–97.
Ball, D. L., and Bass, H. 2000. Making believe: The collective construction of public
    mathematical knowledge in the elementary classroom. In D. C. Phillips (Ed.),
    Constructivism in education: Opinions and second opinions on controversial issues (pp.
    193–224). *Ninety-ninth yearbook of the National Society for the Study of Education.*
    Chicago: University of Chicago Press.
Beach, K. 1995. Activity as a mediator of sociocultural change and individual devel-
    opment: The case of school-work transition in Nepal. Mind, Culture, and Activity,
    2, 285–302.
———. 1999. Consequential transitions: A sociocultural expedition beyond transfer
    in education. *Review of Research in Education, 26.*
Belenky, M. F., Clinchy, B. M., Goldberger, N. R., and Tarule, J. M. 1986. *Women's
    ways of knowing.* New York: Basic Books.
Boaler, J. 1997. *Experiencing school mathematics: Teaching styles, sex and setting.* Buck-
    ingham, England: Open University Press.
———. 2001. Opening the dimensions of mathematical capability: The develop-
    ment of knowledge, practice, and identity in mathematics discourse. In R. Speiser,
    C. A. Maher, and C. N. Walter (Eds.), *Proceedings of the Twenty-Third Annual Meet-*

ing of the International Group for the Psychology of Mathematics Education (vol. 1, pp. 3–21). Columbus, OH: Eric Clearinghouse for Science, Mathematics, and Environmental Education.

Boaler, J., and Greeno, J. G. 2000. Identity, agency, and knowing in mathematics worlds. In J. Boaler (Ed.), *Multiple perspectives on mathematics teaching and learning* (pp. 171–200). Stamford, CT: Elsevier Science.

Bowers, J., Cobb, P., and McClain, K. 1999. The evolution of mathematical practices: A case study. *Cognition and Instruction*, 17, 25–64.

Brown, A. L., and Campione, J. C. 1994. Guided discovery in a community of learners. In K. McGilly (Ed.), *Classroom lessons: Integrating cognitive theory and classroom practice* (pp. 229–70). Cambridge, MA: MIT Press.

Clark, H. H. 1996. *Using language*. Cambridge, England: Cambridge University Press.

Clark, H. H., and Schaefer, E. F. 1989. Contributing to discourse. *Cognitive Science*, 13, 259–94.

Di Sessa, A. A. 1985. Learning about knowing. In E. L. Klein (Ed.), *Children and computers* (pp. 97–124). *New Directions for Child Development*, no. 28. San Francisco: Jossey-Bass.

Dunbar, K. 1995. How scientists really reason: Scientific reasoning in real-world laboratories. In R. J. Sternberg and J. E. Davidson (Eds.), *The nature of insight* (pp. 365–95). Cambridge, MA: MIT Press/Bradford.

Duncker, K. 1945. On problem solving. *Psychological Monographs*, 58 (Whole No. 270). (Originally published in German, 1935.)

Dweck, C. S., and Legett, E. L. 1988. A social-cognitive approach to motivation and personality. *Psychological Review*, 95, 256–73.

Eckert, P. 1989. *Jocks and burnouts*. New York: Teachers College Press.

Engle, R. A., and Conant, F. 2002. Guiding principles for fostering productive disciplinary engagement: Explaining an emergent argument in a community of learners classroom. *Cognition and Instruction*.20, no. 4, 399–483.

Engle, R. A., and Greeno, J. G. 1994. Managing disagreement in intellectual conversations: Coordinating social and conceptual concerns in the collaborative construction of mathematical explanations. *Proceedings of the Sixteenth Annual Conference of the Cognitive Science Society*. Hillsdale, NJ: Lawrence Erlbaum.

Fine, M. 1991. *Framing dropouts*. Albany, NY: State University of New York Press.

Gentner, D., Holyoak, K. J., and Kokinov, B. N., eds. 2001. *The analogical mind: Perspectives from cognitive science*. Cambridge, MA: MIT Press/Bradford.

Godfrey, L., and O'Connor, M. C. 1995. The vertical hand span: Non-standard units, expressions, and symbols in the classroom. *Journal of Mathematical Behavior*, 14, 327–45.

Goffman, E. 1959. *The presentation of self in everyday life*. New York: Doubleday/Anchor.

———. 1981. *Forms of talk*. Philadelphia: University of Pennsylvania Press.

Goodwin, C. 1995. Seeing in depth: *Social Studies of Science*, 25, 237–74.

Gordon, E. W. 2000. Pedagogy and the development of intellective competence. Presented at the College Board National Forum, October, New York.

Graham, S., and Taylor, A. Z. 2002. Ethnicity, gender, and the development of achievement values. In A. Wigfield and J. S. Eccles (Eds.), *Development of achievement motivation*. San Diego, CA: Academic Press.

Greeno, J. G. 1991. Number sense as situated knowing in a conceptual domain. *Journal for Research in Mathematics Education,* 23, 170–218.

Greeno, J. G., Benke, G., Engle, R. A., Lachapelle, C., and Wiebe, M. 1998. Considering conceptual growth as change in discourse practices. In M. A. Gernsbacher and S. J. Derry (Eds.), *Proceedings of the Twentieth Annual Conference of the Cognitive Science Society* (pp. 442–47). Mahwah, NJ: Erlbaum.

Greeno, J. G., and Engle, R. A. 1995. Combining analyses of cognitive processes, meanings, and social participation: Understanding symbolic representations. *Proceedings of the Seventeenth Annual Conference of the Cognitive Science Society,* Pittsburgh, PA.

Greeno, J. G., Sommerfeld, M. C., and Wiebe, M. 2000. Practices of questioning and explaining in learning to model. In L. R. Gleitman and A. K. Joshi (Eds.), *Proceedings of the Twenty-second Annual Conference of the Cognitive Science Society* (pp. 669–74). Mahwah, NJ: Lawrence Erlbaum Associates.

Gutiérrez, K. D., Baquedano-López, P., and Tejada, C. 1999. Rethinking diversity: Hybridity and hybrid language practices in the third space. *Mind, Culture, and Activity,* 6, 286–303.

Hall, R., and Rubin, A. 1998. There's five little notches in here: Dilemmas in teaching and learning the conventional structure of rate. In J. G. Greeno and S. V. Goldman (Eds.), *Thinking practices in mathematics and science learning* (pp. 189–235). Mahwah, NJ: Lawrence Erlbaum Associates.

Hanks, W. 1996. *Language and communicative practices.* Boulder, CO: Westview Press.

Hatano, G., and Inagaki, K. 1991. Sharing cognition through collective comprehension activity. In L. B. Resnick, J. M. Levine, and S. D. Teasley (Eds.), *Perspectives on socially shared cognition* (pp. 331–48). Washington, D.C.: American Psychological Association.

Hayes, J. R., and Simon, H. A. 1974. Understanding problem instructions. In L. W. Gregg (Ed.), *Knowledge and cognition.* Hillsdale, NJ: Lawrence Erlbaum Associates.

Holland, D., Lachicotte, W., Skinner, D., and Cain, C. 1998. *Identity and agency in cultural worlds.* Cambridge, MA: Harvard University Press.

Hutchins, E. 1995. *Cognition in the wild.* Cambridge, MA: MIT Press.

Just, M. A., and Carpenter, P. A. 1980. A theory of reading: From eye fixations to comprehension. *Psychological Review,* 87, 329–54.

Kintsch, W. 1998. *Comprehension: A paradigm for cognition.* Cambridge, England: Cambridge University Press.

Lampert, M. 1990. When the problem is not the question and the solution is not the answer: Mathematical knowing and teaching. *American Educational Research Journal,* 27, 29–63.

———. 2001. *Teaching problems and the problems of teaching.* New Haven: Yale University Press.

Lave, J., and Wenger, E. 1991. *Situated learning: Legitimate peripheral participation.* Cambridge, England: Cambridge University Press.

Lipka, J., with Mohatt, G. V., and the Ciulistet Group. 1998. *Transforming the culture of schools: Yup'ik Eskimo examples.* Mahwah, NJ: Lawrence Erlbaum Associates.

Mead, G. H. 1934. *Mind, self, and society from the standpoint of a social behaviorist* (C. W. Morris, ed.). Chicago: University of Chicago Press.

Mehan, H. 1979. *Learning lessons: Social organization in the classroom.* Cambridge, MA: Harvard University Press.

Meier, D. 1995. *The power of their ideas.* Boston: Beacon Press.

Moll, L. C., and Greenberg, J. B. 1990. Creating zones of possibilities: Combining social contexts for instruction. In L. C. Moll (Ed.), *Vygotsky and education: Instructional implications and applications of sociohistorical psychology.* Cambridge, England: Cambridge University Press.

Moses, R. P., and Cobo, C. E. 2001. *Radical Equations: Civil Rights from Mississippi to the Algebra Project.* Boston: Beacon Press.

Moses, R. P., and Cobb, C. E., Jr. 2001. *Radical equations: Math literacy and civil rights.* Boston: Beacon Press.

Ochs, E., Jacoby, S., and Gonzalez, P. 1994. "When I come down I'm in the domain state": Grammar and graphic representation in the interpretive activity of physicists. In E. Ochs, E. A. Schegloff, and S. A. Thompson (Eds.), *Interaction and grammar* (pp. 328–69). Cambridge, England: Cambridge University Press.

O'Connor, M. C., and Michaels, S. 1996. Shifting participant frameworks: Orchestrating thinking practices in group discussion. In D. Hicks (Ed.), *Discourse, learning, and schooling* (pp. 63–103). Cambridge, England: Cambridge University Press.

Okada, T., and Simon, H. A. 1997. Collaborative discovery in a scientific domain. *Cognitive Science,* 21, 109–146.

Olsen, L. 1997. *Made in America: Immigrant students in our public schools.* New York: New Press.

Packer, M. In press. The problem of transfer, and the sociocultural critique of schooling. *Journal of the Learning Sciences.*

Packer, M. J., and Goicoechea, J. 2000. Sociocultural and constructivist theories of learning: Ontology, not just epistemology. *Educational Psychologist,* 35, 227–41.

Pickering, A. 1995. *The mangle of practice.* Chicago: University of Chicago Press.

Polya, G. (1954). *Induction and analogy in mathematics.* Princeton: Princeton University Press.

Quine, W. V. 1981. *Theories and things.* Cambridge, MA: Harvard University Press.

Rosebery, A., Warren, B., and Conant, F. 1992. Appropriating scientific discourse: Findings from language minority classrooms. *Journal of the Learning Sciences,* 2, 61–94.

Schoenfeld, A. H. 1998. Making mathematics and making pasta: From cookbook procedures to really cooking. In J. G. Greeno and S. V. Goldman (Eds.), *Thinking practices in mathematics and science learning* (pp. 299–319). Mahwah, NJ: Lawrence Erlbaum Associates.

Schwartz, D. L. 1995. The emergence of abstract representations in dyad problem solving. *Journal of the Learning Sciences,* 4, 321–54.

———. 1999. The productive agency that drives collaborative learning. In P. Dillenbourg (Ed.), *Collaborative learning: Cognitive and computational approaches* (pp. 197–241). Amsterdam: Elsevier Science/Pergamon.

Stein, M. K., Grover, B. W., and Henningsen, M. 1996. Building student capacity for mathematical thinking and reasoning: An analysis of mathematical tasks used in reform classrooms. *American Educational Research Journal,* 33, 455–88.

Stein, M. K., Smith, M. S., Henningsen, M. A., and Silver, E. A. 2000. *Implementing standards-based mathematics education: A casebook for professional development.* New York: Teachers College Press.

Stenning, K., Greeno, J. G., Hall, R., Sommerfeld, M., and Wiebe, M. 2002. Coordinating mathematical with biological multiplication: Conceptual learning as the development of heterogeneous reasoning systems. In P. Brna, M. Baker, K. Stenning, and A. Tiberghien (Eds.), *The role of communication in learning to model* (pp. 3–48). Mahwah, NJ: Lawrence Erlbaum Associates.

Stipek, D. 1998. *Motivation to learn: From theory to practice.* Boston: Allyn and Bacon.

Strom, D., Kemeny, V., Lehrer, R., and Forman, E. 2001. Visualizing the emergent structure of children's mathematical argument. *Cognitive Science,* 25, 733–73.

Tudge, J., and Rogoff, B. 1989. Peer influences on cognitive development: Piagetian and Vygotskian perspectives. In M. H. Bornstein and J. S. Bruner (Eds.), *Cognition: Conceptual and methodological issues* (pp. 17–40). Hillsdale, NJ: Lawrence Erlbaum Associates.

Vygotsky, L. S. 1987. *Thinking and speech.* In R. W. Rieber and A. S. Carton (Eds.), *The collected works of L. S. Vygotsky. Volume 1: Problems of general psychology* (pp. 37–285). New York: Plenum. (Original work published in Russian, 1934.)

Weiler, J. D. 2000. *Codes and contradictions: Race, gender identity, and schooling.* Albany, NY: State University of New York Press.

Wenger, E. 1998. *Communities of practice: Learning, meaning, and identity.* Cambridge, England: Oxford University Press.

Wexler, P. 1992. *Becoming somebody: Toward a social psychology of school.* London: Falmer Press.

Woolgar, S. 1990. Time and documents in researcher interaction: Some ways of making out what is happening in experimental science. In M. Lynch and S. Woolgar (Eds.), *Representation in scientific practice* (pp. 123–52). Cambridge, MA: MIT Press.

Yackel, E., and Cobb, P. 1996. Sociomathematical norms, argumentation, and autonomy in mathematics. *Journal for Research in Mathematics Education,* 27, 458–77.

NOTES

1. Holland et al.'s (1998) examples of figured social worlds included the collection of interactions, feelings, and beliefs regarding heterosexual romance in the lives of women students on some American college campuses, the system of caste and gender in Nepal, membership in Alcoholics Anonymous, and a system of beliefs and interactions involving mental illness. They emphasize that figured social worlds afford different ways of participating, or *positional identities,* that characterize different individuals' interactions in the system. For example, there were significant differences individual women's identities in the social world of romantic attractiveness, with some women conforming to the prevalent values of striving to be attractive to men, and others resisting those values and constructing identities organized in opposition to them. In Alcoholics Anonymous, members differed in their levels of advancement in the organization's program, with more advanced members having capabilities, expections, entitlements, and obligations

that exceeded those of newcomers. (Lave and Wenger, 1991, used this as a prime example of transitions from peripheral toward full membership in a community of practice.) Individuals also differed in their degree of engagement and commitment in the organization, with some members developing identities organized mainly by their engaged participation in the activities of being a recovering alcoholic, and others whose participation was sporadic and insufficiently committed to the values of sobriety to support the transformation of identity that Alcoholics Anonymous is organized to try to bring about. Holland et al. also reported examples of *authoring*, particularly in Nepal, in which individuals complied with constraints of the caste and gender system creatively and joined with others in constructing transformations of their social world.

2. To say that agency is turned over to the material apparatus is not to deny that scientists exert considerable agency in determining whether any specific running of an experiment satisfied the conditions that are required for the results to count as data (Woolgar, 1990).

3. This is a view of the "transfer problem" that differs from the usual cognitivist version in which the question is whether someone acquires knowledge in one setting and then may or may not retrieve and use that knowledge in another situation. The situative view that emphasizes development of identities focuses, instead, on ways in which patterns of participation, including positioning, that an individual has learned in one setting are supported in a different community that the individual enters. This view has received considerably less attention, except from a few investigators, notably Beach (1995; 1999), and Packer (in press).

4. Traditionally, the trip taken for this purpose involves public transportation, such as the "T" in Boston, and the sites that are points along the trip line are stations. In this case, to save time and expense, a trip to the science museum did double duty. The sites chosen for the trip included exhibits at the museum, such as dinosaurs, as well as landmarks, such as a fountain.

5. Of course, professional biologists harbor no real uncertainty about the proper classification of orcas. The students' attribution was not unreasonable, however. In the texts they consulted, orcas were sometimes characterized as dolphins and sometimes as whales. In the accepted classification, orcas are members of the family Delphinidae, often referred to collectively as dolphins, but orcas and dolphins are included in the order Cetacea, often referred to collectively as whales.

3

Intelligence as a
Socialized Phenomenon

Robert J. Sternberg
Yale University

Elena L. Grigorenko
Yale University and Moscow State University

Beatrice L. Bridglall
Teachers College, Columbia University

HISTORICAL CONCEPTIONS OF
INTELLIGENCE AND EDUCABILITY

The history of man, and in particular, the history of education and theories of educability is marked by a continuous struggle for more and better education for more people. In the battle between the educational "haves" and the "have-nots" (who are usually identified with the economic "haves" and "have-nots"), every gain is countered by another obstacle to the realization of its full benefits.

Schwebel, 1968:5

Jencks and Phillips (1998), Miller (1995), Reardon (2003), and others document the persistent academic underachievement of many students of color when compared with many of their European and Asian American counterparts. Implicit in these researchers' work is the idea that the current, qualitative state of education for many students of color is plagued by mediocre performance and an exaggerated focus on governance and accountability that is punctuated by some efforts at nurturing academic excellence that is not the norm. Some of the possible explanations for this distressing situation are also elaborated. One of the more deep-seated explanations, however, may be the implicit theory of intelligence that continues to operate among some people in the United States and elsewhere, despite scientific evidence to the contrary: This implicit theory of intelligence suggests that the cognitive ability of those in the lower stratum of society, many African Americans in this instance, is genetically inferior to that of European Americans (Brand, 1996; Herrnstein and Murray, 1994; Jensen, 1998; Rushton and Jensen, 2005; but see Sternberg, 2005; Sternberg, Grigorenko, and Kidd, 2005). This implicit theory concerning the distribution of intelligence was also used earlier in the twentieth century to question the cognitive abilities of various immigrant groups in the United States, all of them "white" (Sarason and Doris, 1979).

Our review of various conceptions of educability in the history of the Western world indicates that for over 2,500 years, intellectual leaders have divided education into the manual and the mental, with the assumption that most people would benefit from vocational training and few from the cultivation of intellectual abilities (Kozol, 1991). Although the introduction of democratic theories and processes caused some reluctant yielding under great pressure, it also spawned barriers to education based on the rationale that the lower socioeconomic classes are thought to be cognitively limited. This implicit theory of the distribution of intelligence was related to, although not necessarily directly resulting from, Plato's categorization of the various socioeconomic classes.

One of the modern concomitants of this theory is the intelligence (IQ) test. Although this test is not intrinsically good or bad, when misused or its data misinterpreted it has been shown to negatively impact students' self-expectations and sense of agency in addition to parents' and teachers' expectations (Beaujean, 2005; Resnick, 1979). It is still used by some to rationalize differentiated curriculum and instruction for high-achieving students, usually from high-status groups, and low-quality general or vocational education for those in the lower stratum of society (Schwebel, 2003; Sarich and Miele, 2004). Overreliance on IQ testing and similar measures has led not only to the segregation of high socioeconomic status students from their low socioeconomic status counterparts in different districts across the country, but also to segregation within the same school building, often by socially defined race. That is, based on test scores and some even more questionable indicators, European American students from the higher socioeconomic strata typically are provided with more rigorous curricula and better-prepared teachers than are African-American students from lower socioeconomic strata (Miller, 1995; Sternberg, 2000; College Board, 1999). Some users of these tests maintain the belief that they measure static ability, that is, ability that is fixed and largely unmodifiable from birth.

We believe that the prevailing theory of the unmodifiability of abilities is unfounded. Moreover, it contributes to our failure to modify teaching and learning appropriately into effective mechanisms for improving the lot of the many diverse students in this country (Sternberg, 1997). We are not suggesting that genetics plays no role in cognitive ability; rather, we assert that genes do not determine absolute boundaries of intelligence for individuals or populations (Martinez, 2000). Relative to the thorny problem of the persistent academic achievement gap between majority and minority students, genes apparently play an important role in explaining differences *within* socially defined races, while environment accounts for most of the gap *between* blacks and whites, leaving relatively little role for genetics (Dickens, 2005).

One of the assumptions undergirding the preponderance of views that support environment as explaining some of the differentials in academic achievement between majority and minority students is that certain experiences influence what is defined and valued as intelligence in different societies (Sternberg, 2004; Sternberg and Grigorenko, 1997). In the West, these experiences include cognitive stimulation during infancy, early childhood interventions, rigorous and demanding curricula throughout the pre-K–16 continuum, supplementary educational services (i.e., quality health care, adequate nutrition, exposure to travel, music, and art), and meaningful employment (Bridglall and Gordon, 2002; Gordon, Bridglall and Meroe, 2005). Interventions that provide these and other experiences (that are thoughtfully conceived, implemented, and assessed with a view to adapting to changing contexts), can also modify intelligence (Martinez, 2000). In this chapter, we support our argument that as a socialized phenomena, intelligence is inherently modifiable, with evidence that (1) the heritability coefficient of intelligence needs to be understood for what it is, not for what it sometimes appears to be (Sternberg and Grigorenko, 1999a, 1999b; Sternberg, Grigorenko and Kidd, 2005); (2) intelligence is a socialized phenomenon (Sternberg and Suben, 1986); and (3) intelligence means different things in different cultures. Again, we are not denying the influence of genetic mechanisms but rather pointing out that they function in more complex and variegated ways than is often believed.

HERITABILITY

Heritability (also referred to as h^2) is the ratio of genetic variation to total variation of an attribute *within* a population. Thus the coefficient of heritability tells us nothing about sources of between-population variation. Moreover, the coefficient of heritability does *not* tell us the proportion of a trait that is genetic in absolute terms, but rather, the proportion of variation in a trait that is attributable to genetic variation *within* a specific population. Observable trait variation in a population is referred to as phenotypic variation, whereas genetic variation in a population is referred to as genotypic variation. Heritability is a ratio of genotypic variation to phenotypic variation.

Heritability has a complementary concept, that of environmentality. Environmentality is a ratio of environmental variation to phenotypical variation. Both heritability and environmentality apply to populations, however, not to individuals. There is no way of estimating heritability for an individual, nor is the concept meaningful for individuals. Consider a trait that has a heritability of .70; it is nonsense to say that the development of the trait in an individual is 70 percent genetic. Rather, this figure means that 70 percent of the variation in a trait within a population appears to be due to genetic factors, including, in broad heritability, gene-environment covariation.

Heritability is typically expressed on a 0 to 1 scale, with a value of 0 indicating no heritability whatsoever (i.e., no genetic variation in the trait) and a value of 1 indicating complete heritability (i.e., only genetic variation in the trait). Heritability and environmentality add to unity.[1] In conjunction, they tell us the proportion of variation in an attribute that appears to be attributable to genetic versus environmental sources of variation within a population. Thus, if IQ has a heritability of .50 within a certain population, then 50 percent of the variation in scores on the attribute within that population is due (in theory) to genetic influences. This statement is completely different from the statement that 50 percent of the attribute is inherited.

An important implication of these facts is that heritability is *not* tantamount to genetic influence. An attribute could be highly genetically influenced and have little or no heritability. The reason is that heritability depends on the existence of individual differences. If there are no individual differences, there is no heritability (because there is a 0 in the denominator of the ratio of genetic to total trait variation in a given population). For example, being born with two eyes is 100 percent under genetic control (except in the exceedingly rare case of severe dismorphologies, which we do not address here). Regardless of the environment into which one is born, a human being will have two eyes. But it is not meaningful to speak of the heritability of having two eyes, because there are no individual differences. Heritability in this case is not 1: It is meaningless and cannot be sensibly calculated.[2] Consider a second, complementary example: occupational status. It has a statistically significant heritability coefficient associated with it (Plomin, DeFries, and McClearn, 1990), but it certainly is not under direct genetic control. Clearly there is no gene or set of genes for occupational status. How can it be heritable, then? Heredity can affect certain factors that in turn lead people to occupations of higher or lower status. Thus, if things like intelligence, personality, and interpersonal attractiveness are under some degree of genetic control, they may lead in turn to differences in occupational status. The effects of genes are at best indirect (Block, 1995). Other attributes, such as divorce, may run in families, that is, show familiality, but again, they are not under direct genetic control; in fact, the familiality may be because they are culturally "inherited."

Heritability Can Vary within a Given Population

Heritability is not a fixed value for a given attribute. Although we may read about "the heritability of IQ" (e.g., Herrnstein and Murray, 1994), there really is no single fixed value that represents any true, constant value for the heritability of IQ or anything else, as Herrnstein and Murray (1994) and most others in the field (e.g., Bouchard, 1997) recognize. Heritability depends on many factors, but the most important one is the range of environments. Because heritability represents a proportion of variation, its value will depend on the amount of variation. As Herrnstein (1973) pointed out, if there were no variation in environments, heritability would be perfect, because there would be no other source of variation. If there is wide variation in environments, however, heritability is likely to decrease.

When one speaks of heritability, one needs to remember that genes always operate within environmental contexts. All genetic effects occur within a reaction range, so that, inevitably, diverse environments will have differential effects on the same genetic structure. The reaction range is the range of phenotypes (observable effects of genes) that a given genotype (latent structure of genes) for any particular attribute can produce, given the interaction of environment with that genotype. For example, genotype sets a reaction range for the possible heights a person can attain, but childhood nutrition, disease, and many other factors affect the adult height that is realized. Moreover, if different genotypes react differently to the environmental variation, heritability will show differences depending on the mean and variance in relevant environments (Lewontin, 1974). Thus, the statistic is not a fixed value. There are no pure genetic effects on behavior, as would be shown dramatically if a child were raised in a small closet with no stimulation. Genes express themselves through covariation and interaction with the environment, as discussed below.

Heritability and Modifiability

Because the value of the heritability statistic is relevant only to existing circumstances, it does not and cannot address a trait's modifiability. A trait could have zero, moderate, or even total heritability and, in any of these conditions, be not at all, partially, or fully modifiable. The heritability statistic deals with correlations, whereas modifiability deals with mean effects. Correlations, however, are independent of score levels. For example, adding a constant to a set of scores will not affect the correlation of that set with another set of scores. Consider height as an example of the limitation of the heritability statistic in addressing modifiability. Height is highly heritable, with a heritability of over .90. Yet height also is highly modifiable, as shown by the fact that average heights have risen dramatically throughout the past several generations.

As an even more extreme example, consider phenylketonuria (PKU). PKU is a genetically determined, recessive condition that arises due to a mutation in a single gene on chromosome 12 (with a heritability of 1), and yet its effects are highly modifiable. Feeding an infant with PKU a diet free of phenylalanine prevents the mental retardation that otherwise would become obvious. This type of mental retardation was once incorrectly thought to be purely genetic, but it is not. Rather, the mental retardation associated with PKU is the result of the interaction with an environment (a "normal" diet) in which the infant ingests phenylalanine. Take away the phenylalanine and you reduce the level of, or in optimal cases, eliminate mental retardation. Note that the genetic endowment does not change; the infant still has a mutant gene causing phenylketonuria. What changes is the manifestation of its associated symptoms in the environment. Similarly, with intelligence or any other trait, we cannot change (at least based on our knowledge today) the genetic structure underlying manifestations of intelligence, but we can change those manifestations, or expressions of genes in the environment. Thus, knowing the heritability of a trait does not tell us anything about its modifiability.

Within-population Effects versus Between-population Effects

One of the worst intellectual slips that has been made by investigators of heredity and environment (or rather, most often, by interpreters of findings on heredity and environment) is to generalize the effects of within-population studies between populations. For example, some investigators have made attributions about effects of racial or ethnic group differences on the basis of behavior-genetic studies (Herrnstein and Murray, 1994), even while admitting that such conclusions are sometimes flawed. All of the behavior-genetic designs in the studies noted above can ascertain effects of genetic variation only within populations. For example, they may tell us something about the extent to which individual differences in the measured intelligence of people in a particular group are associated with genetic factors. They say nothing about sources of between-population differences in levels of measured intelligence.

Lewontin (1972, 1982) illustrated the impossibility of making between-population claims from within-population data. In a study using a set of protein markers (blood groups, serum proteins, and red blood cell enzymes) as indicators of genetic differences between populations, Lewontin estimated that roughly 85 percent of the genetic variance occurs between any two individuals within any socially identified racial group, roughly 9 percent occurs among different populations within a socially identified race, and only the remaining 6 to 7 percent occurs between socially identified races. Other researchers arrived at the same conclusions using more powerful data sets obtained with more technologically advanced methodologies (Barbujani et al., 1997; Kidd et. al., in press; Rosenberg et. al., 2002; Tishkoff and Kidd, in press) or through simulation analyses (Templeton, 1999).

Different populations—racial, ethnic, and religious for example—may encounter quite different environments, on average. Whatever the heritability of intelligence or other attributes within a given setting, no conclusions can be drawn about heritability as a source of differences across settings. The fact that IQs have increased so much over the years (Flynn, 1984, 1987; Neisser, 1998) suggests that environments differ widely over time. They likely differ substantially as well for members of different groups at a given time.

Nisbett (1995, 1998) reviewed published studies investigating sources of differences in cognitive abilities between white and black individuals. These studies, using designs unlike the behavior-genetic studies described above, have directly sought to investigate genetic and environmental effects on intelligence. For example, one design investigated black children adopted by white parents. Of seven published studies, six supported primarily environmental interpretations of group differences, and only one study did not; the results of this one study (Scarr and Weinberg, 1976, 1983) are equivocal. The Scarr and Weinberg study did show that IQs of adopted children were more similar to those of their biological mothers than to those of their adopted mothers. Less clear however, were the "racial" implications of their findings.

Moreover, there is increasing evidence that heritability estimates vary across populations. For example, estimates of the heritability of IQ in Russian twin studies conducted in the Soviet era tended to be higher than comparable estimates in the United States (Egorova, 1988; Grigorenko, 1990; Iskoldsky, 1988). This observation made sense: Environmental variation in Russia under the Soviet regime was constrained; consequently, heritability estimates were higher. Most of the IQ heritability studies until recently have been carried out in various countries of the developed world. Relatively little information exists concerning the heritability of IQ in the developing world, although some studies suggest that heritability may be substantial, at least outside the Western countries most often studied (Bratko, 1996; Lynn and Hattori, 1990; Nathwar and Puri, 1995; Pal, Shyam, and Singh, 1997). Recently, Turkheimer and colleagues (2003) showed that heritabilities differ radically across socioeconomic groups. Obviously, without knowing much about estimates of the heritability of IQ in different populations, we cannot speculate at this point about differences across these populations. At this juncture, heritability estimates do not explain the genetic regulation of behavior and do not provide accurate estimates of the strength of the genetic regulation. Heritabilities are like snapshots of a dancer; they do not tell us either what the dance is about or what is coming next in the dance. The true genetic nature of humans is far from being defined. What *is* absolutely clear is that genes do not act in a vacuum; they act in the environment, and their actions can be altered by the environment. Thus, what are sometimes viewed as genetic differences between groups actually reflect socialization differences (Sternberg, 2004; Sternberg and Suben, 1986). How is intelligence socialized?

INTELLIGENCE IS SOCIALIZED

Below we examine a number of factors regarding how intelligence is socialized.

Children Develop Contextually Important Skills That May Be More Relevant to One Context Than to Another.

Many times, investigations of intelligence conducted in settings outside the developed world can yield a picture of intelligence that is quite at variance with that obtained from studies conducted only in the developed world. In a study conducted in Usenge, Kenya (near the town of Kisumu), Sternberg, Grigorenko and their colleagues devised and administered a test of practical intelligence in adaptation to the environment to examine school-age children's ability to adapt to their indigenous environment (Sternberg and Grigorenko, 1997; Sternberg et al., 2001). Their test of practical intelligence measured children's informal tacit knowledge of natural herbal medicines that they and the villagers believe can be used to fight various types of infections. Sternberg and his colleagues found that the village children used their knowledge of these medicines an average of once a week in medicating themselves and others. This knowledge appears to be essential since more than 95 percent of the children suffer from parasitic illnesses. Consequently, tests of how to use these medicines constitute effective measures of one aspect of practical intelligence as defined by the villagers relative to the contexts of their life circumstances. Middle-class Westerners may find it a challenge to thrive or even survive in these contexts, or for that matter, in the contexts of urban ghettos that are often not far from their comfortable homes. They would not know, for example, how to use any of the natural herbal medicines to treat the diverse and abundant parasitic illnesses they may acquire in rural Kenya.

Sternberg, Grigorenko, and their colleagues measured the Kenyan children's ability to identify the medicines, where they come from, what they are used for, and how they are dosed. Based on work they have done elsewhere, they expected that scores on this test would not correlate with scores on conventional tests of intelligence. In order to test this hypothesis, they administered the Raven Coloured Progressive Matrices Test (Raven, Court, and Raven, 1992), a measure of fluid or abstract-reasoning-based abilities, and the Mill Hill Vocabulary Scale (Raven, et al., 1992), a measure of crystallized or formal-knowledge-based abilities, to their sample of eighty-five children. Additionally, they gave the children a comparable test of vocabulary in their own language, Dholuo, which is spoken in the home, while English is spoken in the schools. As expected, these researchers did not find a correlation between the test of indigenous tacit knowledge and scores on the fluid-ability tests. To their surprise, however, they found statistically significant correlations of the tacit-knowledge tests with the tests of crystallized abilities. The correlations, nevertheless, were *negative*. That is, the higher the children scored on the test of tacit knowledge, the lower they scored, on average, on the tests of crystallized abilities.

Although this surprising result can be interpreted a number of ways, the ethnographic observations of the anthropologists on their team (P. Wenzel Geissler and Ruth Prince) led to these scholars' collective conclusion that a plausible interpretation takes family expectations for their children into account. Apparently, many children, for financial or other reasons, drop out of school before graduation. Some of the reasons for this practice may hinge on the low value placed on Western schooling by many families in the village. From the perspective of the villagers, there are not many viable reasons to revere Western schooling. A contextual analysis by Sternberg, Grigorenko, and their colleagues suggest that there is no reason Western schooling should be valued since the children of many families will for the most part spend their lives farming or engaged in other occupations that make little or no use of Western schooling. Indeed, these families prefer that their children are taught the indigenous informal knowledge that they believe will help them to successfully adapt to the environments in which they will really live. Children who spend their time learning the indigenous practical knowledge of the community generally do not invest themselves heavily in doing well in school; whereas children who do well in school generally do not invest themselves as heavily in learning the indigenous knowledge—hence the negative correlations.

The Kenya study suggests that the identification of a general factor of human intelligence may tell us more about how abilities interact with patterns of schooling and society and especially Western patterns of schooling and society than it does about the structure of human abilities. In Western schooling, children typically study a variety of subject matters from an early age and thus develop skills in a variety of skill areas. This kind of schooling prepares these children to take a test of intelligence, which typically measures skills in a variety of areas. Often intelligence tests measure skills that children were expected to acquire a few years before taking the intelligence test. But as Rogoff (1990, 2003) and others have noted, this pattern of schooling is not universal and has not even been common for much of the history of humankind. Throughout history and in many places still, schooling, especially for boys, takes the form of apprenticeships in which children learn a craft from an early age. They learn what they will need to know in order to succeed in a trade, but not a lot more. They are not simultaneously engaged in tasks that require the development of the particular blend of skills measured by conventional intelligence tests. Hence it is less likely that one would observe a general factor in their scores, much as we discovered in Kenya. Almost thirty-five years ago, Vernon (1971) pointed out that the axes of a factor analysis do not necessarily reveal a latent structure of the mind but rather represent a convenient way of characterizing the organization of mental abilities. Vernon (1971) believed that there was no one "right" orientation of the axes, and that mathematically, an infinite number of orientations of axes can be fitted to any solution in an exploratory factor analysis. This important point seems to have been forgotten or at least ignored by later theorists.

Children May Have Substantial Practical Skills That Go Unrecognized in Academic Tests.

The context-specificity of intellectual performance does not apply only to countries far removed from North America or Europe. One can find the same on these continents, as Grigorenko and her colleagues (Grigorenko, Meier, Lipka, Mohatt, Yanez, and Sternberg, 2004) did in their studies of Yup'ik Eskimo children in southwestern Alaska. In this study, these researchers assessed the importance of academic and practical intelligence in rural and urban Alaskan communities. The practical skills of the 261 students in the sample were rated by adults or peers in the study. (Sixty-nine of the students were in grade 9; 69 were in grade 10; 45 in grade 11; and 37 in grade 12. With respect to gender and location, 145 females and 116 males came from 7 different communities, 6 rural and 1 relatively urban.) Grigorenko and her colleagues measured academic intelligence with conventional measures of fluid and crystallized intelligence and practical intelligence with a test of tacit knowledge (as acquired in rural Alaskan Yup'ik communities). Although the urban children generally outperformed the rural children on a measure of crystallized intelligence, the rural children generally outperformed the urban children on the measure of Yup'ik tacit knowledge. The test of tacit knowledge was superior to the tests of academic intelligence in predicting the practical skills of the rural children (for whom the test was created), but not of the urban ones. Similar to the Kenya study cited above, this study suggests the importance of practical intellectual skills for predicting adaptation to everyday environments. These and other studies done by

Sternberg, Grigorenko, and colleagues examined whether similar results can be found in cultures that are urban and somewhat less remote from the kinds of cultures familiar to many readers.

Dynamic Testing May Reveal Cognitive Skills not Revealed by Static Testing.

Dynamic testing is similar to conventional static testing in that students are tested and inferences about their abilities are made. But dynamic testing differs in that children are given some kind of feedback in order to help them improve their performance. This strategy emphasizes the formative use of testing to promote deep conceptual understanding and mastery of concepts that make up a discipline. This approach should ideally result in substantive knowledge and skill development. Vygotsky (1978) suggested that students' ability to profit from the guided instruction they receive during a testing situation could serve as a measure of children's zone of proximal development (ZPD), or the difference between their developed abilities and their latent capacities. In other words, testing and instruction are considered symbiotic rather than distinct processes. This integration makes sense relative to traditional definitions of intelligence as the ability to learn (Symposium on intelligence and its measurement, 1921; Sternberg and Detterman, 1986). Testing dynamically directly measures the processes of learning in the context of testing rather than measuring these processes indirectly as the product of past learning. Such measurement is especially important when not all students have had equitable opportunities to learn.

A study done in Tanzania (see Sternberg and Grigorenko, 1997, 2002b; Sternberg et al., 2002) points out the risks of giving tests, scoring them, and interpreting the results as measures of some latent intellectual ability or abilities. A form-board classification test (a sorting task), a linear syllogisms test, and a twenty questions test ("find a figure"), which measure the kinds of skills required on conventional tests of intelligence, were administered to 358 school children between the ages of eleven and thirteen years near Bagamoyo, Tanzania. Although Sternberg and Grigorenko obtained baseline scores that could be used to analyze, evaluate, and rank the children in terms of their supposed general or other abilities, they administered the tests dynamically rather than statically (Brown and Ferrara, 1985; Feuerstein, 1979; Grigorenko and Sternberg, 1998; Guthke, 1993; Haywood and Tzuriel, 1992; Lidz, 1991; Sternberg and Grigorenko, 2002a; Tzuriel, 1995; Vygotsky, 1978).

In the assessments, all children in the sample were first given the ability tests, whereupon children in the experimental group were given an intervention while those in the control group were not. The intervention consisted of a brief period of instruction in which children were able to learn skills that could potentially enable them to improve their scores. In the twenty-questions tasks, for example, children were taught how a single true-false question has a 50 percent chance of being correct, and this knowledge could increase the probability of possible correct solutions by half. After the intervention, all children from the experimental and control groups were tested again. The total time for instruction was less than an hour, and Sternberg and his colleagues did not expect dramatic gains. They found, however, that on average, the gains from pretest to posttest in the experimental group were statistically significant and significantly greater than those in the control group.[3]

Of course, the more important question is not whether the scores changed or even correlated with each other, but rather, how they correlated with other cognitive measures. In other words, was the pretest or the post-test score a better predictor of transfer to other cognitive performances on tests of working memory? These scholars found the posttest score to be the better predictor of working memory in the experimental group. Children in the dynamic-testing group improved significantly more than those in the control group.

Educability and Learning in Different Cultural Settings

Heath (1983) examined language development in three communities (Trackton, lower class black; Roadville, lower class white; and Gateway, middle class white) in the Piedmont Carolinas. It is possible to present here only a fraction of the observations she has made on the effects of the incongruency between what constitutes intelligent behavior from the school's perspective and from the community's perspective in which a given child was raised, but several examples suggest that educability and learning are functions of the characteristics that adhere to specific cultural practices and values.

Children in Trackton seem to be at a disadvantage from the school's perspective when they are not able to indicate whether they are present in class. For example, Trackton children did not generally expect adults to ask them questions nor were the children perceived as information-givers or as question-answerers (Heath, 1983:103). As a result, children consider being asked a question strange. For example, when Heath (1983) asked these children to engage in certain tasks or jobs, the children often protested because they saw no reason for doing these tasks. It appeared that these children particularly have trouble handling indirect requests such as, "It's time to put our paints away now." These unfamiliar kinds of statements may not even be perceived as requests (Heath, 1983: 280). These children also have difficulty with "Why?" questions, possibly because adults in Trackton do not engage children in conversations in which such questions are asked.

This practice is in stark contrast to typical middle class upbringing (Heath, 1983:109).

In Roadville and Gateway, however, children usually have had considerable experience with both direct and indirect requests. Adults also saw themselves as teachers who ask and answer questions including "Why?" questions (Heath, 1983:129). Differences in these towns were seen in the lack of persistence by Roadville parents in asking and answering their children's questions. Heath (1983) documented that once Roadville children started school, parents more or less abdicated their role as teachers to the school. From the parents' perspective, their days as teachers were over. Heath suggests that there was an implicit conflict in terms of resource allocation across the three communities she has examined. One of the ways middle class American schools prepare children for a schedule-dominated adulthood is through the expectation that the schools' fairly strict schedules will be observed. Place constraints are also equally important. Things are expected to be in their proper place at the proper time. In Trackton, however, Heath (1983) found that the flow of time was casual. There were no timed tasks at home, and few tasks that were even time-linked (Heath, 1983: 275). For example, people ate when they were hungry, and there were few constraints on those parts of the meal that preceded or followed each other. There were few scheduled activities, and routines, such as going to bed, happened at very different times on different days (Heath, 1983: 167). Children from Trackton thus found it difficult to adhere to a schedule that appeared essentially arbitrary and capricious. Timed tests also seemed even stranger than school schedules. These children's impressions concerning timed exams may also be a factor of literally having no experience with being timed in the performance of a cognitive task.

Children in Trackton also seemed to have similar difficulties with space allocation. Being told to put things in a certain place had little or no meaning to the Trackton child (Heath, 1983: 273). Heath suggested that although most of these children put their materials away after use, the place varied from time to time. She speculated that these children had so few possessions that it was generally not a problem finding the object later. Teachers, however, did not understand why Trackton children handled time and space poorly and were thus unfavorable in their judgments when these children started school.

Children from Roadville and Gateway had a very different sense of time and place. Roadville parents wanted their children to grow up with a very strict sense of everything having in its time and place (Heath, 1983: 137). In Roadville, even the stories emphasized certain sequences of events in a strict chronological order (Heath, 1983). In Gateway, life was strictly scheduled, and even babies were expected to adhere to this fairly strict scheduling (Heath, 1983: 243). Things had a time and a place. Children were expected to learn these rules just as they were later expected to adhere to them in school.

From the perspective of the dominant society, Trackton children were at a disadvantage when they started school because they did not understand similarities and differences among objects and skills that were important in school and critical on typical intelligence tests. Heath (1983) observed that Trackton children never spontaneously volunteered to list the attributes of two objects that were similar to or different from each other. Instead, they seemed to view objects holistically and compared objects as wholes rather than attribute by attribute. Although they may have been sensitive to shape, color, and size, they did not use these attributes to make judgments as to how the two objects were similar or different. This unfamiliarity with abstraction, and their viewing of things in holistic contexts, impeded their progress in reading as well as in reasoning. Some Trackton children experienced a holistic coherence with respect to printed words, such that if the print style, type font, or even the context of a given word changed, the child noticed the change and became upset. At the same time, some children failed to realize the symbolic equivalence of the print under these transformations, which, although relevant to the child, were irrelevant to the meaning of the printed word. Each new appearance of a word in a new context resulted in the perception of a different word.

The holistic perceptual and conceptual style of the Trackton child also interfered with the child's progress in mathematics, where one object plus another may be perceived as yielding one object, in that the two objects were viewed as a new whole rather than as composed of two discrete parts resulting from the summation. Rather than applying rules from one problem to another, children may have perceived each problem as a distinct whole that needed new rules rather than the transfer of old ones (Heath, 1983: 291).

The situation was quite different in Roadville. Adults encouraged children to label things and talked to them about the attributes of these things (Heath, 1983). A primary goal in adults' play with children was to encourage them to define the attributes of the play stimuli, and the toys the adults gave the children encouraged them to match attributes such as color, shape, size, and so on (Heath, 1983: 136). Gateway parents also gave their children educational toys from an early age. Children were encouraged to note points of similarity and difference between objects, and to label these differences as they were encountered (Heath, 1983: 351). Gateway parents talked to children about the names of things in books as well as in the world and discussed matters of size, shape, and color as they arose.

Like the Trackton children who sometimes perceived things in a holistic way, the Kpelle tribe in Africa viewed certain kinds of problems holistically, which inhibited the transfer of problem-solving skills to other contexts that appeared to be dissimilar. Cole and his colleagues showed that the

Kpelle were completely stymied by a problem in inferential combination that utilized an unfamiliar apparatus, but successfully solved an analogous problem that involved familiar objects (Cole, Gay, Glick, and Sharp, 1971). The American apparatus consisted of a box with three compartments. When a button was pushed on one of the compartment doors, a marble would be released. Pushing a button on a second door resulted in the release of a ball. Insertion of a marble into a hole in the third door led to the release of a piece of candy. Even though the Kpelle learned how to obtain the item from each compartment individually, they were almost always unable to figure out how to start with nothing and end up with a piece of candy (i.e., by pushing the button to get the marble and then inserting the marble into the hole in the other door). The second version of the problem was constructed so as to require the identical steps for its solution. In this case, the candy was in a box locked with a red key. Each of two nearby matchboxes contained a key; one key was red, the other, black. To solve this problem, the red key had to be removed from its matchbox and used to unlock the box containing the candy. After learning what the individual containers held, nearly all the Kpelle subjects solved this problem spontaneously. The lack of transfer to the American version of the problem can be attributed to the subjects' failure to compare the problems on a point-by-point basis. Holistically viewed, the American version seemed to be a totally new and different problem.

Trackton children's attitudes toward reading in addition to their perception of reading material placed them at additional disadvantage in the school setting. In their community, reading was strictly a group affair. An individual who chose to read on his or her own was viewed as antisocial, while solitary reading was considered for those who were unable to make it in the Trackton social milieu (Heath, 1983). Further, Heath (1983) observed that children had little opportunity to practice reading or to be read to since there were few magazines, books, or other reading materials in Trackton. In contrast, Roadville parents frequently read to their children, especially at night. McDermott (1974) noted that reading is an act that aligns the black child with the wrong forces in the universe of socialization. Whereas reading is a part of the teacher's agenda and a game the teacher wishes the students to play, it is not a part of the black students' agenda and the games they wish to play. Not reading is accepting the peer group's games over the teachers' games, and Trackton children were likely to make just this choice. This behavior in turn may impede the development of literacy skills.

Attitudes toward reading were also different in Roadville and Gateway. As indicated above, once children started school, parents in Roadville generally stopped reading to their children, partially because they expected the school to take on this task. Adults encouraged children to watch *Sesame Street*, one way for the children to pick up reading, but they were not themselves examples to model. Heath noted that in Roadville, everyone talked about the importance of reading but few people actually engage in it or follow up on what they have read (Heath, 1983: 220). Unlike households in Trackton, Roadville homes did have reading matter such as magazines. However, the magazines usually piled up unread and were then thrown away in periodic cleanings of the house (Heath, 1983). Attitudes toward reading were also different in Gateway. In this town, children were coached before entering school in both reading and listening behaviors. Children were encouraged to read; learn the structures of stories; and use what they learned in their lives.

Crosscultural studies of classification, categorization, and problem-solving behavior illustrate the effects of three processes Sternberg (1985a) has labeled selective encoding, combination, and comparison (see also Davidson and Sternberg, 1984). *Selective encoding* is at issue in studies of attribute preference in classification tasks. In these tasks, a subject may be shown a red triangle, a blue triangle, and a red square, and asked which two objects belonged together. Western literature shows a consistent developmental trend, such that very young children choose color as the decisive (or relevant) stimulus attribute, whereas older children shift their preference to form by age five (Suchmann and Trabasso, 1966). Crosscultural studies, on the other hand, often fail to show this color-to-form shift (Cole et al., 1971). Cole and Scribner (1974) suggest that the preference for form versus color may be linked to the development of literacy (where alphabetic forms acquire tremendous importance), which differs widely across cultures.

Luria (1976) provides an illustration of *selective combination* in a categorization task. Shown a hammer, a saw, a log, and a hatchet, an illiterate (by Western standards) Central Asian peasant was asked which three items were similar. He insisted that all four fit together, even when the interviewer suggested that the concept "tool" could be used for the hammer, saw, and hatchet, but not for the log. The subject in this instance combined the features of the four items that were relevant in terms of his culture and arrived at a functional or situational concept (perhaps one of "things you need to build a hut"). (In his failure to combine the "instrumental" features of the tools selectively into a concept that excluded the log, however, the subject was not performing intelligently—at least, from the perspective of the experimenter's culture.)

In many of Luria's studies, the unschooled peasants have great difficulty in solving the problem given them. Often, they appear to be thrown off by an apparent discrepancy between the terms of the problem and what they know to be true. For example, take one of the math problems: "From Shakimardan to Vuadil it is three hours on foot, while to Fergana it is six hours. How much time does it take to go on foot from Vuadil to Fergana?" The subject's response to this problem was, "No, it's six hours from Vuadil to

Fergana. You're wrong. . . . it's far and you wouldn't get there in three hours" (Luria, 1976: 129). In terms of *selective comparison*, performance suffered precisely because the subject was comparing incoming data to what he knew about his world, which was irrelevant to the solution of the problem. As Luria indicated, the computation could readily have been performed, but the condition of the problem was not accepted. Inherent in the referenced examples concerning how intelligence is socialized is the assumption that intelligence is defined differently in different cultures.

INTELLIGENCE MEANS DIFFERENT THINGS IN DIFFERENT CULTURES

There is growing evidence and consensus that intelligence is defined differently between and within different cultures (see reviews in Serpell, 2000; Sternberg and Kaufman, 1998). These differences are important because cultures evaluate their members as well as those in other cultures in terms of their own conceptions of intelligence. Yang and Sternberg's (1997a) review of Chinese philosophical conceptions of intelligence documents that the Confucian perspective emphasizes benevolence and doing what is right. In this view, the intelligent person spends a great deal of effort learning, enjoying the process of learning, and persisting with a great deal of enthusiasm in lifelong learning. The Taoist tradition, in contrast, emphasizes the importance of humility, freedom from conventional standards of judgment, and full knowledge of oneself as well as of external conditions. Generally in the West, when we talk about intelligent people, we implicitly refer to those who have developed certain kinds of ability or can do certain kinds of things

The difference between Eastern and Western conceptions of intelligence may persist even today. A recent study of contemporary Taiwanese Chinese conceptions of intelligence suggests that Taiwanese Chinese people believe in a general cognitive factor, much like the *g* factor in conventional Western tests; interpersonal intelligence (i.e., social competence); intrapersonal intelligence; intellectual self-assertion; and intellectual self-effacement (Yang and Sternberg, 1997b). Alternatively, Chinese conceptualizations of intelligence were undergirded by nonverbal reasoning ability, verbal reasoning ability, and rote memory (Chen, 1994). This difference may be attributed to different subpopulations of Chinese; differences in methodology; or, possibly, differences in the timing of the referenced studies.

The factors uncovered in Taiwan differ substantially from those identified by Sternberg and his colleagues (1981) in a study of conceptions of intelligence (as perceived by people in the United States). These factors include practical problem solving, verbal ability, and social competence. In both Taiwan and the United States, however, people's implicit theories of intelligence seem to go beyond what conventional psychometric intelligence tests measure.

Studies in Africa also provide another window on the substantial differences in conceptions of intelligence across cultures. Ruzgis and Grigorenko (1994) argued that, in Africa, conceptions of intelligence revolve largely around skills that help to facilitate and maintain harmonious and stable intergroup relations. It appears, however, that intragroup relations are probably equally important and may, at times, be more important. For example, Serpell (1974, 1996) found that Chewa adults in Zambia emphasize social responsibilities, cooperativeness, and obedience as important to intelligence. Children considered intelligent in this culture are expected to be respectful of adults. Kenyan parents also emphasize responsible participation in family and social life as important aspects of intelligence (Super and Harkness, 1982, 1986, 1993). In Zimbabwe, the word for intelligence, *ngware*, actually means to be prudent and cautious, particularly in social relationships. Among the Baoule, service to the family and community and politeness toward and respect for elders are considered key to intelligence (Dasen, 1984).

It is difficult to separate linguistic differences from conceptual differences in crosscultural notions of intelligence. In Sternberg and Grigorenko's research, the investigators used converging operations in order to achieve some separation. That is, they have used different and diverse empirical operations in order to ascertain notions of intelligence. In a given study, they may ask study participants to identify aspects of competence; in another, their sample may be asked to identify competent people; in a third, to characterize the meaning of "intelligence"; and so forth.

The emphasis on the social aspects of intelligence is not limited to African cultures. Notions of intelligence in many Asian cultures also emphasize the social aspect of intelligence (more so than does the conventional Western or IQ-based notion [Azuma and Kashiwagi, 1987; Lutz, 1985; Poole, 1985; White, 1985]). However, neither African nor Asian notions exclusively emphasize social notions of intelligence; they also recognize the importance of cognitive aspects. In a study of Kenyan conceptions of intelligence, Grigorenko and her colleagues (2001) found that there were four distinct terms constituting conceptions of intelligence among rural Kenyans—*rieko* (knowledge and skills), *luoro* (respect), *winjo* (comprehension of how to handle real-life problems), *paro* (initiative)—with only the first directly referring to knowledge-based skills (including but not limited to academics). This phenomenon can also be found in the United States (Okagaki and Sternberg, 1993). For example, different ethnic groups in San Jose, California, had rather different conceptions of what it means to be intelligent. Latino parents, for instance, tend to emphasize the importance of social-competence skills in their conceptions of intelligence, whereas Asian and Anglo parents tend to focus rather heavily on the importance of cognitive skills. Teachers, representing the dominant culture, also emphasized cognitive rather than social-competence skills. The rank order of children from these ethnic groups (including subgroups within the Latino and Asian groups) can be perfectly predicted by the extent to which their parents shared the teachers' conception of intelligence (Okagaki and Sternberg, 1993). That is, teachers tend to reward those children who were socialized into a view of intelligence that happened to correspond to the teachers' own.

Comparative studies of intelligence and the history of the study of this social construction suggest that there is considerable plasticity in the development of the phenomenon that we call intelligence, as well as in prevailing conceptions of it. It appears, then, that intelligence is not only a malleable phenomenon, but also that the character and quality of the construct may be dependent upon the connotation assigned to it by those who shape it as well as those making the judgment. What is being referred to and the value assigned to it are obviously determined by the cultural and social contexts in which it is developed, expressed, and evaluated. Despite its apparent protean status, uninformed debate continues relative to its origins in nature as opposed to nurture as its genesis. More sophisticated students of intelligence and its manifestation as educability agree that the character and quality of mental activity and its product are a function of the *interaction* between whatever is given in nature of the organism and what is nurtured through experience and environmental encounters.

CONCLUSION

Intelligence is largely socialized. Even genetic factors play their part through the mediation of socialization. Behavioral genetic and molecular genetic studies, as well as other biologically oriented work, play an important part in understanding intelligence. But reductionist attempts to understand intelligence solely at these levels are bound to fail not because they are wrong, but because they are incomplete. Intelligence is best understood at a multiplicity of levels of analysis, including the interactions of those levels with each other. In this chapter, we seek to describe some of the ways in which the interactions may be addressed. If we wish to understand schooling properly, we need to understand it as, in part, a society's attempt to socialize the intelligence of its members. The choices we make in education are heavily influenced by implicit theories of what intelligence is. To the extent these theories favor the behaviors, mores, and values of certain groups over others, so will our education practices. Meanwhile, many of our children will be held back in their intellectual development.

REFERENCES

Azuma, H., and Kashiwagi, K. 1987. Descriptions for an intelligent person: A Japanese study. *Japanese Psychological Research*, 29, 17–26.

Barbujani, G., Magagni, A., Minch, E., and Cavalli-Sforza, L. L. 1997. An apportionment of human DNA diversity. *Proceedings of the National Academy of Science*, 94, 4516–19.

Beaujean, A. A. 2005. Heritability of cognitive abilities as measured by mental chronometric tasks: A meta-analysis. *Intelligence* 33(2):187–201.

Block, N. 1995. How heritability misleads about race. *Cognition*, 56, 99–128.

Bouchard, T. J., Jr. 1997. IQ similarity in twins reared apart: Findings and responses to critics. In R. J. Sternberg and E. L. Grigorenko (Eds.), *Intelligence, heredity, and environment* (pp. 126–60). New York: Cambridge University Press.

Brand, C. 1996. *The g factor: General intelligence and its implications*. Chichester, England: Wiley.

Bratko, D. 1996. Twin study of verbal and spatial abilities. *Personality and Individual Differences*, 21, 621–24.

Bridglall, B. L., and Gordon, E. W. 2002. The idea of supplementary education. *Pedagogical Inquiry and Praxis*. New York: Teachers College, Columbia University.

Brown, A. L., and Ferrara, R. A. 1985. Diagnosing zones of proximal development. In J. V. Wertsch (Ed.), *Culture, communication, and cognition: Vygotskian perspectives* (pp. 273–305). New York: Cambridge University Press.

Chen, M. J. 1994. Chinese and Australian concepts of intelligence. *Psychology and Developing Societies*, 6, 101–117.

Cole, M., Gay, J., Glick, J., and Sharp, D. W. 1971. *The cultural context of learning and thinking*. New York: Basic Books.

Cole, M., and Scribner, S. 1974. *Culture and thought: A psychological introduction*. New York: Wiley.

The College Board. 1999. *Reaching the top*. Report of the task force on minority high achievement. New York: The College Board.

Dasen, P. 1984. The cross-cultural study of intelligence: Piaget and the Baoule. *International Journal of Psychology*, 19, 407–434.

Davidson, J. E., and Sternberg, R. J. 1984. The role of insight in intellectual giftedness. *Gifted Child Quarterly*, 28, 58–64.

Dickens, W. T. 2005. Genetic differences and school readiness. *The Future of Children* (15)1. Princeton University and The Brookings Institution.

Egorova, M. S. 1988. Genotip i sreda v variativnosti kognitivnykh phunktsii [Genotype and environment in the variation of cognitive functions]. In I. V. Ravich-Shcherbo (Ed.), *Rol' sredy I nasledstvennosti v formirovanii individual'nosti cheloveka* (pp. 181–235). Moscow: Pedagogika.

Feuerstein, R. 1979. *The dynamic assessment of retarded performers: The learning potential assessment device theory, instruments, and techniques*. Baltimore, MD: University Park Press.

Flynn, J. R. 1984. The mean IQ of Americans: Massive gains 1932 to 1978. *Psychological Bulletin*, 95, 29–51.

———. 1987. Massive IQ gains in 14 nations: What IQ tests really measure. *Psychological Bulletin*, 101, 171–91.

Gordon, E. W., Bridglall, B. L., and Meroe, A. S. 2005. *Supplementary education: The hidden curriculum of high achievement.* New York: Rowman & Littlefield.

Grigorenko, E. L. 1990. Esperimental'nor issledovanie protsessa vydvizheniia I proverki gipotez [Experimental study of hypothesis-making in the structure of cognitive activity]. Unpublished doctoral dissertation, NIOPP APN SSSR.

Grigorenko, E. L., Geissler, P. W., Prince, R., Okatcha, F., Nokes, C., Kenny, D. A., Bundy, D. A., and Sternberg, R. J. 2001. The organization of Luo conceptions of intelligence: A study of implicit theories in a Kenyan village. *International Journal of Behavioral Development,* 25(4), 367–78.

Grigorenko, E. L., Meier, E., Lipka, J., Mohatt, G., Yanez, E., and Sternberg, R. J. 2004. Academic and practical intelligence: A case study of the Yup'ik in Alaska. *Learning and Individual Differences,* 14, 183–207.

Grigorenko, E. L., and Sternberg, R. J. 1998. Dynamic testing. *Psychological Bulletin,* 124, 75–111.

Guthke, J. 1993. Current trends in theories and assessment of intelligence. In J. H. M. Hamers, K. Sijtsma, and A. J. J. M. Ruijssenaars (Eds.), *Learning potential assessment* (pp. 13–20). Amsterdam: Swets and Zeitlinger.

Haywood, H. C., and Tzuriel, D. (Eds.) 1992. *Interactive assessment.* New York: Springer-Verlag.

Heath, S. B. 1983. *Ways with words.* New York: Cambridge University Press.

Herrnstein, R. J. 1973. *IQ in the meritocracy.* Boston: Atlantic Monthly Press.

Herrnstein, R. J, and Murray, C. 1994. *The bell curve.* New York: Free Press.

Hudson, W. 1967. The study of the problem of pictorial perception among the unacculturated groups. *International Journal of Psychology,* 2, 89–107.

"Intelligence and its measurement": A symposium. 1921. *Journal of Educational Psychology,* 12, 123–47, 195–216, 271–75.

Iskoldsky, N. V. 1988. Vliianie sotsial'no-psikhologicheskikh factorov na individual'nye osobennosti bliznetsov i ikh vnutriparnoe skhodstvo [The influence of social-psychological factors influencing twins' individual characteristics and their similarity on psychological traits]. Unpublished doctoral dissertation, NIOPP APN SSSR.

Jencks. C., and Phillips, M. (1998). *The black-white test score gap.* Whashington, D.C.: Brookings Institution.

Jensen, A. R. 1998. *The g factor.* Westport, CT: Praeger/Greenwood.

Kidd, K. K., Pakstis, A. K., Speed, W. C., and Kidd, J. R. In press. Understanding human DNA sequence variation. *Journal of Heredity.*

Kozol, J. 1991. *Savage inequalities: Children in America's schools.* New York: Crown Publishers Inc.

Lewontin, R. C. 1972. The apportionment of human diversity. *Evolutionary Biology,* 6, 381–98.

———. 1974. Annotation: The analysis of variance and the analysis of causes. *American Journal of Human Genetics,* 26, 400–411.

———. 1982. *Human diversity.* New York: Freeman.

Lidz, C. S. 1991. *Practitioner's guide to dynamic assessment.* New York: Guilford Press.

Luria, A. R. 1976. *Cognitive development: Its cultural and social functions.* Cambridge, MA: Harvard University Press.

Lutz, C. 1985. Ethnopsychology compared to what? Explaining behaviour and consciousness among the Ifaluk. In G. M. White and J. Kirkpatrick (Eds.), *Person, self, and experience: Exploring Pacific ethnopsychologies* (pp. 35–79). Berkeley: University of California Press.

Lynn, R., and Hattori, K. 1990. The heritability of intelligence in Japan. *Behavior Genetics*, 20, 4, 545–46.

Martinez, M. E. 2000. *Education as the cultivation of intelligence*. New Jersey: Lawrence Erlbaum Associates, Inc.

McDermott, R. P. 1974. Achieving school failure: An anthropological approach in illiteracy and social stratification. In G. Spindler (Ed.), *Education and the cultural process*. New York: Holt, Rinehart, and Winston.

Miller, L. S. 1995. *An American imperative: Accelerating minority educational advancement.*. New Haven: Yale University Press.

Nathwar, S., and Puri, P. 1995. A comparative study of MZ and DZ twins on Level I and Level II mental abilities and personality. *Journal of the Indian Academy of Applied Psychology*, 21, 87–92.

Neisser, U. (Ed.) 1998. *The rising curve*. Washington, D.C.: American Psychological Association.

Nisbett, R. E. 1995. Race, IQ, and scientism. In S. Fraser (Ed.), *The bell curve wars*. New York: Basic Books.

———. Race, genetics, and IQ. 1998. In C. Jencks, M. Phillips (Eds.), *The Black-White test score gap* (pp. 86–102). Washington, D.C.: Brookings Institution.

Okagaki, L., and Sternberg, R. J. 1993. Parental beliefs and children's school performance. *Child Development*, 64(1), 36–56.

Pal, S., Shyam, R., and Singh, R. 1997. Genetic analysis of general intelligence 'g': A twin study. *Personality and Individual Differences*, 22, 779–80.

Plomin, R., DeFries, J. C., and McClearn, G. 1990. *Behavioral genetics: A primer*. New York: Freeman.

Poole, F. J. P. 1985. Coming into social being: Cultural images of infants in Bimin-Kuskusmin folk psychology. In G. M. White and J. Kirkpatrick (Eds.), *Person, self, and experience: Exploring Pacific ethnopsychologies* (pp. 183–244). Berkeley: University of California Press.

Raven, J. C., Court, J. H., and Raven, J. 1992. *Manual for Raven's Progressive Matrices and Mill Hill Vocabulary Scales*. Oxford: Oxford Psychologists Press.

Reardon, S. 2003. *Sources of Educational Inequality: The growth of racial/ethnic and socioeconomic test score gaps in kindergarten and first grade*. Population Research Institute Paper No. 03-05R.

Resnick, L. B. 1979. The future of IQ testing in education. *Intelligence* 3(3), 241–53.

Rogoff, B. 1990. *Apprenticeship in thinking. Cognitive development in social context*. New York: Oxford University Press.

———. 2003. *The cultural nature of human development*. London: Oxford University Press.

Rosenberg, N. A., Pritchard, J. K., Weber, J. L., Cann, H. M., Kidd, K. K., Zhivotovsky, L. A., Feldman, M. W. 2002. Genetic structure of human populations. *Science*, 298, 2381–85.

Rushton, J. P., and Jensen, A. R. 2005. Thirty years of research on race differences in cognitive ability. *Psychology, Public Policy, and Law*, 11(2), 235–94.

Ruzgis, P. M, and Grigorenko, E. L. 1994. Cultural meaning systems, intelligence and personality. In R. J. Sternberg and P. Ruzgis (Eds.), *Personality and intelligence* (pp. 248–70). New York: Cambridge.

Sarason, S. B., and Doris, J. 1979. *Educational handicap, public policy, and social history*. New York: Free Press.

Sarich, V., and Miele, F. 2004. *Race: The reality of human differences.* Boulder, CO: Westview Press.

Scarr, S., and Weinberg, R. A. 1976. IQ test performance of black children adopted by white families. *American Psychologist,* 31, 726–39.

———. 1983. The Minnesota adoption studies: Genetic differences and malleability. *Child Development,* 54, 260–67.

Schwebel, M. 1968. *Who can be educated?* New York: Grove Press

———. 2003. *Remaking America's schools: Now separate and unequal.* New York: Rowman & Littlefield.

Serpell, R. 1974. Aspects of intelligence in a developing country. *African Social Research,* No. 17, 576–96.

———. 1996. Cultural models of childhood in indigenous socialization and formal schooling in Zambia. In Hwang, C. P., Lamb, M. E. (Eds.), *Images of childhood* (pp. 129–42). Mahwah, NJ: Lawrence Erlbaum.

———. 2000. Intelligence and culture. In R. J. Sternberg (Ed.), *Handbook of intelligence* (pp. 549–80). New York: Cambridge University Press.

Sternberg, R. J. 1985. *Beyond IQ: A triarchic theory of human intelligence.* New York: Cambridge University Press.

———. 1997. *Successful intelligence.* New York: Plume.

———. 2000. *Handbook of intelligence.* New York: Cambridge University Press.

———. 2004. Culture and intelligence. *American Psychologist,* 59(5), 325–38.

———. 2005. There are no public policy implications: A reply to Rushton and Jensen. *Psychology, Public Policy, and Law,* 11(2), 295–301.

Sternberg, R. J., Conway, B. E., Ketron, J. L., and Bernstein, M. 1981. People's conceptions of intelligence. *Journal of Personality and Social Psychology,* 41, 37–55.

Sternberg, R. J., and Detterman, D. K. (Eds.) 1986. *What is intelligence?* Norwood, NJ: Ablex Publishing Corporation.

Sternberg, R. J., and Grigorenko, E. L. 1999a. Genetics and intelligence. *Journal of American Academy of Child and Adolescent Psychiatry,* 38, 486–88.

———. 1999b. Myths in psychology and education regarding the gene environment debate. *Teachers College Record,* 100, 536–53.

———. 2002a. *Dynamic testing.* New York: Cambridge University Press.

———. 2002b. Just because we "know" it's true doesn't mean it's really true: A case study in Kenya. *Psychological Science Agenda,* 15(2), 8–10.

Sternberg, R. J., and Grigorenko, E. L. (Eds.) 1997. *Intelligence, heredity, and environment.* New York: Cambridge University Press.

Sternberg, R. J., Grigorenko, E. L., and Kidd, K. K. 2005. Intelligence, race, and genetics. *American Psychologist,* 60(1), 46–59.

Sternberg, R. J., Grigorenko, E. L., Ngrosho, D., Tantufuye, E., Mbise, A., Nokes, C., Jukes, M., and Bundy, D. A. 2002. Assessing intellectual potential in rural Tanzanian school children. *Intelligence,* 30, 141–62.

Sternberg, R. J., and Kaufman, J. C. 1998. Human abilities. *Annual Review of Psychology,* 49, 479–502.

Sternberg, R. J., Nokes, K., Geissler, P. W., Prince, R., Okatcha, F., Bundy, D. A., and Grigorenko, E. L. 2001. The relationship between academic and practical intelligence: A case study in Kenya. *Intelligence,* 29, 401–418.

Sternberg, R. J., and Suben, J. 1986. The socialization of intelligence. In M. Perlmutter (Ed.), *Perspectives on intellectual development. Vol. 19, Minnesota symposia on child psychology* (pp. 201–235). Hillsdale, NJ: Lawrence Erlbaum Associates.

Suchmann, R. G., and Trabasso, T. 1966. Color and form preference in young children. *Journal of Experimental Child Psychology*, 3, 177–87.

Super, C. M., and Harkness, S. 1982. The infants' niche in rural Kenya and metropolitan America. In L. L. Adler (Ed.), *Cross-cultural research at issue* (pp. 47–55). New York: Academic Press.

———. 1986. The developmental niche: A conceptualization at the interface of child and culture. *International Journal of Behavioral Development*, 9, 545–69.

———. 1993. The developmental niche: A conceptualization at the interface of child and culture. R. A. Pierce, M. A. Black (Eds.), *Life-span development: A diversity reader* (pp. 61–77). Dubuque, IA: Kendall/Hunt Publishing Co.

Templeton, A. R. 1999. Human races: A genetic and evolutionary perspective. *American Anthropologist*, 100, 632–50.

Tishkoff, S., and Kidd, K. K. In press. Biogeography of human populations: Implications for "race." *Nature Genetics*.

Turkheimer, E., Haley, A., Waldron, M., D'Onofrio, B., and Gottesman, I. I. 2003. Socioeconomic status modifies heritability of IQ in young children. *Psychological Science*, 14, 623–28.

Tzuriel, D. 1995. Dynamic-interactive assessment: The legacy of L. S. Vygotsky and current developments. Unpublished manuscript.

Vernon, P. E. 1971. *The structure of human abilities*. London: Methuen.

Vygotsky, L. S. 1978. *Mind in society: The development of higher psychological processes*. Cambridge, MA: Harvard University Press.

White, G. M. 1985. Premises and purposes in a Solomon Islands ethnopsychology. In G. M. White and J. Kirkpatrick (Eds.), *Person, self, and experience: Exploring Pacific ethnopsychologies* (pp. 328–66). Berkeley: University of California Press.

Yang, S., and Sternberg, R. J. 1997a. Conceptions of intelligence in ancient Chinese philosophy. *Journal of Theoretical and Philosophical Psychology*, 17, 101–119.

———. 1997b. Taiwanese Chinese people's conceptions of intelligence. *Intelligence*, 25, 21–36.

NOTES

1. This assumes that the error variance related to measurement of the trait is blended into the environmental component.

2. Again, this is because there is a 0 in the denominator of the ratio.

3. In the control group, the correlations between pretest and posttest scores were generally at the .8 level. Sternberg and his colleagues expected a high correlation because there was no intervention and hence the retesting was largely a measure of alternate-forms reliability. More importantly, scores on the pretest in the experimental group showed only weak although significant correlations with scores on the posttest. These correlations, at about the .3 level (which were significantly less than those in the control group), suggested that when tests are administered statically to children in developing countries, they may be rather unstable and easily subject to influences of training. The reason could be that the children are not accustomed to taking Western-style tests, and so profit quickly even from small amounts of instruction as to what is expected from them.

4

Affirmative Development as an Alternative to Affirmative Action

Beatrice L. Bridglall

Affirmative action is defined as public or private interventions that increase the representation of women and minorities historically denied these opportunities or benefits in employment, business, and education. Affirmative action, however, is not only conceived of as benefiting certain ethnic groups, but also as benefiting society as a whole by enabling diversity and equality. Serious affirmative action efforts for the benefit of ethnic groups began in the 1960s, led by Presidents John F. Kennedy and Lyndon B. Johnson to assist people of color in achieving equal employment opportunities. Later, state and local governments and private businesses joined in this effort. In the late 1960s, the federal government added affirmative action stipulations to federal support given to educational institutions. This was followed by executive orders from the Department of Labor which changed the way affirmative action policies were implemented in colleges and universities in the early 1970s. These orders mandated the setting of goals and timetables for the proportional representation of protected classes of people, including women and minorities.

Despite the colloquial perception that ethnic minorities and women were the principal foci of affirmative action, our nation has had a long history of such targeted action on behalf of specified groups. When it was determined that cheap transportation was essential to the building and unification of the United States as a nation, the fledgling railroad industry was targeted for special attention and support. When the nation's need for "expert training in up-to-date agricultural and industrial methods was becoming an urgent matter, . . . Congress [through the 1862 Morrill Act] provided federal land grants . . . (30,000 acres for each of its senators and representatives) for the purpose of establishing colleges 'to teach such branches of learning as are related to agriculture and the mechanic arts'" (Delbanco 2005:19 quoting Meyer 1972:68). For a brief time after the Emancipation Proclamation, formerly enslaved people were the beneficiaries of small land grants, a mule, education, and specialized social services through the Freedman's Bureau. The GI Bill is perhaps the best known and most widely used affirmative action program that this nation has implemented.

In the current period, references to affirmative action and its many connotations provoke strong feelings from both endorsers and opponents. The divisiveness of seemingly contradictory values that (1) fairness means treating everyone the same, and (2) that our political, economic, and educational institutions are responsible for helping the underserved and underrepresented to overcome past discrimination and provide equal opportunities, and the actual practices of these ideas, were reflected in the 2003 Supreme Court decisions in *Gratz vs. Bollinger* and *Grutter vs. Bollinger*. This divisiveness, however, is not particular to the early twenty-first century but reflects, rather, continuing historical tensions between the referenced ideas of equality and equity. In this chapter, we situate the implications of the Supreme Court decisions in 2003 in a brief historical review of the origins of affirmative action in general and as it relates to education in particular. A discussion of the backlash and challenges to affirmative action follows. The chapter concludes with a discussion of an affirmative development policy, which places emphasis on developing and nurturing intellective competencies for those whose homes, communities, and schools do not naturally provide them, as an alternative to affirmative action.

AFFIRMATIVE ACTION: A HISTORICAL PERSPECTIVE

By most accounts, official movements in the United States to reduce discrimination and injustice against certain racial and ethnic groups (in this instance, African Americans) began with the Civil Rights Act of 1875, 256 years after the first enslaved Africans landed at Old Point Comfort, Virginia ("now an Army base with no commemoration at all of what some call the Black Mayflower. A park there memorializes Jefferson Davis, not the slaves"). For over two and a half centuries before this act, it was unlawful to teach enslaved Africans to read; they could be sold away from family and friends at their masters' inclination; and neither their murder nor mutilation was considered a crime. The systematic denial of human rights for those unlike themselves was etched into the European Americans' first attempts at establishing self-government. That is, even as the colonists launched efforts to protect their own freedom and equality, the Declaration of Independence implicitly protected slavery, while the Constitution explicitly considered a slave as three-fifths of a person for purposes of allocating taxes and representatives among the states (Article I: Section 2: Clause 3: 1788). The Constitution also stipulated that the "migration or importation" of slaves into the existing states would be legal until at least 1808 (Article I: Section 9: Clause 1: 1788). Further, a fugitive slave clause stipulated that when a slave escaped to another state, he must be returned on the claim of his master (Article IV: Section 2: Clause 3: 1788). In these founding documents, the Framers made it clear that their phrase, "we the people" did not include those unlike themselves.

During the 1830s, a number of slaveholding states established the Slave Codes, a set of slave laws designed to (1) prevent the teaching of literacy skills (spelling, reading, and writing) to slaves; (2) limit the assembly of (more than five male) slaves with a free Negro or person of color without the permission of their owner, master, or overseer; and (3) secure the property interest of the owner in his slave (www.wfu.edu/~zulick/340/slavery-notes.html). These state mandates were validated in 1857 when the U.S. Supreme Court ruled that the Negro slave was mere property in *Dred Scott v. Sanford* (60 U.S.: 1857). The court held, further, that Negroes were not considered citizens under the Constitution. As such, they were "beings of an inferior order . . . altogether unfit to associate with the White race, either in social or political relations; and so far inferior, that they had no rights which the White man was bound to respect" (60 U.S.: 1857:407).

While the end of the Civil War resulted in freedom of blacks from slavery, it did not result in equality or citizenship in any meaningful way. Rather, a system of laws in many Southern states bent on re-legalizing slavery (Slaughter-House Cases, 16 Wall. 36, 70, 1873); the passage of the Black Codes (similar to the Slave Codes) which restricted the rights of blacks to rent or own property and imprisoned those who were thought to breach employment contracts; and the systematic denial of rights by the passage of the Thirteenth, Fourteenth, and Fifteenth Amendments severely restricted and disenfranchised black Americans through poll taxes, obscure balloting processes, and property and literacy qualifications. In response to the legal obstacles imposed upon African Americans by the Southern states, Congress passed the Reconstruction Acts and the Civil Rights Act in 1875. To its credit, Congress also established the Bureau of Refugees, Freedmen, and Abandoned Lands (the Freedmen's Bureau), to provide food, hospitals, land, and education to the newly freed slaves at the end of the Civil War. This protection for blacks, however, was short-lived as Reconstruction came to a close, and their new civil rights were quickly whittled away by the U.S. Supreme Court's narrow interpretation of the Civil War Amendments (Slaughter-House Cases, 16 Wall. 36, 70, 1873; *United States v. Reese*, 92 U.S. 214, 1876; *United States v. Cruikshank*, 92, U.S. 542, 1876).

Another considerable setback occurred when the Supreme Court suppressed Congress's attempts to support racial equality in the infamous Civil

Rights Cases (109 U.S. 3:1883). In these cases, the Court ruled that certain sections of the Civil Rights Act of 1875 granting black Americans equal access to "inns, public conveyances, theaters and other places of public amusement" were illegal (109 U.S. 10:1883). The Court ruled that the Fourteenth Amendment gave Congress the power to prohibit, not resolve, discriminatory action by states. As such, blacks who were barred from public places were thought by the Courts to experience only an assault on their social rights at the hands of private individuals and that Congress had no power to redress these actions (109 U.S. 24–25:1883). The Court concluded that "When a man has emerged from slavery, and by the aid of beneficent legislation has shaken off the inseparable concomitants of that [438 U.S. 265, 392] state, there must be some stage in the process of his elevation when he takes the rank of a mere citizen, and ceases to be the special favorite of the laws" (109 U.S. 25:1883). Justice Harlan observed in his dissent, however, that the Civil War Acts and Civil Rights Amendments did not make blacks the "special favorite" of the laws but instead "sought to accomplish in reference to that race . . . —what had already been done in every State of the Union for the White race—to secure and protect rights belonging to them as freemen and citizens; nothing more" (109 U.S. 61:1883).

The final blow to black Americans' struggle for equality and the Civil War Amendments occurred in *Plessy v. Ferguson* (163 U.S. 537, 1896) when the Supreme Court upheld a Louisiana law stipulating that railway companies must provide *equal but separate* accommodations for whites and blacks. In this ruling, the Court held that the Fourteenth Amendment was not intended "to abolish distinctions based upon color, or to enforce social, as distinguished from political equality, or a commingling of the two races upon terms unsatisfactory to either" (163 U.S. 537:1896). The Court continued:

> We consider the underlying fallacy of the plaintiff's argument to consist in the assumption that the enforced separation of the two races stamps the colored race with a badge of inferiority. If this be so, it is not by reason of anything found in the act, but solely because the colored race chooses to put that construction upon it.

Justice Harlan's dissent recognized that the "real meaning" of this ruling was "that colored citizens were so inferior and degraded that they cannot be allowed to sit in public coaches occupied by White citizens" (163 U.S. 560:1896). He feared that the repercussions of this ruling would enable states to preserve the power "to interfere with the full enjoyment of the blessings of freedom; to regulate civil rights, common to all citizens, upon the basis of race; and to place in a condition of legal inferiority a large body of American citizens" (163 U.S. 560:1896). Justice Harlan's fears were not unfounded. Following the ruling in *Plessy*, many states broadened their Jim

Crow laws, formerly limited to passenger trains and schools, to include segregation of the races in residential areas, parks, hospitals, theaters, waiting rooms, and bathrooms. Additionally, statutes and ordinances endorsing separate phone booths for blacks and whites and textbooks for the exclusive use of these racial groups were also sanctioned. (These laws enforcing racial segregation were known by the name of a minstrel show popular in the mid-1800s that stereotyped and ridiculed blacks: "Jump Jim Crow".)

Laws limiting the rights of blacks were not peculiar to the Southern states. In many of the Northern states, blacks were barred from theaters, restaurants, hotels, and inns, prohibited from serving on juries, and blatantly denied the right to vote. The federal government under President Wilson curtailed off the desks of black employees; provided separate tables in the cafeterias and separate bathrooms; and even segregated the galleries of Congress. President Wilson suggested that segregation was "not humiliating but a benefit" to blacks when his segregationist policies were attacked. This compulsory segregation of whites and blacks continued into the middle of the twentieth century. In both world wars, blacks were primarily restricted to separate military units. It was not until 1948 that an end to segregation in the military was ordered by President Truman.

AFFIRMATIVE ACTION IN EDUCATION

As most of us are aware by now, black students have had a history of exclusion from well-resourced public grade schools and graduate and professional schools (Orfield 2001). This situation began to change when some of the Jim Crow laws (promoted by the decisions of the Supreme Court) were struck down in a series of decisions (*Morgan v. Virginia*, 328 U.S. 373, 373 [1946]; *Sweatt v. Painter*, 339 U.S. 629, 629 [1950]; *McLaurin v. Okla. State Regents*, 339 U.S. 637, 637 [1950]), leading up to the *Brown v. Board of Education* decision (347 U.S. 483, 483 [1954]). These decisions, however, did not categorically end segregation, nor did they easily help to move blacks from a position of imposed legal inferiority to one of equality. The cases did mark a shift in the Court's thinking. In the 1938 case *Missouri ex rel. Gaines v. Canada*, for example, the Supreme Court found that Missouri's barring of blacks from attending the state university's law school (and its issuing of tuition money instead to these students to enroll in out-of-state law schools) violated the Equal Protection Clause of the Fourteenth Amendment (*Missouri ex rel. Gaines v. Canada*, 305 U.S. 337, 348 [1938]). Twelve years later, the Court held that Texas violated the Fourteenth Amendment by establishing a separate law school for blacks (*Sweatt*, 339 U.S. at 636). These cases led up to the Supreme Court's 1954 decision in *Brown v. Board of Education*, which found school segregation in the South to be unconsti-

tutional (*Brown*, 347 U.S. at 495). The impact of Brown, however, was not
as substantial as initially expected. There was an immediate systematic rejection of the desegregation decision by Southern politicians, local government officials, and enraged white citizens (Bowen and Bok 1998). This bla-
tant disregard for the Court's decision and the continued unconstitutional
enforcement of segregation incited African Americans to organize (Kluger
1975; Thernstrom and Thernstrom 1997). The Montgomery, Alabama, bus
boycott in 1955–1956 is largely considered one of the catalysts of the civil
rights movement. It gave Dr. Martin Luther King Jr. a national platform with
which to help galvanize efforts to desegregate schools, public transportation, and public places throughout the South. Despite these clarion calls
for equality, the federal government did not take decisive action to protect
the rights of black Americans. On one occasion, President Eisenhower did
relent by sending federal troops to Little Rock when Arkansas Governor
Orval Faubus openly defied court orders to integrate the schools. Congress's
actions at this time were also considered ineffectual. It passed a Civil Rights
Act in 1957 (Civil Rights Act of 1957, Pub. L. No. 89-670, 71 Stat. 634,
634–38 [1957]) that was too weak to counteract the systemic obstacles to
black voter registration in the South.

A. The Consideration of Race in Higher Education Admissions Policies

By 1960, the Supreme Court rulings had not altered the educational landscape as expected. African-American students comprised 4.8 percent of all
enrolled college students in the United States in 1965; 7.0 percent by 1970;
and 9.9 percent in 1980 (Hacker 1983). Black females made up 56.6 percent of all black students enrolled in 1980 (Hacker 1983). Among black
twenty- and twenty-one-year-old males, a total of 64.7 percent had graduated from high school, while 74.4 percent of black females in these age
groups had graduated from high school during this time (Hacker 1983). If
a black male finishes high school, he is more likely to attend college than
a black female high school graduate (Hacker 1983). Further, because the
proportion of males who actually finish high school is less than that of females, more black females are represented in college than are black males.
At this juncture in the twenty-first century, there is a growing consensus that
the underrepresentation of black males in higher education has reached
crisis proportions (Smith et al. 2002).

The number of black students in selective colleges and universities was
even more marginal than in higher education as a whole. Although a
few institutions (Oberlin, Antioch College, Rutgers, and the University of
California, Los Angeles) consciously took steps to recruit and enroll black
students, "no selective college or university was making determined efforts
to seek out and admit substantial numbers of African Americans" before

1960 (Bowen and Bok 1998). There were, however, pockets of interest in nurturing African-American students for higher education. For example, the admissions director at Mount Holyoke College began recruitment efforts in 1959 in schools that had a pool of prospective black candidates and the college did in fact admit ten black students who then enrolled in 1964 (Duffy and Goldberg 1998). In 1963, Wellesley College started a junior-year program for African-American students attending colleges supported by the United Negro College Fund (Duffy and Goldberg 1998). Additionally, Dartmouth, Princeton, and Yale all introduced special summer enrichment programs to prepare promising students of color for possible admission to elite colleges (Duffy and Goldberg 1998).

Despite these documented increases in recruitment efforts for black students in the mid-1960s, blacks made up only 1 percent of the total enrollment at selective New England colleges in 1965 (Kendrick 1967–1968). Some of the reasons for this marginal enrollment of black students on the part of selective colleges included demanding academic requirements, high standards for admission, and a level of tuition and fees that many black students could not afford. With respect to the nation's professional schools, scarcely 1 percent of all law students in America were black, with over one-third of them enrolled in all-black schools (O'Neil 1970). African Americans accounted for close to 2 percent of all medical students, with three-fourths of them enrolled at Howard University and Meharry Medical College, two historically black universities (Nickens et al. 1994). This situation prompted Harvard Law School Dean Erwin Griswold to start a summer program in 1965 to interest juniors from historically black colleges in attending law school (O'Neil 1970). Harvard began admitting black students with test scores that were considerably lower than those of their white peers in 1966 (Bowen and Bok 1998). Black enrollment in other law schools began to rise as Griswold's model was replicated (Bowen and Bok 1998).

The civil rights struggle took on a new intensity when black students in North Carolina initiated a series of sit-ins in 1960, in increasing rejection of segregation at Woolworth and other stores. A year later, "Black and white freedom riders boarded buses bound for the deep South to protest continued segregation in buses and other forms of public transportation" (Bowen and Bok 1998). A federal judge ordered the University of Mississippi in 1962 to admit an African-American student, James Meredith. "Violence erupted as Governor Ross Barnett ordered state troopers to block Meredith's entry" (Bowen and Bok 1998). Governor George Wallace followed this precedent when he tried to keep two black students from attending the University of Alabama in 1963. In the midst of a nonviolent and determined uprising by black and some white Americans, President Johnson signed into law the Civil Rights Act of 1964 (Civil Rights Act of 1964, Pub. L. No. 88-352, 78 Stat. 241, 241–68 [1964]) which obligated the federal government to make significant efforts to end state-enforced segregation. This act did not deter Alabama police from responding violently to a peaceful voting rights march in Selma in 1965. Congress reacted to the violent police action in Selma, Alabama, by passing and enforcing a Voting Rights Act of 1965, Pub. L. No. 89-110, 79 Stat. 437, 437–46 (1965) that led to increased levels of black voter registration and election participation throughout the South (Bowen and Bok 1998).

President Johnson took another significant step when he advocated for a shift away from mere nondiscrimination stances to a more determined, affirmative effort to provide opportunities for black Americans. He asserted, in a 1965 speech at Howard University, that "you do not take a person who, for years, has been hobbled by chains and liberate him, bring him up to the starting line of a race and then say, 'you are free to compete with all the others,' and still justly believe that you have been completely fair" (Commencement Address at Howard University: "To Fulfill These Rights," 2 PUB. PAPERS 635, 636 [June 4, 1965]). Johnson's conviction was reflected in the requirement by the Office of Federal Contract Compliance and the Equal Employment Opportunity Commission that federal contractors submit detailed plans, including goals and time frames, for organizing a workforce that reflected the availability of African-American workers in the appropriate labor market (Bowen and Bok 1998). Shortly after, federal contractors had to include Hispanics, Asian Americans, and Native Americans in their recruitment efforts.

African American and other racial/ethnic workers of color were not the only population to assert their rights. Students began protesting on the campuses of colleges, universities, and professional schools across the country. These protests led to targeted interventions to recruit prospective minority applicants and the use of race in the admissions process. Many higher education institutions began to accept black students despite these students' overall lower test scores and grades when compared to the grades of their white peers (Bowen and Bok 1998). These actions by admissions committees were perceived as being in the interest of not only nurturing a diverse student population with different backgrounds, perspectives, and talents, but also in developing a cadre of minority students for leadership roles (Bowen and Bok 1998). The results included increased enrollment of black students in the Ivy League universities, from 2.3 percent in 1967 to 6.3 percent in 1976, and an increase from 1.7 percent in 1967 to 4.8 percent in 1976 for these students' enrollment in other prestigious colleges and universities (Karen 1991). It is sobering but not surprising that, given the litigation against affirmative action and the Bakke decision (Regents of the Univ. of Cal. v. Bakke, 438 U.S. 265, 265 [1978]) in particular, black student enrollment dropped to 5.8 percent and 4.3 percent respectively in the Ivy League universities and other prestigious colleges and universities in 1986 (Karen 1991).

Blackwell (1987:97) speculates that "the pattern of access of black students to medical colleges during the 1970s can best be characterized by initial optimism and success, followed by declines [and] a leveling off." Blackwell's analysis documents that, of the 266 first-year black medical students enrolled in U.S. medical schools in the 1968–1969 academic year, roughly 60 percent were enrolled at Meharry and Howard Medical Colleges (historically black institutions), while fifty-four of the remaining ninety-seven medical institutions enrolled roughly two blacks each in their first-year classes. In the early 1970s, "the 440 black medical school students, who represented 4.2 percent of all first-year classes combined, were still concentrated primarily at the two historically black medical colleges" (Blackwell 1987:97). The proportions of black students reached a peak of 7.5 percent in 1973 and 1974, and it declined noticeably in subsequent years (Blackwell 1987:98). However, the phenomenon of black medical students who repeated their first year was a confounding factor, because they are reported in figures that include enrolled black first-year medical students. In 1978–1979, black students had a repeat rate of 14.4 percent, while students who were Mexican American, Puerto Rican, and Asian/Pacific Islander had repeat rates of 9.2 percent, 4.6 percent, and 2.7 percent, respectively (Blackwell 1987: 101).

Blackwell hypothesizes that:

> Inadequate undergraduate preparation in the basic sciences, weak self-discipline and poor study habits, insufficient time to study because of job commitments, family problems that interfere with conscientious studying, a hostile learning environment, prejudiced behavior by professors disinclined to be fair to minority students, and a whole range of adjustment problems experienced by black students in a substantially new, often overpowering and intimidating environment may explain why black students in particular repeat their first year in medical school. (Blackwell 1987:100)

Despite these problems, the proportional increase in total enrollment for black students from 1969 to 1979 more than doubled (Blackwell 1987:102). This emergent trend was partially the result of rising levels of institutional commitment; increasing availability of financial aid to reduce these students' concerns about finances; and "aggressive recruitment, special admissions, and federal mandates to desegregate all components of post-secondary education" (Blackwell 1987:102). Some of the more intrapersonal reasons included a shift in black students' views that pursuing medicine as a career was not only for the "economically affluent and socially influential" but was also a feasible career regardless of their socioeconomic backgrounds (Blackwell 1987).

The enrollment of black students in law schools during the 1970s included similar issues and successes. In the early 1970s, 1,115 black students were enrolled in J.D. programs in approved law schools, "represent[ing] 3.8 percent of all first-year enrollees" (Blackwell 1987:288). The peak in the enrollment trend (5.9 percent) occurred later for black students in their first year of law school (in 1978–1979) than for black students in their first year of medical school (1973–1974). The total enrollment for all blacks in law school grew to 4.2 percent in 1979–1980 (Blackwell 1987:290). Blackwell documented, however, that the representation of black law school students decreased at the end of the 1970s and attributed this phenomenon to a retreat by law schools in the wake of the Bakke decision (further resulting in a decline in black student enrollment and their attrition in the second and third years of law school). This decrease notwithstanding, many viewed blacks' and other minorities' presence in professional schools, medical and law schools included, as occurring at a great cost to white students. Blackwell's (1987:289) figure of black students comprising 4.2 percent of total enrollment in 1979 is hardly "equivalent [to] or tantamount to equality of opportunity and equality of access in law schools."

Blackwell's argument concerning this decline, however, was more balanced than it was unilateral. He acknowledged that although a larger proportion of able black students could be recruited for law school programs than is currently the case, "the fact remains that all too many black students are still victimized by weak preparation in elementary, secondary, and collegiate education. Too many suffer from deficiencies in oral communication and writing skills. There are problems of personal confidence, of sophistication, and of lack of ease in dealing with others" (Blackwell 1987:294). On an institutional level, "the deliberate intimidation of students by prejudiced . . . professors" does little to foster black students' class participation (Blackwell 1987:294). Moreover, some professors'

> attitudes . . . toward black and other minority students and faculty, . . . deliberate attempts to subject minority students to public embarrassment or ridicule, . . . harsher grading of minorities, . . . unwillingness to make the same kinds of exemptions or special dispensations for black students that they freely grant to white students, and . . . beliefs that all blacks [sic] students are necessarily less competent than even the average white student all appear to contribute to black student attrition. (Blackwell 1987:294).

In addition to these affective and attitudinal factors, Blackwell hypothesizes that the lack of financial capital was a barrier for many black students because relatively few black students were willing to go into debt in order to enroll in law school, especially when other career alternatives were available. When black students do work while enrolled in law school, their grades may not only decline but their professors may also not consider the reasons behind this decline, resulting in further student attrition. This phenomenon of student attrition is not peculiar to medical or law school nor to this period of time. Its prevalence twenty-five years later is documented and evident in the sciences, engineering, and mathematics (Bonous-Hammarth 2000; Hrabowski 2003; Shuman et al. 2002).

THE BACKLASH AND CHALLENGES AGAINST AFFIRMATIVE ACTION

Although the use of race in admissions decisions during the 1960s was of concern to some higher education officials, particularly given the mandate of Title VI of the Civil Rights Act, which prohibited discrimination on the basis of race, color, and national origin in programs funded by the federal government, the requirement by federal officials in the early 1970s that colleges and universities submit affirmative action plans for minority students seemed to sanction admissions criteria that included race. (Colleges and universities were required in 1967 to submit affirmative action plans for the hiring of minority and female faculty members.)

Despite these gains and assumptions that black students could easily assimilate into their new environments, the integration of black students into higher education was indeed a complicated phenomenon (Peterson et al. 1978). Apparently, many black students were not only disappointed with their experiences in predominantly white institutions but also were caught in the sometimes-divisive discussions concerning "admissions criteria, support programs, residential arrangements, and curricular offerings" (Bowen and Bok 1998:7). This period also marked a leveling-off of enrolled black students as many selective colleges and universities dramatically reduced their admission of underprepared or high-risk black students while implementing other strategies for minority recruitment, including information dissemination, using faculty and student role models, arranging for students to visit colleges and universities, and providing financial assistance (Blackwell 1987; Duffy and Goldberg 1998).

In retrospect, the question was not whether the use of race in admissions decisions would be legally questioned, but when. That challenge came in Bakke in 1978 (*Regents of the Univ. of Cal. v. Bakke*, 438 U.S. 265, 265 [1978]). This case defined the boundaries of affirmative action in education. Briefly, the University of California at Davis Medical School had reserved 16 percent of its existing seats for eligible minority students. Allan Bakke, a white student, claimed that he had been illegally disqualified from the medical school "to make room for minority applicants with inferior academic records" (Bowen and Bok 1998:8). In a five to four decision, the Supreme Court ruled that although a quota for minority applicants is illegal in the absence of a history of past discrimination, a student's minority status can be considered in the admissions process (Bakke, 438 U.S. at 307–10). Because the medical school, however, used racial quotas in admissions, the Court ruled that Bakke must be admitted. In his separate opinion, Justice Lewis Powell argued that, although strict racial quotas are unconstitutional, considering race in admissions to achieve a diverse student body is a compelling institutional purpose.

Given this mandate, many selective colleges, universities, and professional schools continued to take race into account in admitting minority students. Between 1975 and 1985, however, black student enrollment did not increase (nor did it decline). As indicated above, the percentage of black students enrolled in medical colleges peaked at 6.3 percent in the same year that Bakke was filed in California (Blackwell 1987). Other factors influencing this decline include the lack of adequate financial aid for black students, the growing reliance on standardized test scores and grade point averages, and "the presumed downgrading of subjective measures" (Blackwell 1987:102). Bowen and Bok (1998) suggested that some of the macro explanations include the repercussions of the oil crisis and stagflation, which resulted in tuition increases and a reduction of recruitment efforts for minority students. While many colleges and universities increased their recruitment efforts in the late 1980s as their economic situations improved, these efforts now included eligible Asian American, Hispanic, and Native American students and women (Duffy and Goldberg 1998). In effect, black students were not only competing with their well-prepared white peers, but also with well-qualified Hispanic, Asian American, and foreign students. Consequently, enrollment increased for Asian American and Hispanic students, while the enrollment of their African-American peers plateaued.

The presidency of Ronald Reagan from 1981 to 1988 marked a period of significant opposition to affirmative action. This included Reagan's appointment of Supreme Court justices who disagreed with the continuation of affirmative action. Reagan also restricted the Equal Employment Opportunity Commission and the Office of Federal Contract Compliance from pursuing discrimination and affirmative action cases by reducing their budgets (Anderson 2004). Despite Reagan's position, the National Association of Manufacturers approved a policy statement supporting affirmative action as good business policy (Norton 1988). Some companies voiced their opposition to the Reagan Administration's attempts to decrease the use of affirmative action (Norton 1988). While the Supreme Court's decisions concerning affirmative action seemed to wax and wane in the 1980s (See, e.g., *City of Richmond v. J. A. Croson Co.*, 488 U.S. 469, 469 [1989]; *Wygant v. Jackson Bd. of Educ.*, 476 U.S. 267, 267 [1986]), a closer examination of these decisions suggests that they appear to reflect the particular contexts of their respective cases. The Court made clear in its 1989 decision in *City of Richmond v. J. A. Croson Co.* that a state or local institution can have a compelling interest in redressing the current impact of its own past discrimination (*Croson*, 488 U.S. at 491–92). At the same time, however, the Court also decided that redressing the enduring effects of societal prejudice and discrimination was too nebulous an objective to sanction a contracting program that considered race as a criterion. Similarly, a plurality of the Court "ruled in *Wygant v. Jackson Board of Education*, that trying to remedy societal discrimination by providing role models for minority students was not a sufficiently compelling interest to justify a race-conscious" layoff policy (Ancheta 2003).

In *Adarand Constructors, Inc. v. Pena*, the Supreme Court ruled for the first time that all government affirmative action programs—whether federal, state, or local—must meet the most exacting standard of analysis under the U.S. Constitution (*Adarand Constructors, Inc. v. Pena*, 515 U.S. 200, 227 [1995]). The "strict scrutiny" test means that any race-conscious program must "further compelling governmental interests" and be "narrowly tailored" to reach that end. This narrow interpretation of affirmative action caused experts to speculate that fewer forms of affirmative action will be judged constitutional (see, e.g., Ana Puga, "Court Hikes Standards for Antibias Programs: 'Strict Scrutiny' Is Required on U.S. Affirmative Action," *Boston Globe*, June 18, 1995, 1). In a partial response to the ruling in *Adarand*, President Clinton gave a major speech in support of affirmative action on July 19, 1995. In this speech, the president called for reforms to "mend [affirmative action], but don't end it" (Remarks on Affirmative Action at the National Archives and Records Administration, 2 *Pub. Papers* 1106, 1113 [July 19, 1995]). He also initiated a review of federal programs that did not stir much interest.

In higher education, the Supreme Court's Bakke decision did not reconcile polarized views that (1) a racially, ethnically, and socially diverse student body is a compelling educational interest, and (2) "that the affirmative consideration of group identity violates both the academic norm and the principles for which this nation stands" (Killenbeck 2004). Rather, the latter perspective fueled opponents and generated significant victories against affirmative action. This polarization is reflected in the March 1996 decision of the United States Court of Appeals for the Fifth Circuit; it held in *Hopwood v. Texas* that not only was the Bakke decision nonbinding, but also that diversity was not a compelling educational interest (*Hopwood v. Texas*, 78 F.3d 932, 944, 948 [5th Cir. 1996]). The University of Texas Law School, in effect, could consider an applicant's race only if doing so was in the interest of redressing past discrimination by the school itself. *Hopwood* is striking in that a majority of the judges asserted that Bakke no longer characterized the Supreme Court's perspective and that the use of race to achieve a diverse student body was not a compelling enough state interest to satisfy the standard of strict scrutiny. It became illegal to take race into account in Texas public colleges and universities. (Colleges and universities in Louisiana and Mississippi adhered to Hopwood because these states are in the Fifth Circuit.) Texas compensated for this decision by stipulating that all students ranking in the top 10 percent in Texas high schools, public or private, are guaranteed entry to Texas colleges and universities. However,

> when institutions say that they have ended affirmative action, they are almost always talking about one part of an interrelated process, while continuing affirmative policies on other fronts, either through direct action or by adopting "race-attentive" recruitment policies focused on largely minority communities and schools. . . .
>
> In fact, simply enacting a percent plan does almost nothing to replace affirmative action. In Florida, for example, where race-conscious affirmative action is outlawed only in admissions, it is actively pursued in other parts of the process. (Horn and Flores 2003:ix)

During this period, the Regents of the University of California declared that the nine universities in the state system were no longer allowed to consider race in admissions decisions. Shortly after this decision, Ward Connerly (a conservative black activist and University of California regent appointee of former California Governor Pete Wilson) headed an initiative in the 1996 elections in California to end affirmative action in contracting, employment, education, and hiring. After a heated debate, California voters ended state affirmative action programs when they passed Proposition 209 (Stall and Morain 1996).

In the last few years of the twentieth century, attempts by selective public institutions to enroll black, Hispanic, and Native American students have been met with lawsuits that challenged the constitutionality of using race in admissions policies. The most prominent cases include those filed against the University of Michigan's College of Literature, Science, and the Arts (*Gratz v. Bollinger*, 539 U.S. 244 [2003]) and the University of Michigan Law School (*Grutter v. Bollinger*, 539 U.S. at 327 and 339 [2003]), whose appeals the Supreme Court heard in the spring of 2003. In *Grutter*, two central questions were considered in the majority opinion written by Justice O'Connor: (1) whether the use of race in higher education admissions decisions is a compelling interest; and (2) whether the consideration of race by the University of Michigan Law School was the only viable way for the school to achieve its goal of increasing diversity.

The University of Michigan argued that its use of race in admissions decisions was necessary to create and sustain a diverse student body. The university grounded its defense in social science findings that diversity not only potently impacts those in the educational enterprise but also the corporate, government, and defense sectors. The Supreme Court ruled on June 23, 2003, that the use of race in higher education admissions decisions in the interest of promoting diversity is constitutional. Justice O'Connor's opinion stressed that the majority was accepting on "good faith" and with "a degree of deference to a university's academic decisions, within constitutionally prescribed limits" that "diversity will, in fact, yield educational benefits" that "are both 'real' and 'substantial.'" Justice Powell's opinion in Bakke, noting that achieving a diverse student body is a compelling governmental interest for higher education institutions, is clearly reflected and fully sanctioned in the Grutter majority opinion.

This ruling effectively clarified discrepant perspectives concerning the nurturing of student diversity as a compelling interest in the lower federal courts and permitted selective colleges and universities across the United States to continue to consider race in admissions decisions. The Court did not accept the plaintiffs' argument (also endorsed by the United States government, the White House, the U.S. Department of Education, and others) that higher education admissions decisions must be race blind. The Court's decisions also changed the nature of the 1996 ruling of the Fifth Circuit in *Hopwood v. Texas* (78 F.3d 932 [5th Cir. 1996]) by permitting colleges and universities in Texas, Louisiana, and Mississippi to consider race in admissions decisions in efforts to increase student diversity. Although state universities in California, Florida, Texas, and Washington are still prevented by state laws from using race in admissions decisions, private universities in these states can implement constitutionally approved race-conscious policies.

In the law school case, *Grutter v. Bollinger*, the Court essentially affirmed that admissions policies and programs in which race is one of several indicators that are considered in the context of individualized weighing of all prospective applicants can satisfy constitutional requirements. In the *Gratz v. Bollinger* decision, however, the Court held that the university's point system (which assigned a fixed number of points for underrepresented minority group members) was inflexible in that it did not provide sufficiently individualized consideration of applicants, nor was it narrowly tailored to promote student diversity. The weakness in the university's case was not the point system per se, but rather "the failure to provide meaningful individualized consideration that doomed the policy at issue in Gratz, an approach that stood in stark contrast to the one employed by the Law School" (Killenbeck 2004:17). The wider implication of the Court's decision in Gratz suggests that admissions policies that mechanically assign advantages predicated on race are constitutionally questionable.

Although the Court's decisions specifically concerned university admissions policies, they are thought to have ramifications outside of higher education. An analysis by a group of leading constitutional law scholars suggests that the "rulings imply that student body diversity supplies a justification for race-conscious recruitment and outreach, as well as for financial aid and support programs" (The Civil Rights Project, Harvard University 2003). These scholars argue further that the Michigan "cases provide constitutional moorings for the defense of such programs when they are designed to advance diversity" although the "outcome of a legal test of such a program in the Supreme Court is uncertain" (The Civil Rights Project,

Harvard University 2003). Killenbeck reminds us that although the debate about diversity and affirmative action, both before and after the Michigan cases, presumably applied only to African Americans, the guidelines at issue in these cases were not constrained to this racial group. He pointed to the University of Michigan Law School's inclusion of Hispanics and Native Americans in its argument for using the criterion of race to create racial and ethnic diversity on its campus.

AN AFFIRMATIVE DEVELOPMENT POLICY

In the wake of the *Grutter* and *Gratz* decisions, the Center for Individual Rights (which initiated the Michigan litigation) asserted that "it is regrettable that the Supreme Court did not see fit to end racial preferences once and for all as a matter of law" (www.cfif.org). This organization regards their efforts over the past ten years as "the most successful assault ever on racial preferences" and vows that they will continue to challenge minority group membership privilege (Center for Individual Rights Annual Report 2003–2004). In all candor, affirmative action is also under attack because of abuses in its practice. Instead of an effort to ensure that qualified persons are not disqualified because of ethnicity or gender, affirmative action is often perceived as a program to privilege "unqualified" persons over those who are "qualified." The preoccupation with race may be a part of the problem. In a racist society all social arrangements are designed to reflect racist values, and explicit efforts to subvert those values are bound to come up against open resistance.

Let us consider a few modifications to the philosophy and policy of affirmative action. Rather than targeting ethnic or gender groups for affirmative action, let us target larger and more diverse groups: those that are low on wealth and wealth-derived capital resources. Education and employment opportunities could be regarded as instruments of human resource development rather than agencies for the credentialing and rewarding of the "ablest." Rather than protecting the opportunity to enter, let us ensure the opportunity to develop and qualify. In addition to a program of affirmative action, let us consider a program of affirmative development.

The largest affirmative action effort in the history of the United States was our veterans' preference program. This was also an affirmative development program. The components of that program ensured that veterans had ample opportunities to improve their economic, education, and health status. They were a protected group with respect to vocational skills development and employment. They were assisted in the acquisition of wealth through subsidized business and home ownership. The social ethos even gave them privileged positions in the political arena where they were able to access political capital through the jingoistic and patriotic biases of the populists. This national effort may have begun as a reward for service in the nation's defense establishment, but it was, in essence, a massive human resource development endeavor that positioned the nation's labor force for the economic and technological expansions of the latter half of the twentieth century. The affirmative development of the nation's underdeveloped human resources proved to be in the best interest of the entire United States.

A national effort at affirmative development to complement continuing efforts at affirmative action should be much broader than the initiatives directed at improving the effectiveness of education. We recommend that the education community embark upon a deliberate effort to develop academic abilities in a broad range of students who have a history of being deprived of resources and are, consequently, underrepresented in the pool of academically high-achieving students. The systemic or affirmative development of academic ability should include more *equitable* access to the variety of capitals below and to such educational interventions as:

(1) Early, continuous and progressive exposure to rigorous pre-academic and academic teaching and learning transactions. This should begin with high levels of language, literacy, and numeracy development.

(2) Rich opportunities to learn through pedagogical practices traditionally thought to be of excellent quality. Benjamin Bloom's Mastery Learning, Robert Slavin's Success for All, James Comer's School Development, Bob Moses' Algebra Project, Vinetta Jones' Equity 2000; the College Board's Pacesetter, and Lauren Resnick's "effort-based" "thinking curriculum" all attempt to nurture achievement.

(3) Diagnostic, customized, and targeted assessment, instructional, and remedial interventions.

(4) Academic acceleration and content enhancement.

(5) The use of relational data systems to inform educational policy and practice decisions.

(6) Explicit socialization of intellect to multiple cultural contexts.

(7) Exposure to high-performance learning communities.

(8) Explication of tacit knowledge, meta-cognition, and meta-componential strategies.

(9) Capitalization of the distributed knowledge, technique, and understanding that reside among learners.

(10) Special attention to the differential requirements of learning in different academic domains.

(11) Encouragement of learner behaviors such as deployment of effort, task engagement, time on task, and resource utilization.

(12) Special attention to the roles of attitude, disposition, confidence, and efficacy.

(13) Access to a wide range of supplementary educational experiences.
(14) The politicization of academic learning in the lives of subaltern communities of learners.

Skin color and other sources of cultural identity continue to be the basis for troublesome social divisions in the United States and elsewhere. However, we are increasingly persuaded that it is the unequal distribution of resources and the perceived threat of loss of "my share" of those resources that enable cultural, gender, racial, and religious bias to surface and flourish. We did not eliminate racism with the civil rights movement, but we did make enormous strides in moving this nation and other parts of the world away from the worst expressions of discrimination based on race. During the early part of the movement, when masses of ethnically diverse people saw their life chances improving and the opportunities increasing for their children to have lives better than their own, most people in this country were more willing to share those broadening opportunities. As the perception that life was getting better or that it would be better for our children began to wane, we saw an increasing backlash aimed at organized labor, equality for women, blacks, Spanish-speaking persons, and others who seemed alien to whatever was passing for "standard American." It is not surprising that a book like *The Bell Curve* (Hernnstein and Murray 1994), with its rehash of the notion of a "genetic inferiority" in some of us, was published in the final decade of the last century. Nor are the tax revolts and the rescinding of affirmative action unexpected. These are the reactions of a restive populace who have been frightened by deindustrialization, the exportation of production jobs, the requirement that two or more members work in the labor force in order to support a family of four; the downsizing of the work force while profits and the economy soar; and by realistic estimates that the next generations will not live as well as many of us do now. DuBois may have been prescient in suggesting that the line between the haves and the have-nots will challenge the color line as *the* problem of the twenty-first century.

To understand the magnitude of this problem, it is necessary that we look more closely at what it is to have and to have not. In many of the available analyses, income distribution has been the variable of focus. For individuals, inequality in the distribution of, and inadequacy in access to, income comprise a critical factor, but for groups the problem of inequality in the distribution of wealth may be even more critical. This may be true because while income may provide limited access to available resources, it is wealth that provides access to power and control. It is also wealth that provides ready access to essential human resource development capital. Some of us are beginning to believe that without the capital to invest in human development, it is impossible to achieve meaningful participation in an advanced technological society. What is the nature of that capital? Bourdieu (1986), Coleman et al. (1966), and Miller (1995) suggest that it includes:

- Cultural capital: the collected knowledge, techniques and beliefs of a people
- Financial capital: income and wealth, and family, community, and societal economic resources available for human resource development and education
- Health capital: physical developmental integrity, health and nutritional condition, etc.
- Human capital: social competence, tacit knowledge, and other education-derived abilities as personal or family assets
- Institutional capital: access to political, educational, and socializing institutions
- Pedagogical capital: supports for appropriate educational experiences in home, school, and community
- Personal capital: dispositions, attitudes, aspirations, efficacy, and sense of power
- Polity capital: societal membership, social concern, public commitment, and participation in the political economy
- Social capital: social networks and relationships, social norms, cultural styles, and values.

Obviously, wealth is more than money. It is the accessibility and control of resources. Schools and other social institutions seem to work when the persons served in them bring to them the varieties of capital that enable and support human development. If we are correct in assuming that the effectiveness of schools and other human resource development institutions is in part a function of the availability of such wealth-derived capital for investment in human development, we may have in this relationship a catalyst for pedagogical, political, and social intervention.

CONCLUSION

Income and wealth have replaced, or greatly reduced, the significance of the color line in our society. Ethnicity continues to be important, but economic, political, and social planning may be more appropriately directed at reducing the growing disparities between the haves and the have-nots. In the twenty-first century, this will require a quantum leap in the development and utilization of all our peoples. It will require the affirmative development of large numbers of persons who, because of the maladaptive distribution of human resource development capital, have undeveloped academic and other abilities that the nation will need. Such an effort would favor the underclasses in which ethnic minorities are congregated but are by no means the majority. It would be wise, however, to remember that this proposed national program of affirmative development would privilege the development of the lower and underclasses in our society. Unfortunately, classism may be an even more recalcitrant illness than racism. It is sometimes acceptable to talk of racial justice. It is generally thought to be subversive to talk about economic justice. In our judgment, however, the pursuit of universal economic justice, together with racial justice, may be the most promising route to universally optimal human development. It may also be a necessary condition for the survival of our democratic nation. We propose to begin the pursuit of justice with the affirmative development of academic ability in those persons whose natural conditions of life do not permit the easy acquisition of intellective competence. In the twenty-first century, professional educators and pedagogical scientists need to fully engage the challenge posed by James Coleman in his 1966 study, *Equality of Educational Opportunity* (Coleman et al. 1966). Coleman challenged the nation to seek deliberately to uncouple academic achievement from the social divisions to which our students are assigned (class, ethnicity, gender, and first language). A national commitment to the affirmative development of academic ability may enable such an achievement.

REFERENCES

Ancheta, A. N. 2003. Revisiting Bakke and diversity-based admissions: Constitutional law, social science research, and the University of Michigan Affirmative Action cases, 9.

Anderson, T. H. 2004. The pursuit of fairness: A history of affirmative action 177.

Blackwell, J. E. 1987. Mainstreaming outsiders: The production of black professionals, 97. 2d ed.

Bonous-Hammarth, M. 2000. Pathways to success: Affirming opportunities for science, mathematics, and engineering majors. Journal of Negro Education, 69(1–2), 92–111.

Bourdieu, P. 1986. The forms of capital. In Handbook of theory and research for the sociology of education, ed. J. Richardson, 241–58. Westport, CT: Greenwood.

Bowen, W. G., and Bok, D. 1998. The shape of the river: Long-term consequences of considering race in college and university admissions. Princeton, NJ: Princeton University Press.

Center for Individual Rights. 2003–2004. Annual Report. Washington, DC. cir@cir.usa.org.

The Civil Rights Project. 2003. Annual Report. Harvard University. Cambridge, MA: The President and Fellows of Harvard College.

Coleman, J. S., Campbell, E. Q., Hobson, C. J., McPartland, J., Mood, A. M., Weinfeld, F. D., et al. 1966. Equality of educational opportunity. Washington, DC: U.S. Government Printing Office.

Delbanco, Andrew (2005). Colleges: An endangered species? In the New York Review of Books 52, no. 4, March 10.

Duffy, E. A., and Goldberg, I. 1998. Crafting a class: College admissions and financial aid, 1954–1994, at 138–39.

Hacker, A. 1983. A statistical portrait of the American people. New York: Viking Press.

Hernstein, R. J., and Murray, C. 1994. *The bell curve: Intelligence and class structure in American life.* New York: Free Press.

Horn, C. L., and Flores, S. M. 2003. Percent plans in college admissions: A comparative analysis of three states' experiences.

Hrabowski, F. A. 2003. Supporting the talented tenth: The role of research universities in promoting high achievement among minorities in science and engineering. Twenty-third David Dodds Henry Lecture, University of Illinois at Urbana-Champaign. November 5, 2003.

Jencks, C., and Phillips, M. 1998. The black-white test score gap. Washington, D.C.: The Brookings Institution Press.

Karen, D. 1991. The politics of class, race, and gender: Access to higher education in the United States, 1960–1986, 99 AM. J. EDUC. 208, 214 (1991).

Kendrick, S. A. The coming segregation of our selective colleges. *College Board Review,* Winter 1967–1968.

Killenbeck, M. R. 2004. Affirmative action and diversity: The beginning of the end? Or the end of the beginning? 3.

Kluger, R. 1975. Simple justice. 749–50. Alfred A. Knopf, Inc.

Meyer, D. H. 1972. The instructed conscience: The shaping of the American national ethic. Philadelphia: University of Pennsylvania Press, 68.

Miller, L .S. 1995. An American imperative: Accelerating minority educational advancement. New Haven: Yale University Press.

Nickens, H. W., Ready, T. P., Petersdorf, R. G. (1994). Project 3000 by 2000: Racial and ethnic diversity in us medical schools. 331 New England Journal of Medicine, 472.

Norton, E. H. 1988. Equal employment law: Crisis in interpretation—survival against the odds, 62. TUL. L. REV. 681, 685–86 n.17, 713.

Orfield, G. 2001. Schools more separate: Consequences of a decade of resegregation, 2–5.

O'Neil, R. M. (1970). Preferential admissions: Equalizing access to legal education. Tol. Law Review 281, 300.

Peterson, M. W., et al. 1978. Black students on white campuses: The impacts of increased black enrollments, 6.

Puga, A. 1995. "Court hikes standards for antibias programs: 'Strict Scrutiny' is required on U.S. Affirmative Action," Boston Globe, June 18, 1.

Reardon, S. 2003. Sources of Educational Inequality: The growth of racial/ethnic and socioeconomic test score gaps in kindergarten and first grade. Population Research Institute Paper No. 03-05R.

L. J. Shuman. (2002). Discussion at the proceeedings if the 32nd ASEE/IEEE Frontiers in Education Conference. T4A-1-T4A-14 (November 6–9, 2002).

Slaughter-House Cases, 16 Wall. 36, 70, 1873.

Smith, W. A., et al. (Eds.). 2002. The racial crisis in American higher education: Continuing challenges for the twenty-first century. 23–40. Rev. ed.

Stall, B., and Morain, D. 1996. "Prop. 209 Wins, Bars Affirmative Action." Los Angeles Times, Nov. 6, A1.

Thernstrom, S., and Thernstrom, A. 1997. America in black and white: One nation, indivisible, 103–104. New York: Simon and Schuster.

5

Meritocracy and the Opportunity to Learn

Aundra Saa Meroe

Within the history and present conditions of U.S. citizenry, the desirable ideals (i.e., equality, fairness, liberty, and justice) have been subject to an ongoing interrogation of their presuppositions by way of meritocratic practices *in actu*. Meritocratic sentiments typically accompany intentions toward "equality" and "fairness." Idealizations of merit also bear family resemblances to the values of individual "freedom" and "liberty." Further, frameworks of meritocratic distribution claim purchase on approximations to democracy and social justice.

One arena in which adherence to meritocratic values gives considerable pause is that of education—and most specifically, the education of children and young adults. More so than the awarding of differential remuneration or position to adults within government, military, and industrial settings, the meritocratic allocation and provision of educational opportunities for the young force examination of meritocracy's background assumptions. For example, which versions of a democratic society are supported or undermined by meritocratic values? What do meritocratic perspectives presume about human ability and intent, conditions for motivation, effort, and achievement, and cultural constructs of value? Can meritocracy provide a just and humane criterion for determining the life chances of children and adolescents, given its presumptions about development and opportunity? When access to the development and education relevant forms of capital is unequal, can the assignment of further opportunity for development on the basis of merit be just?

With regard to the meritocratic distribution of educational resources among the U.S. student population, a number of critics have pointed to the questionable validity of standardized tests as the predominant mode of operation, given inequitable resources for academic development and achievement, class-based variations in access to testing preparation, cultural differences, and a fundamental disavowal of egalitarian principles. Still others have examined the history and logic of meritocratic social ordering and have found its ethical or practical applicability and values suspect in light of its pretensions to a universal standard of just rewards.

For example, in the epilogue to *The Big Test: The Secret History of the American Meritocracy* (1999), Lemann contends that the development of the U.S. meritocracy, from the 1940s to the present, was initially concerned with the designation of an elite class (i.e., the American Mandarins) according to standardized intellectual performance for the purposes of high-end civil service (Lemann 1999). Despite some overtures toward equal opportunity, Lemann argues that egalitarian values were never at the heart of the widespread application of intelligence tests as a universal standard; rather, the architects of this particular system were concerned with constraining access to resources (e.g., university education, etc.) rather than the expansion of opportunity. When Binet was commissioned to design a test of intelligence, the motive of the French government was to identify those children on whom education need not be wasted. Standardized testing, as a mode of scientific rationality, would be the mechanism by which society might curtail arbitrary privilege.

That this particular blueprint for merit has morphed into a national contest for "the good life" indicates the seductive qualities of its simplistic parameters: (1) IQ and academic performance determine worthiness and (2) the demonstration of potential as a young student should translate into high performance as an adult in the workplace. Lemann, among many others, argues that while the demographic characteristics of this Mandarin class might have diversified somewhat, the sociopolitical justification of this elite substratum and the possibility of competing for entry into it are applicable only at the uppermost levels of socioeconomic privilege.

While Lemann's observations are useful in detailing the pitfalls of U.S. practices of educational meritocracy, it is curious that after extensive historical reflection, he suggests an increase in nationalized standardization and the indefinite extension of the contest for goods:

> The chief aim of school should not be to sort out but to teach as many people as possible as well as possible, equipping them for both work and citizenship. Those who like to think of American life as a great race should think of the race as beginning, not ending, when school has been completed. The purpose of schools should be to expand opportunity, not to determine results. . . . To get more people through college, we shall have to establish greater national authority over education. High schools should prepare their students for college

by teaching them a nationally agreed-upon curriculum. Tests for admission to college should be based on mastery of this curriculum—not the SAT or some dreamed-of better, fairer alternative test of innate abilities. Test-prep should consist of mastering the high-school curriculum, not learning tricks to outwit multiple-choice aptitude exams. (1999:348–49)

In short, Lemann seems to criticize the postwar visions (and present-day manifestations) of Harvard administrators Henry Chauncey and James Bryant Conant for not being sufficiently thoroughgoing. Lemann is advocating a greater application of meritocratic competition beyond the clutches of the vilified Educational Testing Service and College Board. Additionally, his fervent yet pragmatically facile prescriptions for national accountability in education (preschool to baccalaureate) are well rehearsed within discourses on educational policy.

To be fair, this rather ineffectual critique is understandable given the trenchant position of meritocratic values within the doxa of Western sociopolitical and ethical thought. As Goldthorpe (1997) notes, there is something perverse in arguing against the "necessary myth" of merit altogether. Nevertheless, our understandings of and expectations for the uses and limitations of educational merit might be sharpened—and sobered—by a modest genealogical investigation of meritocratic values set within the contexts of socioeconomic and political conditions, the practices and effects of schooling, and the range of existential dispositions found among cultural forms and individuals.

Documentation of the contestable meanings and implications of "merit" extend from Plato's *Republic* and Aristotle's *Nichomachean Ethics* through the advent of "enlightened" modernity to the polyvocal present, thereby giving little warrant for the expectation of consensus in the future. As mentioned above, the comprehensibility of idealizations and practical applications of "merit" cannot be separated from the constellation of such equally challenging concepts as democracy, individuality, equality, justice, and rights—all of which comprise the seemingly stable but ever-shifting ground upon which we make social life sensible and tolerable.

Even the briefest sketch of understandings of merit and its attendant notions within modernity indicate another level of presumptions about intentionality, rationality, and the role of schooling and other forms of acculturation with regard to development and performance. The consideration of these issues in light of the life chances of children and young adults (in particular) and contemporary social inequities in the United States behooves us to clarify our positions on relevant criteria for a "good society" or a "good life." The seemingly idealistic cast of the latter statement is nevertheless an integral step in the design of feasible proposals for practice.

BASIS FOR MERITOCRACY

Meritocracy is often the worldview of the moderate upstart, the alternately savvy and simpleminded social climber, or the ambitious and able outsider facing off with arbitrary conditions of privilege. Meritocratic values also are commonly espoused by the guardians and agents of a variant of hegemonic rationality found in modern capitalist and technologically oriented societies. Herein, highly valued motives and activities are characterized by deliberate efficiency, consistent and systematic industry, and an orientation toward profitability. On the other hand, the values more in keeping with communitarian bonds and religio-ethical reverence are relegated to increasingly atomistic, "private" spheres.

As Young's (1961) *The Rise of the Meritocracy* suggests, meritocratic ideals and values are associated with interrelated cultural and political phenomena in Western history: (a) the transition from agrarian, feudalist, and guild economies to industrial capitalism and (b) the bourgeois challenge to aristocratic ("divine") rule with the alternative of democratic equality and liberty. A seminal expression of the modern meritocratic vision is found in the worldviews of the Western bourgeoisie in the seventeenth century. As the masterminds of the American and French Revolutions and proponents and practitioners of industrial production and free market competition, they advocated a selection criteria for achievement and commensurate reward that would undermine the sociopolitical currency of ascribed characteristics (e.g., family of origin, religious affiliations, etc.).

The conflation of merit with the idea of equality is related to the advocacy of democratic political practice as "rule by 'the people'" and "one *man*, one vote." The idea that everyone is equal in the eyes of God has a long history in Judeo-Christian doctrines. However, it is after the disintegration of the rigid hierarchies of the *ancien regime* that "social equality" becomes a practical ideal manifest in the notion of equality in political participation and legal processes. Nevertheless, the earliest contributors to the debate on U.S. democracy maintained competing views of the extent to which "the people" were capable of ruling themselves.

For example, the conservative views espoused by Alexander Hamilton and John Adams harbor considerable mistrust of the intellectual and moral competency of the masses. Universal suffrage is seen to thwart the rightful duty of the government to set limits for social life according to status quo authority. Moreover, in their view, the assumption of human equality is a gravely misguided sentiment given the inevitability of a "natural aristocracy." Alternatively, within a liberal tradition, Thomas Jefferson's vision of democracy assumed the "infinite improveability" (quoted in Parrington 1930) of human and social progress. Arguing against the material and moral adequacy of status quo conditions at the time, Jefferson contends that a democratic government is legitimate only as far as it safeguards opportunities for "life, liberty and the pursuit of happiness"—"happiness" being a benevolent sense of interdependence and mutual obligation.

Commentators on the classical liberalist doctrines (of the seventeenth and eighteenth centuries) point out that the commitment to equality before the law does not rest upon assumptions of the uniformity of human endowment, ability, and initiative. Nor does this type of equality recommend the egalitarian distribution of various capital resources. What is presumed within the notion of equality before the law is the sanctity of the rights of the individual.

Discourses on individualism developed during the Enlightenment emphasize the independence of the individual from the social institutions of the church, state, and other collective bodies. Individualism finds its economic expression in the doctrine of private enterprise. As Adam Smith's *Wealth of Nations* proposes, each individual should have the liberty to pursue her/his self-interests in the forms of economic competition and profit. Society becomes little more than a network of (purportedly) autonomous persons seeking private economic gain. What saves society from a Hobbesian spectacle is the cumulative transformation of self-interest into the common good of prosperity.

Recursively, the fruits of individual initiative and efforts are recognized, valued, and rewarded only by virtue of power-vested collectives. That is, persons are rewarded according to what others find desirable and useful. The rationality that attends technological and industrial sectors demands a greater degree of fit between functional relevance and one's capacities. As such, different abilities and positions garner different rewards based upon the functional import of certain skills. Within a postindustrial economy, highly rewarded positions and intellectually challenging occupations are assumed to attract the most able and talented people.

For those who are able, superior achievement will be met with superior quality of life and the upper echelons of the social order will evidence what Michael Young labels "rule by the cleverest." Meritocracy, as a basis for the distribution of power and goods, creates a cultural rationale for socioeconomic stratification. Inequality, the inevitable fallout of competition, then has a basis for justification and legitimacy according to the liberty to succeed and to fail. To a considerable extent, meritocratic values straddle conservative and liberal perspectives of the nature of the human and the social: Jefferson's dream of progressive development would be fostered by the emergence of Adams and Hamilton's natural aristocracy as evidenced through recognized achievement.

MERIT AND ETHICS OF EQUALITY

Since the middle of the twentieth century, the belief that society should as-
pire to treat its members with greater equality in terms of formal legal and
political practice has come to be taken for granted (especially with regard
to the civil rights of women and ethnic minorities). On the other hand, dis-
sension builds as the ethic of equality is extended to access to and distribution of material resources and opportunities within an increasingly diverse
society. As such, we are faced with critical distinctions between *equality of
opportunity* and *equality of outcome*. Within the specter of merit, such competing formulations of equality, in turn, foreground ongoing reinterpretations
of civil and human rights and social justice.

Equality of Opportunity and Equality of Outcome

Advocates for "social equality" argue that all persons should be treated
equally within every institutional setting that affects one's life chances.
In most Western societies, this would entail the domains of education,
employment, consumption, and access to medical and social services. In
this regard, equality of opportunity refers to the premise that everyone
should have the chance to achieve—within legal means and without special
privileges—the benefits and rewards available within a society. One's social
place in terms of occupation, income, and affiliation should depend solely
upon efforts to develop particular abilities in contexts free of formal discrimination according to ethnicity, gender, and religious expression.

Many would argue, however, that formalized equal access to institutional
venues is insufficient for the realization of equal opportunity for two main
reasons. First, critics call attention to the central relevance of formative
circumstances in the earliest phases of human development (Katznelson
and Weir 1985). The likelihood and extent to which a representative distribution of citizens seize opportunities presupposes equitable levels of
nurturance in childhood. Important factors in this regard would include the
child's physiological and psychological well-being, basic living conditions,
family structure, parental levels of education and employment, as well as
the formal and informal education through which the child develops and
discovers rudimentary skills and abilities. Second, even if "equal access" is
a legal provision, barriers can exist in the form of (a) the subsidiary preferences, regulations, and standards of institutions themselves and (b) unspo-
ken prejudices and informal, discriminatory interactions among the agents
who comprise the institution.

On the other hand, the notion of equality of outcome is even more challenging to civic and ethical discourse in the United States. A number of
fundamental questions arise when applying the outcome standard to the

understanding that individuals are likely to have differential needs, responsibilities, and tastes: (a) Why should we value the equality of outcome? (b) What are the principal conditions for establishing resource equality? (c) By what specifications and measurements will we determine equal outcome? (d) How is one and who is to judge the egalitarian nature of particular distributions of benefits? (e) What is an acceptable range of equal outcomes? (f) Should resources be distributed in such a way to enable each individual to exercise the same set of capacities? (g) Should greater consideration be given to those at the bottom end of the distribution? (See Dworkin 1981; Miller 1990; and Sen 1981 and 1982.) These questions reflect the trouble with creating acceptable criteria of technical measurement as well as core disagreements about how the idea of equality can and should be practiced.

Equality of outcome is more controversial than equality of opportunity because the former value requires extensive social policy interventions and regulations. The conservative standpoint of the current era has deviated little from its historical position: equality is incompatible with freedom, the egalitarian distribution of resources decimates the incentives on which the capitalist market economy depends, and new forms of inequality will always emerge. The classic liberalist position strongly supports the equality of opportunity yet endorses equality of outcome only in the form of minimal provisions. Conservatives and liberals would both concede that, given the role of market forces in the production and distribution of goods and services, inevitable inequalities will arise according to people's relative success and failure in competition.

In the egalitarian or socialist traditions, the equality of outcome is a central value but a limited practice in socialist states; hence, the goal becomes lesser disparities and greater degrees of equality in material conditions. Socialists would agree with conservatives and liberals that people should be rewarded according to the value of their labor. The notion of "complex equality" (Walzer 1983) suggests that modern societies incorporate a number of fields of competition and distribution in which different goods are allocated each by its own independent criterion. The ideal circumstance of such social pluralism would be a kind of equality in which no one decisively outranks anyone. Nevertheless, the practical problem involves containing the power and influence of economic position to acquire other forms of capital such as quality of life, social prestige, education, and political representation.

Formal Justice versus Social/Material Justice

If meritocratic values are sometimes misattributed to certain applications of equality, to be sure, an envisioned meritocracy is also likely to be held up as a practical manifestation of "justice." In fact, the colloquial notion of justice as a person getting her/his due is hard to distinguish from that of merit. Designations of "justice" and "injustice" are largely evaluations of institutional distributions of benefits and burdens. The criteria of justice mainly refers to the deserts or merits of those affected by the distribution in question. Formal justice requires accurate and fair distributions in accordance with extant rules for "due process." Material or substantive justice concerns the alternatives among distributive criteria (e.g., rights, desert, need, or choice) that constitute competing conceptions of justice. Some perspectives on material justice are associated with the idea of "social justice" because they may advocate substantive inequalities of outcome or distribution between different social groups.

For instance, John Rawls's (1973) theory of justice has been central to contemporary debates on the nature of a just society—yet, often as a landmark position from which to think through and against (Taylor 1989). Rawls's formulations combine criteria for acceptable standards of liberty and material justice under the idea of a social contract. He argues that the principles for procedural fairness in central social institutions should adhere to his constructs of "the original position," "the veil of ignorance," and "the difference principle." More a thought experiment than a possible social reality, the original position would find citizens making rational ethical decisions under dispositions of extraordinary impartiality (i.e., the nonsectarian, nonegotistic, unprejudiced "veil of ignorance"). Under the "difference principle," socioeconomic inequalities and a general lowering of average prosperity and privileges would be acceptable as long as these conditions benefited the most disadvantaged. So, while Rawlsian citizens could live under the extant freedoms of the First Amendment of the U.S. Constitution, it should not be the case that someone, fortunate in the "natural lottery" of family of origin, high intelligence, or rare talent, would enjoy a higher standard of living.

This conception of social justice poses a strong (theoretical) challenge to meritocracy and still can incite debate about the prospects of a (materialistically) egalitarian society. However, its failure as a serious political platform has as much to do with academic debate as it does with the hegemonic values of capitalist competition, hedonism, and individuality. Two main critiques of Rawlsian justice suggest that: (1) the idea of distribution in accordance with an egalitarian pattern involves the unwarranted curtailing of individual liberty and (2) from a communitarian perspective, criteria of justice depend upon the sphere in which distributions are being considered and the value structure of the communities to which we belong. Therefore, Rawls's earlier adherence to a Kantian prescription of ethical universality fails to recognize that the view from the original position is rather close to those of secular liberalism. Standards of justice are always relative to the understandings and expectations current in specific societies and subcultures. (See Sandel 1982; Walzer 1983.)

Rights: Natural, Human, and Moral

Discussions of formal and social equality and justice depend upon assumptions of an individual's right to exist and to act in certain ways and to attain and retain certain abilities and resources. In light of these rights, the rest of the community has the duty of tolerance and noninterference (and in some cases, the provision of the desired entity or effect [e.g., respect]). Rights can be posited on a number of grounds and are represented in formal legislation given the degree of collective assent. Typically, legal rights provide logical grounds and prototypes for moral rights yet to be ratified.

In the Lockean sense, certain rights are seen as "natural." That is, in accordance with divine reason, (human) moral beings have an indisputable right to the protection of "life, liberty and possessions." Within the conditions of civilization, governmental rule has limited authority to constrain or interfere with the enjoyment of natural rights (e.g., the Bill of Rights, U.S. Constitution). While commentators argue in favor of or against the transcendent validity of natural rights, others have made a distinction between natural rights as *action*-oriented and human rights as *passive*. Influenced by the horrors of the Second World War, human rights were argued to be entitlements that impose duties on the community at large regardless of the individual's choice. In principle, human rights include access to education, food, medical attention, and shelter.

Matters of civil and human rights become quickly complicated within discussions of inequality, justice, and the welfare of the individual versus the social collective. We might come to an agreement that certain rights should be treated as transcultural and universally applicable, however, attempts to alter meritocracy's individualist assumptions point to the cultural relativism lurking in all such values. So while dominant utilitarian and Kantian (rights-based) traditions share the assumption that ethical appraisal is founded on impartial and universal principles (e.g., individuals and their interests are to be given equal consideration), the particularist stance (central to communitarian and some feminist ethical theories) argues that any ethical appraisal takes place in the context of particular commitment and relationships to other people, traditions, practices, and conceptions of the good (Gilligan 1982; Macintyre 1981, 1988).

Value Relativity in Merit and Justice

In *The Constitution of Liberty*, Friedrich Hayek's (1960) discussion of "equality, value and merit" provides a useful summary of mistaking meritocracy to be transparent codification of equal rights. Further, his (rather conservative) liberal position demonstrates the laissez-faire harshness of meritocracy's criteria of justice—especially when imagined to apply to the life chances and developmental opportunities of the young. Hayek puts forth two main propositions: (1) No one has the ability to fully ascertain another person's potential, their deepest intents, or the extent of effort expended for any particular achievement. (2) One person's development of exceptional skills and talents should always be seen as a benefit for the larger community.

Underpinning these two assertions are a number of constructions regarding individual liberty, the free society, and distinctions between merit and value and equality/inequality in terms of (a) formal versus (b) material/social spheres. As mentioned above, a liberal democratic tradition (and Hayek's position) supports equality before the law and this entails that individual differences will be judged according to a common standard. All people should be treated in a fair manner before the law and within particular social-moral contexts. While the dilemma of socioeconomic inequalities may be cause for ensuring minimal (life) standards, state-mandated egalitarian outcomes are ultimately liberty-threatening solutions. In Hayek's view, "liberty would mean rather little" if we were all truly equal. (Note that he makes no mention of standards of living and opportunity here.)

With special relevance to issues of educational opportunity and competition, Hayek challenges the nurture bias in the nature-nurture debate by arguing that from birth, people have distinct differences in capacity. For Hayek, it is a good-intentioned lie that "all men are born equal." He allows that if people were exposed to identically nurturant conditions, there might be a greater level of homogeneity, but he holds there would still be inequalities. Neither genetic nor material endowment have anything to do with "moral merit." Although either may influence the degree of social value bestowed, genetic endowment is (largely) beyond human control, whereas material conditions conceivably can be altered. He asks, if we were able to do away with inequalities based upon family of origin and inherited wealth, would the unequal distribution of above-average talent and effort be acceptable? The fact that certain advantages rest on human arrangements does not mean that we can provide these conditions for everyone or that if given to some, others will be deprived. Family, inheritance, and education are often cited as contributing factors to socioeconomic inequalities. Hayek notes that we might also consider geographic locale, culture, tradition, moral codes, worldviews, and so on: would these factors be amenable to universalization?

Hayek, dismissing some egalitarian efforts as "nothing better than envy," offers a counter critique of egalitarian perspectives on educational opportunity. Egalitarians voice the desire to secure equality by demanding that the best educational experiences not only go to those who can afford them, but rather be given "gratuitously" and universally. If it is not possible to provide the latter then everyone must be made to take a uniform test of ability to access superior (and limited) resources. In response, Hayek argues:

Enforced equality in this field can hardly avoid preventing some from getting the education they might otherwise get. Whatever we might do, there is no way of preventing those advantages which only some should have, and which it is desirable that some should have, from going to people who neither individually merit them nor will make as good a use of them as some other person might have done. Such a problem cannot be satisfactorily solved by the exclusive and coercive powers of the state. (Hayek 1960: 86–87)

For Hayek, the transformation of the ideal of equality from the demand that all humanly imposed barriers to success be removed to the desire that all be given an equal start and comparable prospects results in an affront to liberty. This new vision of equality is dangerously close to the opinion that the government knows what is best for all and that the citizenry at large has a duty to gratify the disgruntled.

In a further deconstruction of the connection between merit and egalitarianism, Hayek notes that proponents for greater equality are often justified in pointing out the arbitrary relation between the unequal distribution of goods and any discernible difference in merit. It is his contention that this arbitrariness is the mark of a free society because it would be unbearably constraining if everyone's position was determined by the extent to which they performed according to what others esteemed. He suggests that a rigorous distinction be made between merit and value. Meritorious actions are varieties of conduct deserving of praise: something done according to an accepted rule of conduct that has precipitated the pain of effort. Therefore, merit has to do with the moral character of the action and not the value of the achievement. The "value" of the performance or the capacity of the person has no necessary connection with its ascertainable merit. Merit is a matter of subjective effort and not objective outcome: "A decision of merit presupposes that we can distinguish between that part of their achievement which is due to circumstances within their control and that part which is not" (Hayek 1960:89). The question then becomes whether it is desirable that people should enjoy advantages in proportion to the benefits derived by the larger community.

Goldthorpe's (1997) contemporary application of the work of Hayek and Schaar to the issues of meritocracy in education reaffirms the conclusion that the notion of merit may be "a necessary myth" for individual motivation as well as any degree of faith in a just society. Any rigorous attempt to judge the validity and empirical efficacy of meritocratic selection demonstrates its culture-bound variety of understandings. He comments:

As Schaar (1967) has observed, the idea of merit as the basis of selection and reward has a wide appeal in the culture of modern societies; to question its viability or desirability is thus always likely to appear perverse. Apart from anything else, such questioning would seem to leave the way open for a return to ascriptive criteria, or worse, to all manner of discriminatory practices in education and employment alike.(Goldthorpe 1997: 676)

MERIT AND SOCIAL STRATIFICATION

Allegiance to meritocratic values is supportable within assumptions of an "open society." In more theoretical terms, Henri Bergson (1932) and Karl Popper (1945) define the "closed society" as a small, tightly knit, face-to-face community. Bergson characterizes it as static and centralized social organization in accordance with an authoritarian and absolutist orientation to religious belief and practice, morality, and everyday customs. Predictably, Popper saw the closed society as tribalist and anti-scientific. Current theoretical understandings of the open society assume that such an environment: (a) supports the exploration of new ideas, (b) views education as a formal venue for intellectual development as opposed to indoctrination, (c) makes political processes subject to public scrutiny and critique, (d) promotes the freedom of international relations, and (e) tolerates no ideological or religious monopoly.

In more colloquial political discourse, the closed society is one in which privilege, power, and prestige are determined by birth and maintained by law and custom. The openness of a society depends upon the extent to which access to power and resources depend solely upon individual ability and achievement. Meritocratic views affirm the legitimacy of these latter prescriptions for an open society, given that distributional justice privileges socially valued abilities and achievements over the safety nets and straightjackets of class, ethnicity, family origin, and gender.

In empirical and historical terms, the attainment of an open society is in the same class as that of utopian experiments. It is not to be taken as an absolute term; rather, it is an ideal standard according to which we might judge social life by degrees. However, even the most modest assessments of societal openness may not account for the extent to which the kernels of individual ability and achievement are themselves brought into being and conditioned by pre-existing circumstances of social and material resources.

The "elite theories" originating with Gaetano Mosca (1965) and Vilfredo Pareto (1919) and surfacing in the work of Weber, Aron, and C. W. Mills, strike at the tenability of social equality and fully realized democracy. The basic premise of elite theory reaffirms the inevitability of social inequality and competition for capital resources. The attainability of "classlessness," equality, and democracy within capitalist or socialist contexts is impossible given the perennial existence of a ruling constellation of minority groups distinguished by their superior abilities and formidable maneuvers of economic, political, and social networking. For Weber, democracy in practice devolves simply into "competition for political leadership" and Aron's (1964) synthesis of class and elite theory concludes that a classless society has little bearing on the fact that any feasible government must reside "in the hands of any but a few."

Education, Social Stratification, and Merit

Modern commentators have repeatedly noted the haphazard trajectory of certain ideals found in Plato's *Republic* (for example, see Charles Taylor and N. Lemann). According to Plato's vision of the just society, exclusive levels of education in preparation for rulership would culminate in a class of civic devotees ("guardians") led by a philosopher-king. Gone would be the oligarchy of the wealthy; so, too would this intellectual aristocracy displace the debased tendencies of mass rule (i.e., democracy) (Rouse 1984). Out of the three Socratic principles of civic unity—the egalitarian distribution of wealth, restrictions for the size of the populace, and the recognition of merit despite contingencies of birth—it is the latter that has been most tenaciously embraced. Intellectual promise and educational rigor, the necessary materials for the ascendance of "Reason," would be held in the highest regard. Even as Socrates advocates universal provision of basic education, he describes the attainment of philosopher status as a hard-won and rare impartiality to and transcendence of baser material concerns.

The practical realization of the ideal of universal (rudimentary) education as human right/responsibility and the groundwork of a social order is a relatively modern-era phenomenon. Like social rule, the benefits of an extensive education have been typically assumed to belong "in the hands of a few." Conceived of as a limited resource, education had long been held to be wasted on "the masses" (be they women, people of color, the working classes, the poor, and so on). Educational opportunity and intellectual development bear a strong, positive correlation with socioeconomic status in most modern societies. In terms of Weber's tripartite analysis of social stratification, educational resources can play a role in terms of: (a) economic class, that is, one's life chances; (b) social power as the extent to which one can manifest one's desires in matters of conflict and competition; and (c) the status or prestige bestowed by peers according to commonly held values. Although these three aspects of stratification are interrelated phenomena, it is possible for a person to hold varying levels of privilege according to these indices.

In most Western cultures, central criteria for social rank include family and ethnocultural background, income and wealth, occupation, educational attainment, and social esteem and power. As discussed above, education and occupation have been viewed as those aspects of socioeconomic status (SES) most amenable to individual and social policy initiatives. Nevertheless, in the case of the United States, both historical and statistical portraits repeatedly demonstrate the clustering of high-status employment and superior educational resources within the traditionally dominant social groupings of European American men and the upper to upper middle classes.

Equal opportunity policies in education (e.g., affirmative action and desegregation) in the past half-century have led to a wider distribution of academic development and attainment across gender and ethnic membership. However, socioeconomic status—often conflated with ethnocultural membership—is strongly associated with the quality of educational inputs made available within different communities, subcultural practices and values regarding the relevance of education, and hence, levels of academic performance and educational attainment. Children in the lowest SES groups are more likely to be exposed to the most inadequate educational inputs and to rank lowest in distributions of standardized academic assessment and less likely to graduate from high school, attend four-year colleges and universities, or pursue graduate or professional training. As such, it follows that the children of the highest SES groups benefit most from and perform best within the culture and structural processes of schooling.

These patterns can be explained according to three general social perspectives that, in turn, have a bearing on how the validity of educational meritocracy is determined. The conservative or hereditarian view would attribute the coincidence of inequalities in terms of SES and educational attainment and performance to differential genetic endowment and psychological dispositions. For hereditarians, poverty does not cause ignorance; rather, various types of social and mental incompetence cause poverty. Educational inputs fail to significantly help the poor because such persons do not possess the innate capacity to benefit from these resources.

Placing great emphasis on the results of intelligence testing, it is argued that a correlation between high IQ score and high socioeconomic status supports the validity of meritocratic distribution of goods (see Jensen 1969 and Herrnstein 1973). For example, Herrnstein, in *I.Q. in the Meritocracy*, explains the pragmatic logic of rewarding higher levels of skill with enhanced remuneration and status: "To the extent that high intelligence confers a competitive advantage, society thereby expresses its recognition, however imprecise, of the importance and scarcity of intellectual ability" (1973:61). As painful as it may be for some to accept, Herrnstein maintains that the processes of social stratification successfully sort people out according to their initiative and ability. Both high intelligence quotients and superior educational opportunities are seen as limited resources. From this posture, major policy initiatives to increase educational inputs for the lower classes and other underperforming groups should not extend beyond tracking into lower skills training for lower status occupations.

The classic liberalist view on educational meritocracy would concur with the conservative view that stratification is a result of meritocratic distribution and that competition is conducive to individual and social progress. However, the acquisition of academic merit has more to do with individual effort instead of genetic endowment. In the liberal view, talent is widely distributed throughout the population and can be profitably developed and employed when not stifled by the lack of equal opportunity due to class, ethnicity, or gender (Bell, 1977; Berger, 1977). Although educational opportunities in the United States have not attained the status of a true meritocracy, a classic liberal perspective would not eschew merit as a guiding principle. Liberal policies would advocate equity in the access to and quality of public institutions of education; however, consensus breaks down with regard to government policies such as affirmative action and forced school busing. At this point, classical liberals begin to balk against mandated efforts constructed according to group-based rights and preferences.

"New Egalitarian" or radical positions have little faith in the validity of meritocratic ideals within a society severely divided along lines of socioeconomic and political privilege. An egalitarian view of disparities in educational attainment would point to the deleterious impact of poverty, racism, and sexist discrimination within institutional procedures and mundane social life. Academic assessment and testing—the heart of the educational meritocracy—is charged with dividing children into those with or without academic potential. Often these assessments (formal and informal) are powerfully influenced by the experiences made available to children given parents' levels of education, occupational status, and income. These initial assessments of "ability" in turn shape the expectations held for the student's future (on the part of influential others and the child her/himself). As these expectations are typically realized throughout the career of schooling, these now young adults are prepared to take their places within a status system in which skin color, class affectations and affiliations, and college credentials hold more sway than knowledge, ability, or ethical character (Jenks et al. 1972; Jenks et al. 1979; Sewell and Shah 1967; Bowles and Gintis 1972).

Radical/egalitarian perspectives in the United States are sometimes characterized as a reaction to the disappointing results of liberal educational opportunity policies during the Kennedy and Johnson administrations. When compensatory education programs did not deliver on the hopes that education was the gateway to middle-class security, many concluded that factors other than education were causing inequality (Webb and Sherman 1989). From this understanding, educational efforts alone would not be sufficient to contend with systemic inequalities. The notion of equal and fair competition is reduced to a farce in the context of socioeconomic inequities; therefore, radicals advocate (with little success) for the mass redistribution of wealth alongside the dissemination of an emancipatory curriculum rich in critical analysis and political activism (Aronowitz and Giroux 1985).

MODERN CONSTRUCTS OF THE PURPOSES OF EDUCATION: INDIVIDUAL VERSUS COLLECTIVE, STATUS QUO VERSUS TRANSFORMATION

To speak of these various positions on educational meritocracy begs the question of what the general and substantive aims of education as a social institution are from the start. Here again, tensions between the preeminence of the individual and/or the collective sociocultural order are at stake. Certainly, schools are charged with the inculcation and transmission of substantive knowledge bases, skills, and values deemed necessary for negotiating the demands of modern society and finding one's functional role within it. Nevertheless, as culturally prescribed understandings and abilities are presented to young people for their internalization, there is another aim to circumvent unthinking conformity, and even further, to encourage the discovery and development of singular talents within a smaller "gifted" population. The modes of grading, ranking, selection, and tracking of students all make reference to a common standard with an eye toward exceptionalism.

In theoretical terms, many of these themes are borne out in the formalized visions of the proper role of education in the work of educational theorists such as Durkheim, Dewey, Rogers, and Freire. In Durkheim's pedagogical sociology, the functional well-being of the individual and the social order depend upon the dissemination of a homogenous set of worldviews, substantive understandings, and practices (Durkheim 1922/1956). Education as a social institution is a national resource and responsibility for promoting a (secularized) moral order based upon rational choice (Durkheim 1925/1973). Like Durkheim, Dewey sees the individual as a product of society—the notion of a person's full autonomy and independence is a mythic byproduct of the modernization process. At the same time, this dualism between the individual and the social collective is unnecessary as the society is equally dependent upon the agency (solitary and cooperative) of its members.

For Dewey, education is a means to foster a productive sense of interdependence between the member and the group and a balance between social cohesion/stasis and innovation by the careful development of various capacities of human intelligence (Dewey 1916/1966). Intelligence is not an innate ability but rather a habitual phenomenon acquired through extensive socialization. The processes of reasoning, the identification and resolution of problems, and judgment both emerge from and can transform existing knowledge bases, technological modes, and sociocultural perspectives and practices. As "the key to freedom," Dewey's conception of "social intelligence" is a mélange of democratic principles and elements of the scientific method that provides an ideal model for intellectual discovery, problem solving (academic, practical, sociopolitical, etc.), and greater interpersonal regard (Dewey 1916/1966).

The notions of "freedom" and "liberation" with regard to the educational process also figure prominently in the work of Carl Rogers and Paulo Freire, albeit with certain differences. The psychologist Rogers views traditional educational institutions as a central culprit in the propagation of "inauthenticity" and alienation given schooling's emphasis upon constraint and conformity (Rogers 1969). Rogers argues that education should be in service to the individual as opposed to the social collective. The freedom he seeks via education is resolutely individual. Children need not be instructed in social cohesion and cooperation as these are innate capabilities. Further, students should not be directed by "teachers" but allowed to discover their "real selves" and to explore their own values and interests with the support of "facilitators."

Paulo Freire's agenda for education also takes aim at the social order as a site of domination and dehumanization. Like Rogers, Freire would argue for greater individual freedom through more egalitarian and dialogic modes of interaction; however, Freire is also concerned with forces of economic and political oppression that thwart the agency of individuals as well as particular classes within a society (Freire 1985). A liberatory education takes on the challenge of unshackling the consciousness of one's sociopolitical "limit situations," furnishing the individual with a vocabulary of "true words" and the intellectual capacity for critical reflection (and distancing from received worldviews), and prompting transformative action (Freire 1971).

As C. A. Bowers (1987) notes in his volume, *Elements of a Post-Liberal Theory of Education*, many of the perspectives reviewed above do not fundamentally question the classical liberal notions of personal autonomy, individualism, freedom, and faith in progress and reason within modern Western culture. In particular, both Dewey's "progressive" and Freire's "liberatory" education privilege the individual's capacity for self-directed investigation, critical reflection, and participation within spheres of political/civic discourse. In Bower's view, the idiom of liberalist thought, as incorporated within educational theory, effaces each individual's "embeddedness" [within a] "social ecology":

> The "language of individualism" is not the only threat to the social ecology; the ability to maintain the commitments and moral understandings essential to a viable community is also threatened by excessive concentrations of wealth in the hands of a privileged few, by distortions in the work place, and by the progressive corruption of the democratic process. A common denominator among these threats to shared moral understanding, social practices, and institutional supports of community is the pursuit of short-sighted interests—economic, technological, and personal. (1987:137)

But even Bower's insights only take us so far, given his argument's preoccupation with language and discourse. When relating conceptualizations about the social purposes of education with the guiding principles and practice of educational meritocracy, we are speaking of more than the necessity to equip students with critical thinking skills and effective discourses. These educational ideals simultaneously presume a widely held commitment to egalitarian principles and rest upon an assumption of access to adequate educational resources and living conditions.

As Lemann's account of the recent history of educational merit in the United States details, the last century of thinking about educational aims and opportunities took a variety of forms, which included but were not exhausted by Dewey's progressive program. Specifically, Lemann cites four camps: (1) Dewey's and The Progressive Education Association's programs whereby schools would become less authoritarian, rigid in terms of curricula, and dependent upon credentialization, and would instead emphasize creative individualism and rational critique and inquiry to be tested with innovative assessments for college admission; (2) the findings of William Learned's and Ben Wood's Pennsylvania Study, which prescribed a more rigorous and universal standard of academic mastery among high school students in determining one's access to the privilege of a college education; (3) Robert Yerkes' IQ testing experiments which, after being used to identify officer material among army recruits, were offered as a means of limiting higher education to the (presumably innately) intellectually gifted; and (4) E. F. Linquist's efforts to use the diagnostic Iowa test to guide teachers in maximizing their students' potential and ability to benefit from higher education.

In Lemann's view, it was only Linquist's efforts that aimed at something close to greater educational access for the majority of American students, while the former three perspectives, to varying degrees, upheld the relevance of and became increasingly vigilant against the inherent elitism residing in traditional constructs and operationalizations of educational merit. This would entail a reconceptualization of the preeminent status of academic ability and expertise (as opposed to other social resources among the populace), a reevaluation of the universal validity and applicability of the national assessments (e.g., SAT, GRE) developed within the cultures of ETS and The College Board (with more emphasis placed on the mastery of a nationally prescribed curriculum), and a mitigation of the cultural adoption of these measures as bureaucratic proxies for moral worthiness and entitlement to socioeconomic privileges. Lemann, among a large community of scholars and educational advocates, points as well to the paramount priority of renewing and reformulating our national commitment to ensuring equitable access to high-quality educational resources—across SES and ethnic groups—from the start of one's career as a student.

REAPPROACHING MERITOCRACY:
THE IDEA OF AFFIRMATIVE DEVELOPMENT

Lemann ends his analysis by citing Thomas Jefferson's and Horace Mann's efforts to establish public education and the implementation of the GI Bill as peak moments in which educational goals and expansive sociopolitical visions of social equality and human potential were effectively joined. Our proposal for "affirmative development" is among the newest generation of educational visions for contributing to both the common good and individual achievements. Reflecting upon the cultural, political, bureaucratic, and practical mishaps and victories of the affirmative action programs of the past fifty years, Gordon suggests a comprehensive response to the cultural precedent of meritocracy while also addressing the significant discrepancies in the availability and distribution of socioeconomic, cultural, and intellectual resources—background factors which ultimately determine the moral validity of meritocratic judgments.

While affirmative action programs largely are associated with expanding educational and employment opportunities for people previously excluded due to gender and ethnic group affiliation, Gordon argues that this social experiment was most effective in achieving greater gender equity, and in facilitating the development of the largely white male veterans of military service. On the other hand, fluctuations in the national economy and labor market and, in turn, U.S. citizens' relative sense of fiscal and employment security, severely undermined the continued and widespread support of affirmative action programs, especially those that targeted members of ethnic minority groups. Incorporating observations of the primacy of economic status within the interdependent web of racism and classism in sociopolitical structures (e.g., see the scholarship of Cox, DuBois, and Wilson), Gordon suggests that the next generation of equity-seeking public policies mount a larger assault against economic disparities. Further, he argues, in line with the theoretical constructs of Becker, Bourdieu, and Coleman, that we broaden our scope for assessing socioeconomic needs to include various forms of human capital resources (e.g., cultural, health, financial [wealth and income], political, social, and so on).

From this position, Gordon then addresses the issues of educational access and meritocratic distribution: "Education and employment opportunities could be regarded as instruments of human resource development rather than agencies for the credentialing and rewarding of the 'ablest.' Rather than protecting the opportunity to enter, let us ensure the opportunity to develop and qualify" (2001, 5). Herein, Gordon challenges meritocracy's ethos of entitlement as well as the construction of education and other forms of ability/talent development as prize or reward. His program of affirmative development reaffirms Dewey's position that intelligence, or more precisely, intellective competence, is comprised of a host of capacities dependent upon social milieux of pedagogical, material, and socioemotional supports.

In the worldview of meritocracy, ability, initiative, and effort are important to the designation of worthiness. However, when judging the talents and potential of children, can we validly apply the standard of purposive, instrumental, rationalist intent according to one's performance on standardized assessments or realm of tasks for which a young person may have yet to generate personal significance? In contrast to the assumption of inherent and largely inalterable intelligence quotients, Gordon's affirmative development assumes a wealth of potential among the majority of the student population. Given that students arrive at school with different abilities, sensibilities, and human capital resource supports, one mandate for schooling should involve the realization of "diversity as input—homogeneity as output" in terms of academic performance (e.g., content mastery, specified problem solving, investigation and creativity, metacognitive skills, and the like).

The individualist assumptions of the meritocratic paradigm are undermined by the idea of affirmative development. The interventions of affirmative development are to begin with exposure—from the earliest ages—to those pedagogical initiatives that have proven most effective. As opposed to tracking and ranking of individuals within cohorts, the use of various assessments are envisioned to be most effective as diagnostic instruments for targeted remediation or acceleration according to the abilities and needs of students and teachers. A large component of affirmative development involves the "hidden" incubators of high achievement: sufficient material resources (as well as effective strategies of resource utilization), socialization to the values of academic labors, and social bonds (with peers, family, mentors, and others) and networks that support personal development in general and the pursuit of academic excellence in particular. As such, academic development is to be given multiple existential relevancies (i.e., socioeconomic, cultural, political, etc.). Affirmative development assumes that the very will to achieve can and should be learned, fostered, and protected long before we begin the process of determining a child's initial promise and her subsequent worth to society as an adult.

REFERENCES

Aron, R. 1964. *German Sociology* (M. Bottomore and T. Bottomore, trans.). New York: Free Press of Glencoe.

Aronowitz, S., and Giroux, H. 1985. *Education under siege: The conservative, liberal and radical debate over schooling.* South Hadley, MA: Bergin and Garvey Publishers.

Bell, D. 1977. *The coming of a post-industrial society*. New York: Basic Books.

Berger, P. 1977. *Facing up to modernity: Excursions in society, politics and religion*. New York: Basic Books.

Bowers, C. A. 1987. *Elements of a post-liberal theory of education*. New York: Teachers College Press, Columbia University.

Bowles, S., and Gintis, H. 1972. I.Q. in the US class structure. *Social Policy*, 3, 65–96.

Dewey, J. 1916/1966. *Democracy and education*. New York: The Free Press.

Duckworth. 1939. *Intelligence in the modern world*. New York: Random House.

Durkheim, E. 1922/1956. *Education and sociology*. Glencoe, IL: The Free Press.

———. 1925/1973. *Moral education*. New York: The Free Press.

Dworkin, R. 1981. Equality of resources. *Philosophy and Public Affairs*, 10, 283–345.

Freire, P. 1985. *The politics of education: Culture, power and liberation*. South Hadley, MA: Bergin and Garvey.

———. 1971. *Pedagogy of the oppressed*. New York: Herder and Herder.

Gilligan, C. 1982. *In a different voice*. Cambridge, MA: Harvard University Press.

Goldthorpe, J. 1997. Problems of meritocracy. In A. Halsey, H. Lauder, P. Brown, and A. Wells, *Education: Culture, economy, society*. New York: Oxford University Press.

Hayek, F. 1960/1984. Equality, value and merit. In M. Sandel (Ed.), *Liberalism and its critics* (pp. 80–99). New York: New York University Press.

Herrnstein, R. 1973. *I.Q. and the meritocracy*. Boston: Little, Brown and Co.

Jefferson, T. n.d. Reproduced in Vernon Parrington, 1930. *Main currents in American thought: The colonial mind, Volume I*. New York: Harcourt Brace Jovanovich.

Jenks, C., Smith, M., Ackland, H., Bane, M., Cohen, D., Gintis, H., Heyns, B., and Nichelson, S. 1972. *Inequality: A reassessment of family and schooling in America*. New York: Harper and Row.

Jenks, C., et al. 1979. *Who gets ahead?* New York: Basic Books.

Jensen, A. 1969. How much can we boost I.Q. and scholastic achievement? *Harvard Educational Review*, 39, 1–23.

Katznelson, I., and Weir, M. 1985. *Schooling for all: Class, race, and the decline of the democratic ideal*. New York: Basic.

Lemann, N. 1999. *The big test: The secret history of the American meritocracy*. New York: Farrar, Strauss, and Giroux.

Macintyre, A. 1981. *After virtue*. London: Duckworth.

———. 1988. *Whose justice? Whose rationality?* London: Duckworth;

Miller, D. 1990. Equality. In G. M. K. Hunt (ed.), *Philosophy and politics*. Cambridge: Cambridge University Press.

Mosca, Gaetano. 1965. *The Ruling Class*. New York: McGraw-Hill.

Pareto, V. 1916–1919. *The Mind and Society: A Treatise on General Sociology*. New York: Dover.

Popper, K. 1945. *The Open Society and its Enemies*. 2 vols., 5th ed. London: Routledge and Kegan Paul.

Rawls, J.. 1973. *A theory of justice*. Oxford: Oxford University Press.

Rogers, C. 1969. *Freedom to learn: A view of what education might become*. Columbus, OH: Merrill.

Rouse, J. C. G. (Trans.).1956/1984. *Great dialogues of Plato*. New York: New American Library.

Sandel, M. 1982. *Liberalism and the limits of justice.* Cambridge and New York: Cambridge University Press.

Sen, A. 1981. *Poverty and families: An essay in entitlement and deprivation.* Oxford: Clarendon Press.

———. 1982. *Choice, welfare and measurement.* Oxford: Blackwell.

Sewell, W., and Shah, V. 1967. Socioeconomic status, intelligence and attainment in higher education. *Sociology of Education,* 40, 1–23.

Taylor, C. 1989. *Sources of the self.* Cambridge, MA: Harvard University Press.

Walzer, M. 1983. *Spheres of justice.* Oxford: Martin Robertson.

Webb, R., and Sherman, R. 1989. *Schooling and society.* New York: Macmillan.

Young, M. 1961. *The rise of the meritocracy: 1870–2033: An essay on education and equality.* Baltimore, MD: Penguin Books.

6

Cultural Experience, Academic Cultures, and Academic Ability

Edmund W. Gordon

The end of the twentieth century is an exciting period for the field of pedagogy and the science of behavior. In both fields, perspectives that, in an earlier period, were considered to be divergent are being recognized for their interrelatedness, while others are becoming more coherent and still others are even beginning to converge. This period is marked by changing conceptions of pedagogy and changing conceptions of psychology. Many of us now think of pedagogy as referring to the transactions by which humans teach *and* learn. Some of us claim that psychology is the science that is concerned with the study of the mechanisms *and* the meanings of human behavioral expression. Let us examine for a moment some specific changes in both.

CHANGING CONCEPTIONS OF PEDAGOGY

1. Perhaps the most important change in the way that we think about pedagogy is to be found in the distinction between training and education. Traditionally, *education* and *training* were used fairly synonymously to refer to the process by which values, knowledge, and skills are transferred from more knowledgeable and competent persons to persons with less well-developed abilities. The traditional teacher used didactic presentation and modeling, primarily, to transfer to the learner that which the teacher knows. In modern conceptions of pedagogy, this transfer function that I associate with training has receded in importance and has been replaced by the stimulation of thought and intellective growth. *Training* is now associated with the transfer by the teacher and absorption by the student of that which is to be learned, while *education* is associated with the development of intellect.

2. In this process of intellective development it is the learning activity of the learner rather than the teaching activity of the teacher that is given greatest emphasis. The teacher gives less attention to didactic instruction and demonstration, and more attention is given to mediation, resource acquisition and management, motivation, and support.

3. Without neglecting the authority and power of accumulated knowledge and technique (subject matter content and skills), the learner is encouraged to discover through active and vicarious engagement with the environment and to uncover in her own experience and thinking, representations of the mechanisms by which the phenomena of the world can be understood and their meanings explained.

CHANGING CONCEPTIONS OF PSYCHOLOGY

1. In psychology it is perhaps the change in the definition of behavior that is most important for education. Rather than limiting this construct to the overt and observable manifestations of human expression, we now think of behavior as being inclusive of all that emanates from the activity of the organism—overt motor, verbal, and attitudinal activity, feelings, and thought. Vygotsky (1978) would speak of social consciousness as the product of engagement in activity.

2. Unlike the knowledge acquisition, stimulus/response, and trait theorists, students of modern psychology are revisiting constructs like intentionality, attribution, existential states, and hermeneutical (interpretative) mental activity.

3. Modern psychology has not ended its romance with genetic determinism, but it is increasingly embracing epigenetic phenomena, and interactionist and transactionist conceptions of behavioral determinism; and possibly of even greater importance is the growing acceptance of contextualist and perspectivist approaches to the understanding of human learning and behavioral development.

These and other changes in these two fields have critical implications for the development of a science of pedagogy. In recent years, this author has referred to the knowledge base for education as the pedagogical sciences. I begin with the assumption that the subject matter knowledge in pedagogy, at any particular time, is a given. One can neither teach nor learn without attention to that content. I also consider subject matter content to be discipline-based knowledge; process knowledge concerning the disciplines; skill in the application of such knowledge, processes, and related techniques and technologies; and appreciation for the meaning of, and the values which adhere to, knowledge and its applications.

Pedagogy has to do with the design and management of the teaching and learning transactions involving pedagogical content. So it is that in this chapter I have little to say about subject matter or content knowledge, not because it is unimportant, but because my concern here is with the identification of that knowledge, which is essential to the design and management of teaching and learning transactions, what Schulman has called pedagogical knowledge.

In my view, pedagogical knowledge is best represented by the disciplines encompassed by the behavioral and social sciences, as they are amplified by the arts and humanities. Those behavioral sciences are anthropology, biology, and psychology. The social sciences are economics, history, political science, and sociology. This classification of the disciplines is somewhat arbitrary in that many of these disciplines overlap, and some could be called behavioral, social, or both. What is important is that in their totality they represent the knowledges and methodologies essential to pedagogical understanding and practice. Yet when one examines the literature of these disciplines, the seminal work tends not to be conducted by educational research scientists, and the cutting edges of knowledge production and application are underrepresented in the curriculums of our schools of education.

To make matters worse, postmodern thought and the politics of changing demography have resulted in changed perspectives with respect to the knowledge represented in these disciplines. Concepts once thought to be invariant and universal are now thought to be much more susceptible to contextual and situational phenomena. Realities once taken as granted are increasingly recognized to be mediated by particularistic attributions and existential states. Cultural diversity, once entertained for its exotic appeal, is beginning to be recognized as essential to the integrity of most epistemological endeavors. Let us examine this phenomenon within the context of the intersect between culture and the behavioral sciences.

I turn to two of our most seminal pedagogical scientists—Piaget (1952) and Vygotsky (1978) —radically different in their perspectives, almost contradictory, but complementary in the processual implications of their thinking. Piaget's notions posit the genesis of cognitive functions within the developing person, so much so that the proponents of the heritability of intellect can cite his formulations in support of the idea that cognitive capacities are more or less preprogrammed in the genetic material of the person. Operating from a cognitive-structural perspective on cognitive development, Piagetians emphasize the structural nature of human cognition, and the ordered sequence of increasingly sophisticated logical mental structures that are genetically programmed to unfold in response to experiences over significant periods of life (Case, 1985; Feldman, 1980; Piaget, 1952). Piaget maintained that there are four major stages of cognitive development, and unique structural features that enable qualitatively different modes of cognitive functioning characterize each stage. To account for the mechanisms through which development occurs, Piaget posited four constructs: assimilation, accommodation, equilibration, and schema. Assimilation and accommodation and the movement from concrete to formal operations are represented as the unfolding of natural processes as a function of maturation.

By contrast, Vygotsky purports that nascent cognitive abilities emerge, develop, and are displayed within a sociocultural milieu (Bronfenbrenner, 1979; Gardner and Rogoff, 1982; Palinscar and Brown, 1984; Wersch, 1979; Whiting, 1980). Geertz (1962) assumes, with Vygotsky, interdependence of context and cognition when he states, "the human brain is thoroughly dependent upon cultural resources for its very operation; and those resources are, consequently, not adjuncts to, but constituents of mental activity" (730). Followers of Vygotsky posit the genesis of intellective function outside the developing person in the interactions between the person and the social environments to which she is exposed. It is through these interactions that intellective behavior and capacity are developed, that nascent cognitive abilities are cultivated, that knowledge and cognitive skills are transmitted, and that the development and expression of cognitive behavior are encouraged and rewarded.

When we ignore the implicit genesis of cognitive capacities and focus on the processual features implied by their theories, these two pedagogical scientists appear to be elaborating different features of the same process. Assimilation and accommodation are what the developing person does with the content and meanings of environmental encounters. These encounters are the vehicles by which knowledge and skills are transmitted. It is through these encounters that cognitive behavior is encouraged, cultivated, and rewarded.

Embedded in these encounters are Vygotsky's social scaffoldings, which enable movement from concrete to formal (abstract) operations. The mental activities that enable this cognitive growth have been called "generalized event representations" (Nelson 1978) or signs and scripts used in social interaction, which are similar to the Piagetian concept of schemata. It is to Vygotsky, however, that we generally turn for the functional bridge between culture and pedagogy, but the processual conceptions of both theorists point to the critical role of culture in our understanding of the mechanisms and the meanings of what it is to teach and to learn. Vygotsky takes us further. Vygotsky distinguished between natural mental behavior and cultural mental behavior—the first is associated with the behavior of many forms of animal life, such as attention, perception, and memory. The latter is limited to higher forms of life such as human organisms and includes selective attention, logical memory, secondary and tertiary signal systems, as in complex language production and comprehension, and—of special interest to educators—mediated learning.

Now, the bridge between these human capacities and culture is Vygotsky's psychological tools. Like material tools, which enable humans to manipulate some aspects of nature and the physical world, these psychological tools enable some degree of control over mental behavior as well as the development, preservation, and communication of culture. In an elaborately conceptualized system of psychological thought, Vygotsky has provided us with what he called a unified psychological science and I would call the foundations of a "Cultural Historical Science of Pedagogy."

There are many seeds from which this notion grows. Cultural historical psychology can be conceptualized as existing along a continuum within psychology that extends from experimental psychology through correlational psychology to interpretational psychology. I argue that interpretational psychology requires that we give attention to *context,* to *perspective,* and to *intention;* thus, great importance attaches to these constructs in my thinking about cultural historical psychology.

Let us look at a little bit of the history of my thinking around these problems. In addition to my first exposure to the work of Vygotsky and other Russian psychologists some forty-five years ago, I was also influenced by the work of Kurt Lewin, who advanced the very simple notion that, if we are going to understand behavior, it can best be understood as a function of interaction between environmental forces and personal characteristics. His colleague Murray amplified that notion to talk about something he called the Alpha and Beta Presses of the environment. Murray saw the environment as bifocal: the reality environment (which I call the consensus environment because the "reality" or "real" environment so often consists of those aspects upon which we can agree) and the existential environment. For example, take a podium. All of us can agree that it is a podium. That designation would refer to the Alpha Press of this environmental artifact. But the Beta Press of this artifact would be the special meaning that is assigned to the podium. It may have one meaning for you and another for me. It may have different meanings for each of us depending on what our experience with it has been. This notion suggests that if we are to understand behaviors, we have got to understand them in the context of the characteristics that people bring to situations, the characteristics of those situations themselves, and in addition, the existential states, the attributions that persons bring to and develop in these situations. What Lewin and Murray were writing about, though, was the importance of the examination of the context in which people live their lives, the meanings that those life experiences have for the persons who live them, and the ways in which context and meaning ultimately shape human behavior and consciousness.

Somewhat later than the work of Lewin was that of Cronbach (1957). Lee Cronbach, in his 1957 presidential address to APA, talked about the two disciplines of psychology—the experimental, in which we manipulate things, and the correlational, in which we observe and look for correlations between things. He made the observation that these two approaches tended to go along their separate ways. He was arguing for their integration. It was some six years later when Tom Pettigrew was doing his work on racial desegregation in the United States that he made the case for the use of qualitative data to amplify quantitative data. He was arguing that to understand what was happening in the desegregation of the schools and communities, simply looking at the quantitative data wasn't enough. Looking at the qualitative data wasn't enough. What one needed to do was to bring these ways of knowing together so that they complement each other.

Also important to me have been Barker (1968), Cole, Gay, Glick, and Sharp (1971), and much more recently, William McGuire, whose work I refer to below. What Barker and Cole et al. did was to take seriously the examination of the environment or ecology of human development—the cultural and situational variables, the context, the careful description of the person/environment dyads in which behaviors develop. The more recent of these concerns that have influenced my thinking are those that are reflected in McGuire's contextualism (1983) and perspectivism (1989), Sullivan's critical psychology (1984), and the newest group of folks who are thinking of themselves as cultural historical psychologists, Stigler, Shweder, and Herdt (1990).

There are four basic themes of contextualism that I would like to explore. The first concerns the nature of human activity. Those of us who are thinking in this direction assume that human acts are dynamic, active, and developmental. Reality is no longer considered stable or necessarily ordered. It is continuously changing; it is continuously being constructed and reconstructed by those who experience it. Individuals are no longer considered to be simply passive or reactive. Rather, humans are seen as self-conscious, reflective, intentional, and transformative beings, that is, as reactive beings who are not only reacting to their environments but who are also intentionally creating and changing them. We recognize, then, that one of the characteristics of culture is its capacity to shape our behavior, yet another of its characteristics is its capacity to be created and shaped by human behavior. That is, each of us is born into a culture, but each of us is contributing to the constant reformation, the constant transformation of that culture. So when we think about culture as context, cultural context is by no means a fixed phenomenon. We are in error when we examine human cultures from "photographs," as it were—from still pictures captured at one point in time—without sensitivity to the fact that a photograph captures in static picture form an isolated condition or incident that in all subsequent instances is history (Gergen 1976) and may have changed in some ways.

A second assumption that underlies my thinking in this area pertains to the nature of communicative acts. Since human communicative action takes place in and relates to its surroundings, context must be examined in order to understand communicative acts. We now recognize that most communicative acts have intentions behind them. We also understand that intention is often influenced by the context in which it occurs, even in interactions that have the same reference points. Furthermore, human acts involve relational processes where the act incorporates, reflects, and affects the sociocultural contexts. Things are never constant; they are constantly changing. Human actions are thus dynamic and dialectically related to context. One act influences the subsequent act. That act functions as background of the thing that was initially expressed. And so goes the process in much the same way, as do proprioceptive reactions, in which a response in one part of an organism stimulates a different response in another part of the organism.

The third basic theme of contextualism involves epistemological questions having to do with the nature, origins, and boundaries of our knowledge. The contextualist position holds that there can be more than one theory or perspective applying to human behavior at the same time because of differences in context, circumstance, temporal factors, and, according to Keil (1990), constraints. Keil is a cognitive psychologist who in his work looks at the way in which prior knowledge constrains the development of subsequent knowledge—how a prior condition constrains a subsequent behavior. The fact that all of us know, for instance, that 2 + 2 = 4 limits the kinds of things that we are likely to do with 2 + 2, unless we shift to another number set. Now those of us who are willing to break out of that mind set can do a lot of things with that fact. But within that set, the fact itself forces certain kinds of reactions.

This concern with context suggests that if we are indifferent to the kinds of things that have gone before, the kinds of things that are carried in the mind of the person, we have an incomplete picture. I refer to my earlier reference to the importance of attributional phenomena, whereby insufficient attention to the idiosyncratic meanings of an experience can result in misunderstanding the behavior. No matter how accurately I describe the situation that I am observing, unless I understand it in the same way as those involved understand it, I have missed a crucial part of the situation, since that indigenous perspective is going to influence the behavior observed. The mere fact that I understand it in a way that has gained some consensus, and we call it *reality*, has nothing to do with the appropriateness of the interpreted relationship between my perception of the stimulus and the respondent's behavior, if the respondent's understanding of that stimulus is different from the consensus interpretation.

Principles and theories cannot be seen as universally valid, then, because the contexts to which they refer are constantly changing, and they involve vastly different historical and sociocultural meanings across persons and situations. There are cognitive constraints, because any representation of reality will always be distorted by historical dynamics, since in relating to some aspects of "reality," other aspects are necessarily omitted. In a paper that Fayneese Miller, David Rollock, and I wrote (1990), we used a little phrase that I like to refer to and remind my students of: "When we have developed a way of seeing, we have also developed a way of not seeing." It is terribly important to remember that when I fix my vision and hone my lenses so that I can see one aspect of a thing, there are just loads of other things that I do not and cannot see. My colleague Bill McGuire, who writes about multiple perspectives and multiple contexts, suggests that if this is in fact true, good scientific investigations have to examine the same hypothesis in multiple contexts. You have to run the experiment in a variety of ways because what you want to do is understand the phenomenon, not simply prove your hypothesis.

Edmund Sullivan has written a brilliant little book, *A Critical Psychology* (1984), in which he attempts to apply critical theory to psychology. From this perspective, critical interpretation is a central purpose of psychology as a discipline. He offers critical interpretation not so much as a substitute for empirical work, but as an essential addition to more traditional approaches to knowledge production. Critical interpretation is analytical in that it deconstructs not only the problem, method, and findings but also the purpose, the intent, the underlying values, the knowledge interests served by the phenomenon, and the method by which it is studied. What critical theorists are suggesting is that when we are looking at a piece of research, designing it for that matter, it may not be enough to simply look at the relationship between the problem and the method and the findings. They are arguing that the intentions and the knowledge interests of the folk who do the work are important.

In the Gordon, Rollock, and Miller (1990) paper we argue that the perspective, which an investigator brings to his or her work, can influence the manner in which the question is posed and the investigation is designed. These factors can also influence findings, rendering them not as objective as we are inclined to think. So as a responsible scientist I owe it to you to remind you, and maybe even more important than reminding you, I need to remind myself that I have not been so, that the things that I report, the kinds of conclusions I come to are the products of a specific perspective that I have brought to the problem. Thus, the problem, the method, the findings should never be separated from context. They are synthetic, that is constructive, in the sense that special attention is given to the intentions that drive the behaviors of those who study as well as those being studied. And since intent must be inferred, we do not yet have good ways of measuring it. Concern with it involves interpretation, and that is constructive interpretation.

In their concern for intent, the critical interpretationists are critical of the mechanical and biological metaphors which they assert have guided most behavioral sciences. They are arguing that we may have looked too narrowly for our explanations for behavior. We may have been using excessively the mechanical metaphor, in which we look for one thing causing the other, or the biological metaphor, with its implied unidirectional linear relationships. Both are primarily concerned with explaining how things work. Instead, the critical interpretationists propose that we also have to be concerned about the *why* questions, about why things work. And here we have to focus on meanings. I often refer to the difference between efforts at identifying the mechanisms by which aging can be explained and a search for understanding of the meanings of growing old. When the question is, what are the factors associated with growing old, social scientists can identify these. But if you want to know the meanings of growing old, I'd go to a good novel, a good piece of poetry, or I would talk to a person like myself, who is over eighty-five years old. The *meanings* of growing old are quite different from the *mechanisms*, but both the meanings and the mechanisms are important if one is to understand aging.

Spokespersons for critical interpretation offer as more useful the personal metaphor. They ask, who and what is this person, a question that they claim requires an "I-Thou" dyad. They are arguing that too much of our work has focused on the autonomous person. When we stop to think about it, none of us can exist as an individual outside of relationships to other people. Human beings are essentially social beings. We derive our existence and are able to maintain it; we achieve our survival out of our interactions with other people. It is "I-Thou" rather than just the "me" or "I" or "you." It is the social forces that drive the interactions in and between these dyads that ought to be the subject of our investigations.

It is from such ideas as these that we now see a confluence of thought that could become a new subspecialty in the sciences of behavior. Some people are calling it cultural psychology. Stigler, Shweder, and Herdt in *Cultural Psychology* present a collection of essays by fourteen different writers who are approaching the problems of this area from different perspectives. This is a field that is being born rather than a field that exists. This school of thought asserts that cultural psychology is the psychology of intentional worlds—the intentional worlds of the I-Thou dyads that drive behavior. A cultural psychology aims to develop the principle of intentionality—action responsive to and directed at mental objects or representations—"by which culturally constituted realities (intentional worlds) and reality-constituting psyches (intentional persons) continually and continuously make each other up, perturbing and disturbing each other, interpenetrating each other's identity, reciprocally conditioning each other's existence" (Shweder, 1990). Thus I am constantly in the process of creating you as I try to understand you, because what I have to do in order to understand you is to create an image of you, this vision of you in my mind. It may be perturbing, it may be disturbing, it may be reconciling. You may share my image or parts of it. You may defy it, but my mental images contribute to my identification of you and vice versa. In addition, we may be reciprocally conditioning each other's existence as well as each other's images.

Now if these notions hold, what do they imply for the relationship between a specific context such as that of academic cultures and the cultivation of a specific ability such as academic ability?

In a conceptually provocative book-length review of the then extant research concerning the nature and origins of intelligence, J. McVicker Hunt (1966) argued the case for life experience as a primary determinant of the quality of human intellect. At the time and since, there have been compelling arguments in support of biological and possibly genetic explanations of the nature and source of differences in human intelligence, but Hunt's work stands as the most extensive treatment of the evidence for the causal role played by experience. Since that period in the middle of the twentieth century, many, if not most, scholars of this complex set of issues have concluded that these "nature versus nurture" debates and even those that seek to parcel out the relative contribution of each miss the point. The evidence seems increasingly persuasive that variations in the quality of human intellect are the result of complex and dynamic interactions between whatever is given in the biology of the organism and what is available in the environment of the developing organism (Gordon and Lemons, 1989). Even in the presence of specific genetic indicators (genotype), the phenotypic manifestation (behavior or characteristic) will reflect the impact of environmental encounters on the developing organism. Genotypic phenomena are thought to be characterized by a range of reactive capacity along which a specific phenotypic expression may fall, depending on the nature of the interaction between the genetic material and specific aspects of its environment (Hirsch 1968). Nonetheless, environment/genotype interactions of a specific nature tend to be associated with behavioral outcomes of a specific nature. Learning environments are a case in point.

Gordon and Armour Thomas (1991) have advanced the notion that consistencies in particular cultural environments are associated with the development of particular cultural expressions or behaviors. Through processes of acculturation, adaptation, and socialization, younger members of specific cultural groups come to acquire behavior that is consistent with that of the group with which they identify and in which they have had these experiences. For example, language group members tend to speak the indigenous language, and males who grow up with and identify with male models tend to be proficient in the behavior of other male culture members.

Because schools are so ubiquitous in technologically advanced societies, we tend to forget that schools and other academic institutions are characterized by cultures that serve academic purposes. These are specialized cultures that privilege attitudes, behaviors, beliefs, technologies, and values that are peculiar to schooling and intentionally designed to serve academic purposes. With appropriate encouragement and support, academic ability is the product they tend to produce. Thanks to authors like Seymour Sarason (1992) we are familiar with the "culture of schools." Some of us also know that preparation for and socialization for schooling begins long before some children arrive at school.

Language skills, listening behavior, help seeking, turn taking, socialization to routines, elemental self-care, and self-regulation are learned by many children at home and/or in preschool. Pupils who do not come to school with these developed abilities soon learn that they must be mastered or the pupil begins to fall behind. Since such abilities are instrumental to the acquisition of academic knowledge and skills, and since such acquisition is the work one does in school, most children learn from other children or with direction from their teachers and quickly accommodate to the instrumental and content learning required by the culture of the school. Pupils who enter without these instrumental abilities and do not acquire them through acculturation or directed learning may founder unless this tacit knowledge is made explicit and their use of it is frequently reinforced.

The processes and strategies by which one gets along in school increase in complexity as the student progresses. Students who come from homes where there are adults and/or siblings who have successfully experienced schools may find it easier to become rapidly acculturated than those who do not. Those who are fortunate enough to catch on quickly and to identify with the process are able to avoid the incongruence that is experienced when the streetwise student find that her street smarts do not fly well in school (see Carol Lee's chapter in this volume). The ability to make sense of one's environment and to solve the problems peculiar to that environment may vary in different contexts, especially when the cultural competence honed in one context is inappropriate to the demands of another context. Thus it is that greater attention may need to be given to the explication of the unique demands and rewards of academic cultures as a component of deliberate attempts to develop academic ability in children whose life conditions have not predisposed them to the development of such ability.

REFERENCES

Barker, R. 1968. *Ecological psychology: Concepts and methods for studying the environment of human behavior.* Palo Alto, CA: Stanford University Press.

Bronfenbrenner, U. 1979. *The ecology of human development.* Cambridge: Harvard University Press.

Case, R. 1985. *Intellectual development: A systematic reinterpretation.* New York: Academic Press.

Cole, M., J. Gay, G. Glick, and D. Sharp. 1971. *Cultural context of learning and thinking.* New York: Basic Books.

Cronbach, L. J. 1957. The two disciplines of scientific psychology. *The American Psychologist,* 12, 671–84.

Feldman, D. 1980. *Beyond universal in cognitive development.* Norwood, NJ: Ablex.

Gardner, W., and B. Rogoff. 1982. The role of instruction in memory development: Some methodological/choices. *The Quarterly Newsletter of the Laboratory of Comparative Human Cognition,* 4, 6–12.

Geertz, C. 1962. The growth of culture and the evolution of mind. In J. M. Scher (Ed.), *Theories of the mind.* New York: Free Press.

Gergien, K. J. 1990. Social understanding and the inscription of self. In J. W Stigler, R. A. Schweder and G. Herdt (Eds.), *Cultural psychology.* New York: Cambridge University Press.

Gordon, E. W., and E. Armour-Thomas. 1991. Culture and cognitive development. In L. Okagaki and R. Sternberg (Eds.), *Directors of development: Influences on the development of children's thinking.* Hillsdale, NJ: Erlbaum and Associates.

Gordon, E. W. , and M. P. Lemons. 1997. An interactionist perspective on the genesis of intelligence. In R. J. Sternberg and E. L. Grigorenko (Eds.), *Intelligence, heredity, and environment* (pp. 323–40). New York: Cambridge University Press.

Gordon, E. W., D. Rollock, and F. Miller 1990. Coping with communicentric bias in knowledge production in the social sciences. *Educational Researcher,* 19(3).

Hirsch, J. (1968). Behavior-genetic analysis and the study of man. In M. Mead, et al. (Eds.), *Science and the Concept of Race.* New York: Columbia University Press.

Hunt, J. McVicker. 1961. *Intelligence and experience.* New York, Ronald Press Co.

Keil, F. 1990. Constraints on constraints: Surveying the epigenetic landscape. *Cognitive Science,* 14, 135–68.

McGuire, W. J. 1983. A contextualist theory of knowledge: Its implications for innovations and reform in psychological research. In L. Berkowitz (Ed.), *Advances in experimental social psychology.* New York: Academic Press.

———. 1989. A perspectivist approach to the strategical planning of programmatic scientific research. *The psychology of science: Contributions to metascience.* 214–45. New York: Cambridge University Press.

Nelson, K. 1978. How young children represent knowledge of their world in and out of language. In R. Siegler (Ed.), *Children's thinking: What develops?* Hillsdale, NJ: Erlbaum.

Palinscar, A., and A. L. Brown. 1984. Reciprocal teaching of comprehension-fostering and comprehension-monitoring activities. *Cognition and Instruction,* 1, 117–75.

Piaget, J. 1952. *The child's conception of number.* New York: Norton.

———. 1973. *The psychology of intelligence.* Totowa, NJ: Littlefield and Adams.

Piaget, J., and B. Inhelder 1969. *The psychology of the child.* New York: Basic Books.

Sarason, I. G., G. R. Pierce, and Sarason. 1996. *Cognitive interference: Theories, methods, and findings.* Mahwah, NJ: Lawrence Erlbaum Associates.

Schulman, L. S. 1986. Those who understand: Knowledge growth in teaching. *Educational Researcher,* 15 (2), 4–14.

Schweder, R. 1990. Cultural psychology—what is it? In J. W. Stigler, R. A. Schweder, and G. Herdt (Eds.) *Cultural psychology* (pp.1–46). New York: Cambridge University Press.

Stigler, J., R. Schweder, and G. Herdt (Eds.). 1990. *Cultural psychology: Essays on compensatory human development.* New York: Cambridge University Press.

Sullivan, E. 1984. *Critical psychology: An interpretation of the personal world.* New York: Plenum Press.

Vygotsky, L. S. 1978. *Mind in society. The development of higher psychological processes.* Cambridge, MA. Harvard University Press.

Wertsch, J. V. 1979. From social interaction to higher psychological processes: A clarification and application of Vygotsky's theory. *Human Development,* 22, 1–22.

Whiting, B. 1980. Culture and social behavior: A model for the development of social behavior. *Ethos,* 8, 95–116.

II

AFFIRMATIVE DEVELOPMENT
OF ACADEMIC ABILITY

7

The Curriculum and Its Functions

Edmund W. Gordon

Throughout the history of structured knowledge acquisition (education), curricula have been used to develop specific intellectual processes considered necessary for the achievement of particular knowledge bases, skills, and values. The very substance and certainly the spirit of the curriculum is derived from a projection of the purpose and outcomes of society and its educational facilitators or institutions onto the learning experience. The success of a curriculum is entirely dependent upon the clarity of these goals and the efficiency and effectiveness of the pedagogical practices that emerge from their projections.

PREREQUISITES FOR CRITICAL LITERACY

Critical literacy cannot be taught without a critical pedagogy that seeks to inform, expose, and enable learners to engage in struggles that further their own interests. Such a critical pedagogy focuses on getting students to think critically and to delve deeply into structure and extract meaning from textual material. It adds relevance to the classroom by grounding the learning experience in problems that are a part of students' lives. Given this dynamic, curriculum developers must (1) create instructional materials that reflect the real life experiences of a broader range of students; (2) devise flexible approaches teachers can draw upon; and (3) specify whose interest(s) curriculum materials are to serve.

One of the several purposes and functions of curriculum is the transmission of selective aspects of cumulative knowledge and cultural heritages (Szcszciul, Gordon, and Taylor, 1989). According to the standards of critical literacy, however, this purpose cannot be served for various ethnic or racial groups in American society because the curriculum materials available to them are seriously limited. Yet if we are serious about exposing American students to models of how others perceive the world and engage its problems (enabling critical literacy), we must provide classroom materials and promote discussion that deliberately represents a wider range of perspectives and approaches to solving problems.

Teachers and curriculum materials can further facilitate the mastery of abstract, critical competencies by drawing from students' daily life experiences that can be brought to bear on the knowledge they receive in school. Learning is then enabled when students can use their own cultural currencies as vehicles for education. Additionally, students must be allowed to manipulate and reference learned material by utilizing the information, strategies, or symbols relevant to and established within their own cultures or they will suffer academically. The key to critical literacy, thus, is participation, defined as the full involvement and exchange of systematic thinking between students and teachers.

Teachers must also possess a functional knowledge of their students' cultural codes, or at the very least, they must know how to access those codes. In African-American vernacular, for example, the term *reading* refers to a means of discerning the inner workings of an individual's character by examining his or her demeanor or actions. By applying "reading" to literary analysis, teachers can teach their students how to assess the underlying structure and implicit meanings of a text. This paradigm is useful because it enables students to think both critically and analytically.

However, critical thinking is not taught exclusively by books, and abstract thinking is not the exclusive domain of the academic. Individuals think critically and abstractly in daily life. Everyday speech itself involves a level of abstraction, and teachers can use it as an avenue to critical literacy by engaging students in analysis of their own speech and writing.

Critical thinking is also participatory and involves teaching students to present their thoughts orally and allowing them to discuss their ideas. This exercise creates an avenue for students to discover their styles, backgrounds, and experiences. However, while it is important to build oral competencies, caution is advised when doing so may limit student development. In such instances, the challenge is not merely getting students to talk but getting them to use oral skills in ways that unite them around the subject matter. Critical pedagogy emphasizes that for orality to be useful in the classroom, students must learn to think "out loud," that is, they must learn to present their thoughts in a structured manner. The goal, thus, is not random outbursts but the systematic presentation of ideas.

To help students attain critical orality, teachers must ask relevant contextual questions that stimulate critical thinking rather than reinforce existing stereotypes. Teachers must also be aware that the types of recommended questions guiding critical analysis do not require students to have comprehensive knowledge of the specific subject area; as such, teachers must facilitate students' ability to recognize relationships between available facts or contents. Similarly, to facilitate transfer from oral to written form, students must be taught to formulate ideas orally and present information with a central unifying idea. Curriculum that is designed so that students understand that orality and literacy are interrelated, supportive processes will enable teachers to present orality as a cognitive function and as a means of introducing broad concepts in addition to brief signs and signals. Enabling students to articulate their positions by using both concepts and signals thus becomes the predicate for instruction leading to critical literacy and broader learning outcomes.

Although critical orality is a valid objective of school learning, its attainment is not always made explicit in the curriculum. This obviously has implications for curriculum design and development, the rudiments (goals, objectives, purposes) of critical orality, and outcomes that include creative communication and articulation. Teachers must also be aware that some of the mechanisms, which include open-ended, randomized methods (in which questions arise out of random contexts), may be too unstructured for elementary through junior high school level students, and a question-guided discussion style may be too sophisticated for those groups, but a guided-discovery approach may be appropriate if teachers furnish the proper context. Brainstorming sessions, which provide the strategic moments for teachers to intervene and encourage critical orality, set the stage for creative communication and articulation and provide an avenue for classroom exploration of multicultural differences.

Francis Roberts and I advocated these ideas to inform the polemical discussion of multiculturalism and the social studies curriculum in New York state. We believed that questions focusing on "whose canon?" "whose history?" and "whose voice?" were counterproductive and urged our colleagues to instead ask, "how we can better enable learning and the development of intellect in our students?" And by shifting the focus away from either a Eurocentric or Afrocentric curriculum to an emphasis on meeting the learning needs of students, multiculturalism and multiperspectivism were perceived as vehicles for enhancing intellectual competence in all of our students. Despite the political nature of the educational debate involving social and economic equality, equal opportunity, the centricity of Western civilization, and the inclusion of diverse histories and perspectives, our argument for multiculturalism was perceived as pivotal given its contributions to the enabling of effective pedagogy and to the overarching purpose of education—the nurturance and development of intelligence.

To that end, knowledge, science, and education do not have to be revolutionized before society can become more sensitive to diverse human characteristics, contexts, and perspectives, or before education can be improved. Revolutions are difficult to come by and usually are unselectively destructive. There is, however, room for a great deal of expansion, change, and reform within the current debate concerning the nature of the canon and the curricula through which it is taught. But in what ways? How will society know in which directions to proceed? What is society to use as signposts?

If the integrity of the canon is understood and agreed upon as a reference point that should remain as an anchor, a new set of criteria is needed to guide these changes. In this context, integrity is taken to mean wholeness, soundness, completeness, and the lack of deception. The following, therefore, are offered as criteria by which the integrity of the canon is to be judged:

1. The canon should reflect the comprehensiveness of knowledge. Knowledge should not be context-bound; but rather both universal in its applications and capable of being assigned general applications. Herein lies one of the elusive goals of scientific methodology. Currently, understanding and application are situationally bound, require sensitivity to contextual phenomena, and are often related to the perspective provided by the position from which a phenomenon is investigated. Demands for relativistic knowledge thus seem to conflict with desires for absolute knowledge; similarly, efforts to know and understand seem to require both inclusive and exclusive categories. The result is the emergence of paradoxes that appear both irresolvable and essential to the comprehensiveness of knowledge. Yet, while the criterion of comprehensiveness creates a tension between the absolute and the relative, this tension need not immobilize human thought. It can be the driving energy behind knowledge production and critical interpretation.

2. The canon should contribute to the conservation and stability of knowledge, techniques, and knowledge products. Verbal and written symbol systems and other cultural products are the foundations for the continued development of human societies, and human beings cannot afford to lose access to them. These systems and products deserve to be considered for membership in the human archives; but because such inclusiveness is nearly impossible, some system of selection is justified. However, to avoid arbitrary or chauvinistic exclusion, criteria of measurement and rules for determining validity and acceptability for inclusion must remain flexible and dynamic. At the same time, the core of the canon should remain relatively stable over time to enable replication, reflection, critical analysis, and critical interpretation between multiple investigators and situations.

3. Notwithstanding, the canon must be characterized by the capacity to accommodate change. Its boundaries must be sufficiently permeable

to permit expansion and constriction in response to new or different information, perspectives, or technologies. According to Kuhn (1970), paradigms change as a result of changing experiences and different views of phenomena. Similarly, the canon must respect and accommodate contextualist, existentialist, universalist, and relativist conditions of validity as they may be differentially applicable, depending on the nature of the knowledge and the purpose for which that knowledge is to be used. However, this accommodative capacity of the canon must not be an excuse for the rejection of falsification, because a part of the canon must always demonstrate that a particular assumption, finding, or theory has failed to be confirmed.

4. The contents of the canon must be accessible to a broad range of audiences. No matter how brilliant the findings and statements of scholars, if the means by which those findings are represented to others *prevents* other scholars (and those outside the academy) from understanding, then the findings do not meet a crucial criterion of the canon. The canon should be interpretable by persons who are interested and prepared to use it.

5. The canon must reflect a functional and meaningful relationship between prior knowledge and the requirements of new knowledge recognized as a condition of effective learning. Requirements for inclusion in the canon must be based upon the functional characteristics of the content rather than its ritual characteristics. Thus, the dogmatic nature of new content is insufficient rationale for its inclusion, but a specific bit of dogma may be justifiably included because of its historical significance.

6. The canon must reflect the aesthetic and nutritive value of knowledge, respecting intellectual behavior as an art form and intellectual stimulation as the nutrients of metacognition.

A canon so conceived would be a living document, more variable than concrete, designed not so much to protect and conserve knowledge and technique as to enable learning and the development of intellect.

Three kinds of literature have emerged with respect to curriculum development. First, curricular theory has developed a body of literature that is stimulating the debate regarding curriculum content, the studies that should be referenced, and the rationale for the utilization of each. The theories appear to be guided by a wide range of psychological principles and are generally designed to provide some frame of reference for the curricularist. The second kind of curriculum material involves curriculum implementation. This literature focuses on the "how-tos" for building curricular goals, objectives, and evaluations and is designed for curriculum planners in local school districts who are responsible for creating or modifying existing curriculum plans. The third level are the actual materials used to implement the curriculum, such as textbooks, workbooks, and other related materials that teachers use to teach to the curriculum guide. It appears logical that the first kind or level should inform the second and the second informs the third; however, in practice, it is not uncommon for these three levels to work without one necessarily informing the other. Robert Zais (1976) describes the result of this type of curriculum development:

> Curriculum construction in the United States is generally conducted in a shockingly piecemeal and superficial fashion. "Reforms" are implemented in response to popular clamor and perceived social crisis; "innovations" are often little more than jargon; and the whole process is influenced by mere educational vogue. The results, of course, are school programs characterized by fragmentation, imbalance, transience, caprice, and at times, incoherence.
> There are a number of reasons for this unfortunate state of affairs. One is the overwhelming complexity of the curricular enterprise; the number of interdependent variables that influence curriculum development is disconcertingly immense. A second and related reason for superficiality is the relative infancy of the curriculum field. . . . Finally, the pragmatic nature of the American temperament—as suspicious of reflection and theorizing as it is infatuated with the desire to "do anything" to "get the job done"—has been a continuing source of difficulty. Curriculum workers tend to charge ahead, making decisions and changes without really understanding the basis and nature of curricular phenomena or the effect of their actions on the total curriculum. (p. 244, 1976)

Although Zais has painted a bleak picture, his text makes no attempt to clarify how this problem might be alleviated. The truth in his claims of "fragmentation" may be a matter of degree. Nevertheless, whether one agrees or disagrees with Zais is not the primary issue. His claims are significant in that there has been and continue to be an inherent complexity to the process of curriculum development in part because multiple sources can enter into and influence its development. These complexities are magnified when those who are responsible for writing or revising curriculum act or make decisions without a clear understanding of the implications of their decisions or without a common framework from which to make decisions. According to Elizabeth Vallance (1985):

> Educators are not accustomed to clarifying the conceptual or philosophical lines along which their curriculum choices should be made. Few educators, after all, have the luxury of building a complete curriculum anew; that educators infrequently question the very basis of their enterprise is thus scarcely surprising. But the infrequency of the activity merely underscores the importance of being able to approach problems freshly when the opportunity does arise. It is in the activity of questioning the prevailing conceptions of curriculum that educators can come closest to making genuine changes in the educational system. (p. 201)

Thus, educators need to more fully examine the framework that both informs and guides the decision-making process of curriculum development. The task remains complex.

Arthur Foshay (1986) attempted to characterize or simplify the task of curriculum development by delineating the process into seven decision points or steps which include: (1) the student (his nature and needs); (2) the content (in relation with the student), (3) the learning method (in relation to 1 and 2); (4) purposes (in relation to 1, 2, and 3); (5) context (including materials and the social and physical environment), (6) the governance (who makes the decisions and how they are made); (7) cost (time, talent, and money). Foshay suggests that there is some interdependence between and among variables. Although Foshay did not argue that theories or principles should guide or do guide the decision-making processes, this complex process not only embodies tasks or elements but also multiple levels of theory, philosophy, committee members' intuition, and the powers of social and political concerns. The sequential nature of these steps suggests a hierarchy; if this is the case, however, the "purpose" appears wrongly positioned. The purpose of curricular decisions needs to become more prominent, thereby informing each decision point, and the guiding premise for each decision point should be whether the possible solution is in agreement with or opposed to the intended purpose and the theoretical framework of the curriculum.

It is helpful to review Ralph Tyler's (1950) *Tyler Rationale*, which is an earlier framework of a system for making curricular decisions. *Tyler Rationale* begins with the student, society, and subject matter, and proceeds to screen objectives based upon a philosophy of education and a psychology of learning as sources. Tyler asserts that as an objective survives the screening process and is written in precise measurable behaviors, it eventually becomes a part of the curriculum. The power, therefore, of a particular philosophy of education can significantly impact curricular decisions. Additionally, this approach assumes that the purpose of curriculum is either clearly defined before objectives are screened, or that a clear purpose is of no consequence and need not even be addressed in the curriculum planning process. This approach seems to simplify the process to the point of not considering requisite elements such as the purpose upon which the curriculum is created.

While the process of curriculum development is not easily agreed upon, defined, or even sequenced, certain procedures are inherent in almost every model of curriculum development. According to Geneva Gay (1980), curriculum development includes the identification of goals and objectives, selection and organization of the content, learning activities, teaching processes, and evaluation of student outcomes and the effectiveness of the design process. Additionally, whether implicit or explicit, each model of curriculum development evinces a purpose that influences curriculum decisions. Whatever the processes involved, if the purpose remains implicit and not theoretically informed, curriculum development will remain a loose patchwork collection of coursework that lacks a clear sense of direction or purpose. Hilda Taba (1962) asserted that:

> Any enterprise as complex as curriculum development requires some kind of theoretical or conceptual framework of thinking to guide it. To be sure, theoretical considerations are, and have been, applied in making decisions about curriculum, and possibly more theoretical ideas are available than have been applied in practice. What is lacking is a coherent and consistent framework. (p. 413)

And not only is a conceptual framework significant but so too is a consistency for decision making. The presence of a theoretical framework or guideposts in the decision-making process might adequately address Zais's concerns and inform the curriculum development process, thus allowing for one knowledge base of literature to inform the other and ultimately reach the intended goals or purposes of the curriculum. The curriculum, notwithstanding, can have significantly different outcomes depending upon the theory that guides its development.

What, then, are the models that can guide the curriculum planning process? Gay (1980) has postulated four models for conceptualizing the curriculum-planning process: academic, technical, pragmatic, and experiential (p. 121). While no one model is completely functional on its own, they are designed to provide a framework for curriculum development. Interestingly, each model seems to have an implicit conception of what schools are and should do. At the same time, however, the relationship between school and purpose appears reciprocal and oftentimes it is difficult to determine which force drives which. The following discussion examines Gay's models and suggests the metaphors for schools that are implicit in each. The implications of such models and schools are explored and recommendations for theorists and curricularists are made through a fifth model for curriculum planning.

THE ACADEMIC MODEL

The academic model may be most familiar to scholars and scientists alike. Gay argues that the academic model is "based upon the use of scholarly logic in educational decision-making" (p. 122). The academic model, which praises the wisdom of intellectual maturity and academic rationality, is based somewhat on "Tyler's Rationale." In this model, the important processes include identifying objectives using intellectual rationality in addition to determining the desired learning outcomes. As with any good piece of scholarly or scientific literature, no one source determines those outcomes. According to Gay, the academic model relies on five foundational sources: the learner, society, subject matter disciplines, philosophy, and the psychology of learning. The end product becomes one of balancing the learning outcomes for all five foundations. Like academicians, the curriculum developer working with this model attempts to get as much information as possible to determine what kind of learning is most desirable. Gay argues that:

> The research and theories of such developmental psychologists and learning theorists such as Piaget, Dewey, Maslow, Prescott, Kohlberg, Tanner and Havighurst are used conjunctively to develop composite, general profiles of learners. Anything less than this comprehensive analysis is considered insufficient, in view of the fact that human growth is developmental, organismic, differential, asynchronistic, and cyclical. (p. 123)

Additionally, curriculum specialists in the disciplines advocate the centrality of the traditional academic disciplines; they concede, however, that it is important for students to become adept at not only knowing content but also the generic skills of problem solving, decision making, or any other skill that has an inherent rationality.

Gay stressed the broad-based nature of the academic model approach by noting that:

> When using learning theories to select curriculum objectives, content, and learning activities, academically oriented curriculum workers consult experimental and developmental psychology, as well as anthropological, sociological, and sociopsychological studies. They investigate cognitive, behavioral, gestalt, moral, and sociocultural (or environmental) theories of human growth and development to derive comprehensive and prescriptive principles of learning. The resulting data enable them to identify desired learning outcomes that are developmental in nature, to determine the most appropriate sequence of objectives, and to ascertain the conditions requisite for learning certain types of objectives. (p. 124)

The function of such curriculum development seems driven by "academic rationalism" which emphasizes disciplined approaches of knowing (Eisner and Vallance, 1974). This approach assumes that an appropriate and definitive sequence can and should be determined and learning conditions and outcomes can be fully specified. The academic model suggests that curriculum planning transcends particular school situations or specific school environments, almost assuming that there is one "best" curriculum. William Bennet's (1987) *James Madison High School* or Theodore Sizer's (1964) *Essential School* might be current examples of the use of the academic model for curriculum planning.

While it would appear plausible that almost any philosophy of education and its function and purpose could be supported by this model, Gay suggests that "philosophies which view the fundamental purposes of education as the preservation and transmission of cultural heritage and cumulative knowledge of humankind, and the development of intellect" are more compatible (p. 124). This approach, which seems to have a sterility implicit in the relevant decision-making processes, emphasizes the transmission of content or knowledge versus transaction between the learner and content. This suggests further that the learner is a passive recipient of the imparted knowledge and returns to the original definition of teaching, which is to impart information systematically. Little emphasis is placed on how the learner will interact with the content; the focus instead remains on what the learner will be taught.

Implicit in this model is a conception of the school as a factory, which seems less a metaphor and more a true systematic schema for how the school operates (Foshay, 1986). The concept of a factory school is not new and implies an input-process-output, where the student enters the process of school and leaves school having achieved the specified learning outcomes. The academic rationality and discipline-based approach maintains that the recommended outcomes are those that all children need to learn. It assumes that all children, universally, have the same needs. The model, however, raises the question of the fundamental purpose of educational curriculum planning. In the input-output process, the procedures or how content gets taught to children appears fully predetermined based upon previous analysis about what is best for all children. Additionally, the learner, as with an assembly line approach in a factory, simply appears to move through the curriculum, from content area to content area, absorbing information. It suggests a highly passive learning approach with the purpose focused on the traditional academic disciplines. The Lancaster school in the early nineteenth century is the earliest example.

THE TECHNICAL MODEL

The technical model of curriculum development is essentially an analytic approach, which, however, does not fully separate it from the academic model. The technical model is distinguished by the fact that it perceives instructional planning in terms of "systems," "management," and "production" (Gay, 1980:132). The focus shifts from academic disciplines to maximizing educational program efficiency and performance. This model is implemented by applying principles of scientific management and production and is indicative of the kind and type of operations inherent in corporations and industry. The academic and technical models both involve a process-product approach where the product, or desired learning outcomes, are primary.

According to Gay, the difference seems to be that:

> While the academic model appeals to theoretical logic and academic rationality as the bases for sound decision-making, the technical model uses the logic of "systems analysis," empiricism, scientific objectivity, and managerial efficiency. The stimulus-response and operant conditioning theories of behaviorist psychology comprise the epistemological foundations of technical approaches to curriculum development. Their ontology is fundamentally scientific realism or logical empiricism. This instructional planning model ascribes to the belief that nothing is real or meaningful unless it is observable and is susceptible to objective analysis, using publicly verifiable data. (p. 132)

Given this basis, the purpose appears driven by the notion that: (1) curriculum worth knowing is "preparation for life's functions"; (2) these functions are reducible to constituent parts; and (3) since learning represents a change in behavior which is demonstrative, then all learning is observable and measurable in quantifiable terms. This systematic approach lends itself to careful, exacting, and highly ordered instructional planning. It also involves needs assessment, creation of observable measurable goals, translation of goals into measurable instructional objectives that can be sequenced or hierarchically arranged, synthesis where activities and evaluations are determined, and application of these objectives. Gay's illustrations of this model include IEPs for mainstreaming handicapped children or computer-assisted instruction.

Like the academic model, the technical model implies that the school as a factory is designed to create products. However, unlike the academic model, nothing exists unless it contributes to production. The technical model has characteristics of large-scale management and can forcibly hold the principal qua manager readily accountable to the public consuming the product of an educated or ignorant graduate. Foshay argues that the weakness of this notion of school "offers an illusion of certainty in an area dominated by uncertainty and ambiguity. . . . To act as if jobs could be described adequately and then distributed according to a table of organization is to deceive oneself" (p. 89). Notwithstanding, the model manifests a process-input-product approach through systematic analysis of what needs to be done and regards the student as an object experiencing the process of learning objectives. As with any factory or production line, it is plausible that not all products will meet set standards because the objectives driving the model appear to negate individual needs or differences. While the measurable observable outcomes invite assumed accountability measures, the connotations of the factory metaphor can be markedly negative.

THE PRAGMATIC MODEL

The Pragmatic Model, unlike the academic or technical models, appears less as a model and more as a consequence of how curriculum can be persuaded. It is not clear what the specific processes are in this model, only that the model is school-specific, with no universal principles evident. Gay argues that:

> The pragmatic curriculum model perceives instructional planning as a particularistic, localized process that is specific to the sociopolitical milieu of the school context in which it occurs. . . . Of particular interest are the informal political negotiations, power allocations, and consensus building that take place among different groups. (p. 137)

This "political" perspective of curriculum development involves the regulatory power of the federal government, state officials, local boards of education, and governing bodies. Thus, the political environment of the community often controls school environments. Gay concludes that "what becomes the operational or functional curriculum in local school communities [is a result of] the power, influence, and pressures exerted upon the educational decision-making processes from forces both internal and external to the system" (p. 138). We view this less as a theoretical or practical basis and more as an influence, upon which curriculum decisions are often swayed, which may or may not be informed by theory.

In the pragmatic model, the school appears to be functioning as a bureaucracy, defined by Foshay as "an institution controlled by non-elected government officials" (p. 90). As a bureaucracy, the school's focus has shifted dramatically from the needs of children to the running of an institution. If a school's curriculum is dictated by bureaucratic controls then its purpose seems to be nothing more than a holding port for children or an institution designed to meet the needs of the local, state, and federal governments. Compared with the academic and technical models, which do maintain some focus on the student, this model appears to be driven externally, with the needs of students regarded as secondary to curricular decision making. In the case of the academic and technical models, the focus seems to be on the process and product of the curriculum, which can be universally applied. In the pragmatic model, external forces seem to drive the decision-making processes. In the experiential model, we see a dramatic shift in how the curriculum is defined. Previously, the student was considered at some point in the curricular decision-making process.

THE EXPERIENTIAL MODEL

In the experiential model, the focus shifts definitively to a purpose that is child-centered. According to Gay, the experiential model is:

> subjective, personalistic, heuristic, and transactional. It is a learner-centered, activity-oriented approach to teaching and learning. . . . It theorizes that personal feelings, attitudes, values, and experiences are critical curriculum content, that active involvement of students in planning learning activities is essential to maximizing learning outcomes, that people create their own phenomenal worlds though selective perception, and that people learn only that which has personal meaning to them. (p. 126)

The experiential curriculum model has an ongoing process that seems to emerge from students and their associated needs and realities. This model is based upon inquiry and appears highly situational. Gay cites Arthur Foshay's concept of the "humane curriculum" defined as education focused on the human condition and curriculum content and experiences that are responsive to the qualities essential to the preservation of humanity, including intellectual, emotional, social, physical, aesthetic, and spiritual. The individual's perceived self-worth is a precondition for learning and appears to guide the learning process. Similarly, the cultivation of students' attitudes and their own thoughts and opinions is central. And because students' realities are predicated on their social or cultural backgrounds, they have a certain frame of reference or knowledge base that is significant in the learning process. Given this dynamic, it is important that the cultural background of students should significantly impact and inform curriculum development. The emphasis in this model, as opposed to the academic, technical, and pragmatic models, is not on the product or outcome but rather on the process. Gay suggests that objectives may include:

> learning how to learn and how to think critically and autonomously, valuing, developing positive self-concepts, taking social perspectives, participating in democracy, developing individual creativity and social efficacy. Identifying these outcomes as "education for life," Louis Rubin explains that people should learn to think, to feel, to love, to value, to live, to act, and to find personal meaning in daily activities. (p. 129)

The above objectives do not appear to be ends in themselves; rather, they are skills designed to prepare students for life's challenges. And the outcomes or purposes, which are different from those specified in the academic, technical, or pragmatic models, may have been assumed in curriculum previously but were not specifically stated or addressed. We cannot expect students to be able to make responsible decisions unless they have had meaningful experiences, either real or vicarious. According to Taba (1962), providing experiences for children is significant because:

> People only learn what they experience. Only that learning which is related to active purposes and is rooted in experience translates itself into behavior changes. Children learn best those things that are attached to solving actual problems that help them in meeting real needs or that connect with some active interest. Learning in its true sense is an active transaction. To learn to think logically, one needs to do it—not only absorb logical arguments or master logically arranged material. To pursue active learning the learner needs to engage in activities that are vital to him, in which he can pursue personal goals and satisfy personal needs. Learning occurs during the process of overcoming obstacles in reaching solutions or goals. Some hold, furthermore, that only by pursuing personal problems is it possible to activate motivation and effort and to experience purposeful activity. (p. 401)

Hence, the experiential model is where the learner is actively engaged and knowledge is not merely imparted. Instead, the learner cultivates behaviors through experiences either real or vicarious in which the learned skill or knowledge can be applied. The focus rests on the process, namely, the interaction between learner and content, and when the content is relative to the learner's need, the individual's motivation to learn increases. Taba does not believe that only personal problems should be used to activate motivation in the child; however, purposeful activity appears as a key construct.

The experiential model of curriculum suggests that the school is less a factory or a bureaucracy and more a clinic. If we consider the school as a clinic, with "an intake procedure, a referral procedure [with] specialists who work with individuals according to their needs" (p. 89), the experiential model characterizes school as a clinical prescriptive approach based on the individual's needs in a meaningful and purposeful context. The significance of this approach lies in the intent to diagnose and provide interventions that meet the collective and individual needs of a diverse student population. Specifically, it assumes that one diagnosis en masse is not and should not be sufficient; rather, it is imperative to consider the variety of needs implicit in school populations and prescribe accordingly.

The difficulty with the experiential model is how to fully operationalize it. Gay believes that implementation of this model can be seen in Montessori methods, open education, learning centers and stations, and independent study. The technical and academic models suggest a prevailing sense of neatness or tidiness; that somehow the "solution" could be arrived at, systematized, and successfully implemented. In the experiential model, since the outcomes are less specific and more affective in nature, the task of the curricularist becomes increasingly difficult to specify, particularly on a large scale. With significant consideration given to the individuality of the child, as opposed to determining only psychological principles that can be universally applied to all children, the experiential model becomes increasingly more difficult to apply. Yet, if the purpose of schools is to prepare students for life's challenges, then the level of difficulty in the model is not reason enough to avoid it.

Gay does not assert which model is the best or the right one to use; rather, she asks: "How can conceptual or theoretical models of the curriculum-planning process help curriculum workers better understand and improve the dynamics of the process?" She contends that curriculum planning involves more than selecting and implementing a model because, taken independently, the models do not appear fully functional. The reality is that curriculum developers in local school districts often haphazardly patch together what they know without thoroughly understanding the rationale behind curriculum decisions. Thus, we are back to Zais's concerns about the state of curriculum development.

Decision-making that informs curriculum should not be relegated to an uninformed eclectic approach because of circumstances, influences, or situations. Instead, curriculum developers need a methodology that manipulates the four models (academic, technical, pragmatic, and experiential) into a feasible, functional curriculum. In fact, this strategy may call for a fifth model that can both bridge the gap between theoretical knowledge and the practical needs of curricularists in local districts in addition to the gap between curriculum, curriculum materials, and prescribed methodologies for teachers.

In his essay regarding a practical language for curriculum contends, Joseph Schwabb (1969) argues that:

> no curriculum grounded in but one of these subjects can possibly be adequate [or] defensible. A curriculum based on theory about individual personality which thrusts society, its demands, and its structure far into the background or ignores them entirely can be nothing but incomplete and doctrinaire; for the individuals in question are in fact members of a society and must meet its demands to some minimum degree since their existence and prosperity as individuals depend on the functioning of their society. In the same way, a curriculum grounded only in a view of social need or social change must be equally doctrinaire and incomplete, for societies do not exist only for one's sake but for the prosperity of their members as individuals as well. In the same way, learners are not only minds or knowers but also bundles of affects, individuals, personalities, earners of livings. They are not only group interactors but possessors of private lives. (17)

We postulate and recognize that there are no absolutes and that there is no one best model; however, an eclectic approach drawing on the strengths of each model (academic, technical, bureaucratic, and experiential) may more closely meet the needs of curriculum developers because current models may not be fully functional. The eclectic model assumes that no one point of departure, concept, or construct, such as child-centeredness or discipline-based, is absolute; it is rather a careful selection based upon the purpose of preparing students for the multiplicity and complexity of life's functions.

THE ECLECTIC MODEL

We can analyze the eclectic model by re-examining *Tyler's Rationale* which advocates three sources as points of departure: the student, society, and subject. Given the nature of the eclectic model, a fourth category should be added: enablement, which we define as the process of developing a students' capacity to understand and appreciate learning content. In other words, the prime consideration should be the building of a cadre of skills and experiences that both nurtures knowledge acquisition and forms the basis of academic experiences without which further learning and inquiry becomes difficult or impossible to attain. This concept, for example, which informs the eclectic model, is drawn from the experiential model. Of significant importance is consideration of how we teach children to understand, appreciate, and apply the process of learning content areas. Enablement suggests that curriculum planning and development must have as its purpose teaching children to both apply skills and concepts beyond recall and comprehension levels and to their personal experiences and needs.

Like the academic model, the eclectic model should be based upon psychological principles; however, those guiding a technical model are insufficient. Given the changing population in our schools and the needs of individuals and societal influences, it becomes necessary to consider the application of principles and theories of cognitive psychology, such as Bruner's (1966) perspective of teaching, which is "to penetrate a subject, not to cover it. You do this by 'spiraling' into it: a first pass to get the intuitive sense of it, later pass over the same domain and go into it more deeply and more fully" (Bruner, 1966, p. 8).

This approach suggests that learning must be both meaningful and purposeful to the learner; merely introducing it is not enough. Curricular decisions should be both informed by current theories of intellect and consideration of students' individual needs. Curricularists must also be aware that not all students process information in the same way; nor do all students come to school predisposed to acquire knowledge with the same set of skills. Hilda Taba (1966) argues that:

> If a child's sensory discrimination, language, and cognitive skills are inade-
> quately developed, he is not prepared to cope with the complex and confusing
> stimuli that school offers. He is not capable of handling the many strategies
> of transforming information that make it useable; he can not see sequences,

reverse the order of events, group properties of objects and events into class categories, or develop generalizations from specific data. Yet success in school depends precisely on these cognitive skills: the ability to distinguish the meaning of one word from that of another; the capacity to handle abstractions that organize the physical characteristics of the environment, such as direction, distance, location, scale, etc. This is the mental equipment upon which the performance in school depends. (p. 8)

If the purpose of curriculum is to prepare students for life's functions, then curriculum development should be responsive to the needs of young adults as individuals, not en masse. And while a curriculum may be written to address the needs of the individual, a teacher's response to students can nurture their academic and social success. Florence Stratemeyer (1957) remarks that:

In the selection of the experiences that are to be part of the curriculum, perhaps no area of the teacher's work is more significant than the identification and interpretation of the everyday concerns of learners. Since they are the starting points for curriculum experiences, the teacher's insight into these concerns and needs in essence determines the quality of the learning that will result. (p. 336)

In order for the experiences they provide in their classrooms to be effective, teachers must have an understanding of the diverse experiences children have in addition to methodologies to meet students' diverse needs. Like the technical model, teachers must have objectives upon which they can build lesson plans; however, teachers must be afforded more direction and flexibility about implementing these objectives. It is no longer enough to merely present content for the sake of following it with an examination. The teacher needs to be skilled in not only teaching content, but in helping students to understand, appreciate, structure, and organize their own thoughts, materials, and understandings. This deliberate way of teaching and learning needs to be informed by pedagogy. Enablement has not often been apparent in our schools. The curriculum planning process needs to specify how teachers are to enable children.

For example, in the skill area of quantitative understandings, not all children will arrive at school disposed to handle quantitative relationships. A child may be plagued with mathematics anxiety, having had little or no success or exposure to the content area. This eclectic approach should provide modifications or approaches to address such dispositions so that the child may fully experience the quantitative curriculum and be successful with the material. All children should be provided with an opportunity for success despite their gender, race, ethnicity, or their cultural heritage. For example, in the area of writing, speaking, and listening, while some children are raised in environments that encourage literacy behavior, many others are not exposed to such behavior on a regular basis and need more than what knowledge- and recall-based classrooms can provide. The classroom, thus, needs to be experientially based so that children can have direct or vicarious experiences, compensating them for inadequate preparation.

The various methodologies that teachers use to implement the curriculum should be guided by the principles of learning and incorporate research-based best practices on how to teach enabling skills. For example, for learning to be meaningful, children need to be taught how to positively transfer a particular skill or understanding to another situation. While the notion of transfer has been in existence since the days of Plato and Aristotle, the definition of transfer has changed. Students do not transfer material or use that knowledge in another situation by simply seeing the same material over and over again. Rather, the student needs to learn information in a context in which it will be used again. It is the broader generalization or category of knowledge that may transfer, not an independent piece of information. According to Hilda Taba (1966):

> The problem of transfer is central to all education. Whatever is taught produces some transfer, but that transfer may be either positive or negative. . . . It is hoped that whatever is taught in school is somehow used in the individual's later life—that there is a degree of positive transfer into situations that were not "covered" in school experience and that limited exposure to the materials students learn in school "can be made to count in their thinking for the rest of their lives." Since no program, no matter how thorough, can teach everything, the task of all education is to cause a maximum amount of transfer. The curriculum must always stress those things that promise most transfer, which create a mastery and understanding of matters beyond that which is taught directly. (p.121)

The research confirms that children do not readily transfer learning in one situation to another (Perkins, 1988). Additionally, they often do not conceive of using one skill in another situation, particularly if the perceptions of the two are not blatantly similar. For example, a child who has learned problem solving at a computer terminal may not be disposed to use this skill in another mathematics course. The challenge, therefore, becomes one of designing curriculum that stresses the transferability of skills, enabling students to think independently and apply skills in a variety of contexts.

If students are expected to transfer and apply skills, then the curriculum must provide for teaching and enabling them to perform at higher cognitive levels. For example, if we examine a standard hierarchy such as Bloom's 1964 taxonomy, recall or comprehension only lay the foundation for understanding. And through sophisticated levels of application, analysis, synthesis, and evaluation, students are necessarily required to cultivate a deeper understanding of the content, which provides the basis for positive transfer. If students are expected to know how to get along with people and respect one another's opinions, then they need to be given opportunities, such as working productively in structured cooperative learning groups where they can successfully achieve some goal. This situation, paralleling others in a student's life, may allow the skills of cooperation and active listening to transfer to new situations.

If students are better able to transfer those skills into new situations, then the curriculum truly will have met its function of preparing students for life. Thus, the pragmatic model's objectives may be considered addressed when the outcomes are positive and students leave school enabled to meet the demands of the workplace, home, and society. Given this dynamic, political influences can be better addressed when societal needs are adequately met. Consequently, necessary governmental funding and support can be directed by the guiding principles of the curricular model.

Functionally, curriculum cannot assume total responsibility for the cultivation of all student attitudes and attributes; however, meeting a child's individual needs and helping the child develop a positive self-concept appear as preconditions for learning. Consideration for the child and his or her needs and development of his or her dispositions cannot be overlooked in the framework of curriculum development. Taba comments:

> There is an obvious need for a *rapprochement* between the disciplines studying culture and those studying education, for the real issues that plague schools today are not exclusively rooted in education itself—they spring from the dynamics of the human and social environment. An understanding of what the environment is, what it contains, by what dynamics it operates, and what problems and possibilities it holds should shed light on what education can and must do if it is to play its legitimate role. . . . It must be recognized also that schools themselves are in a sense cultures, and that these cultures educate individuals, possibly in ways which are not part of the conscious goals or design. (p. 47)

Indeed, we educate students to believe that they are not worthwhile when, by omission, we do not build their self-esteem. In the eclectic model the school is culture in and of itself. It is not simply a factory or a bureaucracy, or even a clinic. While each of these concepts may operate at some level, the school as a culture suggests that school environment is important and that students may be educated in ways that are not part of the design. The eclectic curriculum planner, therefore, needs to provide for the building of a supportive climate that fosters the growth of a student's self-esteem. The curriculum needs to address how to cultivate behaviors that include a desire to act and to experiment without fear of failure; a sense of self-reliance; dependability; the benefits of self-control; intellectual curiosity, open-mindedness, and the independent thinking required of a leader; and the pursuit of lifelong learning. The curriculum should address interpersonal relations, such as those built upon mutual self-respect, sensitivity to the needs and opinions of others, and the importance of and ability to reach group consensus. A solid eclectic curriculum needs to address the societal constraints of community expectations, the need for understandings and applications of content. It should incorporate appreciation of historical and ethnic heritage and recognition of the necessity of moral and ethical conduct in addition to how values impact choices and conflict resolutions. Such moral and ethical decisions cannot be assumed.

The eclectic approach to curriculum needs to weave these attitudes and attributes through guided experiences in a range of disciplines and content areas. It cannot be left to chance or be assumed that the child can transfer skills; it must be worked toward. Students must be expected to operate at higher cognitive levels that require a deeper and richer understanding of content that is both purposeful and meaningful. Skills and competencies cannot be ends in and of themselves. Students need to have experiences that allow them to apply concepts. This requires a continuity and interrelationship among the disciplines in addition to transferring skills and applications between and among disciplines. The multiplicity of students' needs must be at the forefront of curriculum decisions and concomitant methodologies.

While no one model can truly be a panacea for curriculum reform, if curriculum planning can be better informed by a theoretical premise and be guided by not only the principles of learning but also the needs of the individual in a transaction with material and content, then the purpose of preparing students for all of the varied demands of life's functions can come closer to reality. Curriculum planning needs a guide. Curriculum planners need to carefully examine that goal or purpose that the curriculum is intended to achieve and build the curriculum based upon those identified purposes. In the preface to the eighty-fourth yearbook of the National Society for the Study of Education, Elliot Eisner indicated that the yearbook was predicated on several assumptions. The assumptions appear to hold true for the curriculum planning process:

> First, the mind is not given at birth, but rather is shaped by the experience a growing human has during the course of his/her life. Second, the potential of the mind is not yet fully understood. What humans have the capacity to think about is related to the context in which they live. Since contexts change, the capacities of mind themselves alter. Third, the roads to knowledge are many. Knowledge is not defined by any single system of thought, but is diverse. What people know is expressed in the cultural resources present in all cultures. Fourth, the school has a special responsibility to develop the mental potential of the young. The major vehicles it employs to achieve this end intentionally or not—are the curriculum of the school and the quality of teaching that the school provides. (1985: 116–32)

Let us carefully inform and shape the curriculum with theoretical frameworks so that the decision-making process will be both a deliberate and informed one.

REFERENCES

Bennet, J. W. 1987. *James Madison High School: A curriculum for American students.* Washington, DC: U.S. Department of Education.

Bloom, B. S. 1964. *Stability and change in human characteristics.* New York: Wiley and Sons.

Bruner, J. 1966. *Toward a theory of instruction.* Cambridge, MA: Belknap Press of Harvard University.

Eisner, E. W. (Ed.).1985. Aesthetic modes of knowing. *Learning and Teaching the Ways of `Knowing* 84 (2). Chicago, IL: Eighty Four Yearbook of the National Society for the Study of Education.

Eisner, E., and E. Vallance. 1974. *Conflicting conceptions of curriculum.* Berkeley, CA: McCutchan Pub. Corp.

Foshay, A. W. (Ed.) 1980. *Considered action for curriculum improvement.* Alexandria, VA: Association for Supervision and Curriculum Development.

Gay, G. (1980). Conceptual models of the curriculum planning process. *Considered Action in Curriculum Improvement.* Alexandria, VA: American Society for Curriculum Development.

Kuhn, T. 1970. *The structure of scientific revolutions.* 3rd ed. Chicago: University of Chicago Press.

Montessori, M.1917. *The advanced Montessori method.* New York: Frederick A. Stokes Company.

Perkins, D. 1988. *Smart schools: from training memories to educating minds.* New York: Free Press.

Schwabb, J. 1970. *The practical: a language for curriculum.* Washington, DC: National Education Association, Center for the Study of Instruction.

Sizer, T. 2003. The Coalition of Essential Schools. www.essentialschools.org.

Stratemeyer, F. 1957. *Guides to a curriculum for modern living.* New York: Teachers College, Columbia University.

Szcszciul, E., E. W. Gordon, and D. Taylor. 1989. *The functions of the curriculum.* Paper presented at the Conference on Human Diversity and Pedagogy. Yale University, New Haven, CT.

Taba, H. 1962. *Curriculum development: theory and practice.* New York: Harcourt, Raced & World.

———. 1966. *Teaching strategies and cognitive functioning in elementary school children.* San Francisco, CA: San Francisco State College.

Tyler, T. W. 1949. *Basic principles of curriculum and instruction.* Chicago: University of Chicago Press.

Vallance, E. 1995. *Business ethics at work.* Cambridge: Cambridge University Press

Zais, R. 1976. *Curriculum: principles and foundations.* New York: Crowell.

8

The Teaching and Learning of Intellective Competence

Carol D. Lee

Gordon's concept of intellective competence is situated, in this chapter, in the current literature on cognition and learning and the assumption that intellective competence is natural to the human species. The problem for many educators and policy makers is not whether African American, Latino/a, Native American, certain Asian American students, and generally students from low-income communities develop intellective competence, but rather whether they develop a quality of intellective competence in particular domains, especially academic domains.

The case for the academic achievement gap between many European and Asian American students and their African-American, Latino/a, and Native American peers is based on decades of accumulated data on national trends of standardized tests in reading, mathematics, and science (Mullis, Dossey, Foertsch, Jones, and Gentile 1991). Specifically, data from the National Assessment of Educational Progress (NAEP) show that African-American and Latino seventeen-year-olds read only as well as white thirteen-year-olds, even though the achievement gap in reading has been declining over the last several decades. At the same time, NAEP data (see table 8.1) show that for the most rigorous reading tasks on that assessment, only 1 percent of African American and Latinos/as score on the advanced level (Campbell, Hombo, and Mazzeo 2000).

However, while achievement on rigorous academic tasks is lacking among particular groups of students, the core problem is national in scope. Historically, problems that are concentrated and fester in low-income inner-city and rural communities eventually come to haunt more affluent communities (e.g. school violence in Columbine High School, HIV/AIDS, early sexual activity, drug use, and so on). The academic achievement gap

Table 8.1.   NAEP Results

	African American	Latino	White
Make Generalizations	95%	97%	98%
Partial Skills	66	68	87
Understand Complicated Information	17	24	46
Learn from Specialized Materials	1	2	8

between the referenced racial/ethnic groups is an explosive issue partially because its enduring presence reifies long-standing assumptions of inferiority about many people of color (Hernstein and Murray 1994). Specifically, many students of color not only underperform in school relative to their majority peers but the prevalence of low expectations and persistent tracking, for example, indicate that they are not expected to do well (Ball 2000; Baron, Tom, and Cooper 1985; Oakes 1985; Varenne and McDermott 1998). Public policy responses to the achievement gap, likewise, tend to emphasize the use of direct instruction, scripted lessons, and basic skills multiple choice assessments, while such instruction is not characteristic of private and public schools aimed at the elite. While direct instruction, per se, is important for developing students' core knowledge and skills, it is used largely for purposes of drill rather than inquiry (Bereiter and Engelmann 1966; House, Glass, and McLean, 1978; Goslee 1998; Piller 1992). This lack of rigorous curriculum and supportive learning environments for many students of color is usually associated with those enrolled in schools with less experienced teachers, fewer resources, low-level basic skills instruction, and greater punitive accountability (Darling-Hammond 1999; Darling-Hammond and Green 1990; Haycock 1998). Students in this situation are also more likely to live in communities with inadequate housing, access to health care, jobs, and human resources, and greater amounts of violence and crime. It is not a surprise, then, that children who live in these communities face greater challenges in their life trajectories.

CONTEXTS OF DEVELOPMENT

Bronfenbrenner's (1989) ecological model can be used to understand life course development. In this model, the child is placed at the center relative to the various contexts in which the child interacts with others who influence his development. The natural starting place, of course, is the home. Within this context, there are multiple relationships: child to parent, child to siblings, child to extended familial networks that may or may not be physically present in the home. Outside the home, the child interacts with adults, older persons, and peers in institutional structures that include peer social networks, the church, community-based organizations (formal and informal), and the school. The adults, particularly the parents, bring into the home environment their experiences in other sites where children are not present. These include the place of work, peer social networks, and other experiences. Then, of course, there are broader, macro-level influences that include public policy, economic conditions, political conditions, and other social influences, all of which directly and indirectly impact the child's life. While it is very clear that the developing child, adolescent, or young adult is influenced by these nested contexts surrounding him or her, those interested in improving education have not clearly understood how to make sense of or effectively use these overlapping contexts (Lee, Spencer, and Harpalani 2003; Rogoff 2003). The field has largely focused on single contexts (family, classrooms, or neighborhoods) and assumptions of linear relationships between these contexts. These narrow foci place us at a disadvantage in understanding the dynamic relationships between people and the referenced nested and interdependent contexts that surround them.

In this context, development is defined as changes in form and quality of participation in activities over time, as well as the range of activities in which one is able to participate over time. Development and the resources within a particular context are thus mutually constitutive of each other. That is, people's opportunities for participation in particular ways are not only made possible by the access to resources in the various contexts of their lives, but their participation also shapes the contexts in which they function. This view of development and context as interdependent suggests several things: (1) most people have an agentic perspective (Bandura 2001); (2) there are different pathways to development; and (3) people's goals and motivations are different, resulting in different development trajectories. While seemingly obvious at one level, these assumptions have important implications for how we think about the question of the teaching and learning of intellective competence. First, if people have agency (including children), is the lack of achievement among particular groups of students due to a lack of intentionality and self-regulation, for example, either among the students, their parents, their teachers, or those in positions to make decisions regarding the allocation of resources available to schools? Second, what does the idea of different pathways to development mean for how instruction is organized? Third, is there congruence in terms of goals for development among students, their teachers, their parents, and policy makers; and what are the consequences of a possible lack of congruence? These questions form some of the scaffolding for the idea of teaching and learning intellective competence.

UNDERSTANDING THE CONTEXTS
OF INTELLECTIVE COMPETENCE:
EVERYDAY THINKING AND ACADEMIC LEARNING

A common folk theory is that students who do not achieve well in school are not "smart." This assumption is influenced by the legacy of IQ testing in schools. The assumption underlying IQ is that human beings are born with nascent capacities that define the outer limits of what they are able to do (Gould, 1981). It was assumed that IQ tests were a scientifically objective measure of those outer limits. The history of IQ tests undermine assumptions of objectivity, as early test designers were known to remove items on which females scored higher because they were presumed to be less intelligent than men. While IQ tests do not carry the weight they once did, the underlying assumptions of innate and fixed abilities are alive and well.

Current views on the capacity to learn acknowledge the context-dependent nature of ability. These views also assert that through experience over the life course, people engage in goal-directed behavior (Bransford, Brown, and Cocking, 1999; Bransford and Johnson, 1972). Infants seek food and comfort and young children seek to fulfill their goals through communicating to others whom they believe can help them. In the process of engaging in goal-directed activity, humans draw on both innate biological resources as well as socially learned behavior (Quartz and Sejnowski, 2002). Over time, these patterns become encoded in long-term memory as schemas and are subsequently used as frameworks for interpreting new experiences in the world (Rumelhart, 1978). The human brain efficiently streamlines diverse experiences into meaningful wholes. This collapsing of individual schemas into larger, more generative explanatory patterns allows humans to encode new experiences across the life course. This includes deducing over time those features of a schema or network of schemas that enable us to understand and adequately respond in relevant ways to new experiences. Intelligent systems such as the human brain must be adaptive to changing circumstances (Holland, 1995).

This perspective on how people learn suggests that (1) we learn by imposing meaning and significance on experiences; (2) the quality of experience, particularly in terms of how a set of experiences affects feelings of either satisfaction (i.e., ego fulfilling) or dissatisfaction, influences both what is stored in long-term memory, and what kinds of connections across experiences are made; (3) what we are able to recognize in new experiences is influenced by the nature and quality of connections we are able to make with prior experience and knowledge. Human beings who do not engage in such activity (i.e., being actively engaged in learning, using one's prior experiences in the world to make sense of new experiences encountered, using strategies to fulfill ego needs of a positive sense of self), on the whole, are not likely to live past infancy. Thus, in one sense, intellective competence is basic to the survival of the human species. In practical terms, this means that the African-American fourteen-year-old boy who is failing eighth grade and scored in the bottom quartile of the Iowa Test of Basic Skills on reading is nevertheless actively engaged in learning, using his prior experiences in the world to make sense of what happens in his daily reading or mathematics lessons and using strategies to fulfill his ego needs for a positive sense of self. The question concerning this boy is not whether he has developed intellective competence, but rather what kind of intellective competence, to be used for what ends? There is no question that there are situations in which this boy's ability to reason and problem solve will be superior to that of his parents or his teachers. The point, here, is that intellective competence is context dependent. Feuerstein (1980), for example, has demonstrated how students with certain mental disabilities are able to carry out learning tasks when they have particular kinds of supports. Vygotsky (1978) referred to this idea as the zone of proximal development, which he defined as the range of what a person can do with help, compared to what he can do alone. What one can do with help is always greater than what one can do alone. The question for those charged with addressing the academic achievement gap is what kind of help is most useful and for whom.

Research, particularly during the 1970s and 1980s, looked at what was called practical thinking in everyday contexts, with an interest in understanding relationships between reasoning in everyday contexts and qualities of reasoning that were the object of western schooling (Rogoff, 1990; Rogoff and Chavajay, 1995). Researchers looked at dieters using informal mathematics to determine portions (Lave, Murtaugh, and de la Rocha, 1984), unschooled Liberian tailors using mathematics to adjust and design patterns (Lave, 1977), and unschooled and semi-schooled street children in Brazil managing the sale of candy to foreigners (Saxe, 1991). Several findings from these studies are relevant to the question of the educability of intellective competence. First, there were differences between the quality of reasoning on these tasks between schooled and unschooled persons. Second, the goals and the nature of social and other supports surrounding a given routine practice influenced the kinds of problems and the kinds of solutions people used. Third, the ability to solve problems depended on the contexts under which the problem was elicited.

For example, Scribner and Cole (1981) studied literacy practices among the Vai people of Liberia, West Africa. Initially, they gave Western-based literacy tasks involving syllogistic reasoning to Vai adults, schooled and unschooled. They found Vai schooled adults did better on these tasks than unschooled adults. However, neither population scored as well as their Western counterparts. However, by observing the Vai in the conduct of their everyday lives, Scribner and Cole reasoned that it made no sense to claim that these people were incapable of complex reasoning, because the complex tasks of Vai life were not ones that Cole and Scribner could themselves do. So, they decided to go further, and investigate how the Vai used literacy. They discovered three literate scripts used among the Vai: Arabic text in the Koran, the Vai script used to write personal communications, and the English they studied in Western-style schools. People could be skilled in any one or a combination of the three literate scripts. Scribner and Cole discovered that each of these scripts was used in different kinds of routine tasks and that each afforded different kinds of literacy skill. They administered problems specific to the kinds of tasks each literate script routinely involved. On memorization tasks, Vai skilled in Arabic literacy and study of the Koran did best. On tasks requiring recall of sentences uttered by syllable (rather than by word), those skilled in Vai literacy outperformed others. (In the Vai script, syllables are written together with no space between words.) On tasks requiring logical and syllogistic reasoning, including verbal explanations of such reasoning, those who attended English schools outperformed others. The overall findings from these studies suggest that literacy is not one capacity. Rather, the particular practices associated with the use of different scripts promote different forms of reasoning. As Cole (1996) notes, "There is no more reason to attribute cases where schooled people excelled at our tasks to their ability to read and write, *per se*, than there is in the cases where Vai or Qur'anic literates excel" (p. 234). He goes on to say, "When people performed poorly in one of our tasks we assumed that it was the task and our understanding of its relationship to locally organized activities, not the people's minds, that were deficient" (p. 80). The many studies of everyday thinking, including the crosscultural studies comparing literate and nonliterate peoples, converge on the following claim. Competence is context dependent and to understand the quality of people's reasoning, one must examine the demands of routine practices in which they engage (Nasir, Rosebery, Warren, and Lee, 2006).

Similar arguments could be imagined for the African-American fourteen-year-old boy who scores in the bottom quartile on the ITBS in reading, but who reads the *Source* magazine to learn more about Run DMC and understands the irony of the song "I Used to Love Her" by Commons. And what may be revealing is that it is most likely that neither his parents nor his teachers understand anything about what knowledge base he brings to bear or what personal goals are invoked as the boy, on his own and with his friends, decides to read the *Source* or make an effort to interpret the figurative lines of "I Used to Love Her." There are likely profound differences between the contexts in which he displays complex reasoning about particular tasks outside school and the contexts of his school experiences.

In another series of studies, Saxe (1991) studied schooled and semi-schooled homeless children who lived on the streets of Recife, Brazil, selling candy to foreigners. Saxe and others discovered that these children were actually managing businesses that included several layers of participation and expertise. Children would purchase candy from wholesalers and then configure portions to sell on the street. They had to figure out how to bundle the candy, how much to sell the candy for, when to change the sale price depending on the wholesale price and quantity, as well as the rate of foreign exchange on a given day. In this practice, there were clear distinctions between experts and novices. Saxe and others (Nunes, Schliemann, and Carraher, 1993) document the mathematical knowledge these children used, most either without benefit of schooling, or with only minimal schooling. Based on these studies, Saxe developed a model to represent how these children developed new goals and attendant planning strategies, and engaged in new forms of buy-sell activities as they developed in expertise. Saxe calls this the Four Parameter Model for Emergent Goals, represented in figure 8.1.

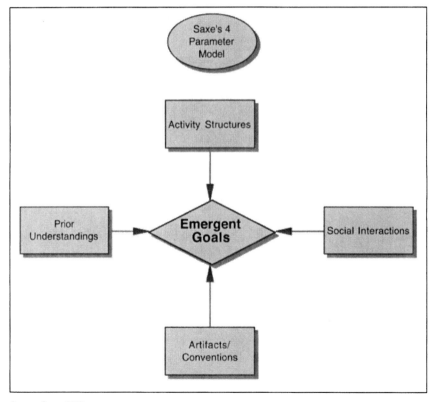

Source: Saxe, 1991.

Figure 8.1. Four Parameter Model for Emergent Goals

The idea is that as we participate in a routine activity over time, new goals emerge out of

- our prior understandings of what's involved in this activity;
- how the activity itself is structured;
- what resources (ideas, tools) are available in the activity and its surrounding setting; and
- the kinds of interactions we have with others engaged in the activity.

What does this mean for the question of the educability of intellective competence? Let's take our fourteen-year-old African-American eighth grader. The site of activity is his classroom. The routine activity is reading from a basal reader a story about dinosaurs. If we want to understand the nature of his participation in the activity, we must understand his perception of the task, his peers, and his teacher. What prior understandings about reading in school, reading in this classroom, reading with this teacher, and reading this kind of text does he bring? What is the nature of his interactions with others in the classroom? What ideas and tools are available to him to carry out the task? Saxe would argue that answers to these questions can help us understand the nature of the boy's participation (or lack thereof) in the reading lesson; that is, understanding what goals emerge for the boy as he participates in the lesson (i.e., to read with understanding and to use what he reads for some meaningful personal goal, or to protect his sense of inadequacy in the immediate task by either psychologically withdrawing or by taking active steps to disrupt the activity).

Remembering that this young man does read outside of school, the question of the context-dependent nature of displays of competence should be foremost in our inquiries about how to influence his emergent goals and those of others like him. Support for this claim can be found in a study by Hall, Reder, and Cole (1975):

> Thirty-two children, age 4 years 6 months, were the subjects for the experiment. Sixteen were black and an equal number were white. Subgroups of four children within each racial group were randomly assigned to the experimental conditions such that order of exposure to experimenter (black and white) and dialects (Standard English vs. Vernacular Black English) were counterbalanced. They found that whites performed better than blacks in SE; blacks performed better than whites in VBE; blacks tested in VBE were equivalent to whites tested in SE; and whites performed better in SE than in VBE. (Hall and Guthrie, 1980: 445)

The purpose for this citation is not to make a case for the efficacy of African-American Vernacular English (although based on my research, I might well make such a case), but rather to illustrate again the context-dependent nature of the display of competence. My position is that this fundamental precept is foundational to any claims that we make about intellective competence and to any decisions we make—whether instructional or policy—regarding how to address the problems of the achievement gap.

QUALITATIVE ATTRIBUTES OF ACADEMIC INTELLECTIVE COMPETENCE

I argue thus far that intellective competence is a hallmark of the human species and that people demonstrate intellective competence in the contexts of everyday lives (Ritchhart, 2002). However, while the studies of everyday reasoning have documented the quality of thinking embedded in such practices, this same body of research has also claimed that Western schooling fosters a particular kind of academic intellective competence (Ceci and Ruiz, 1993).

Academic intellective competence consists of knowledge, skills, and dispositions. The knowledge component is viewed largely as subject matter content (e.g., the English language arts, mathematics, the sciences, and the social studies). Literacy is a skill that crosses each of the subject areas. In a sense, each subject area requires particular literate skills in order to engage in the problem-solving tasks of the disciplines. There is debate about whether a generic set of literacy skills are sufficient for the work of the subject areas, and at what point in a student's development specialized literacies become necessary. With respect to skills and dispositions, there are similar debates as to whether a set of generic dispositions and strategies are sufficient for work across all subject areas or if specialized dispositions and strategies are essential (and if so, at what point in a student's development will they be required). In the cognitive science literature, these tensions are reflected in discussions of the problem of transfer and in distinctions between weak and strong problem-solving strategies (Klausmeier, 1985; Luchins and Luchins, 1970; Singley and Anderson, 1989). Weak problem-solving strategies are general and may apply across domains; whereas strong problem-solving strategies are those specific to a domain and require in-depth domain knowledge. These tensions surface in schools in debates over generic critical thinking curricula versus teaching specific forms of critical thinking within a subject area .

Some of the implications for instruction include:

1. Knowledge is most efficiently stored in long-term memory when it is learned in meaningful packages (Chi, 1978).
2. Knowledge stored in long-term memory can be accessed most efficiently and strategically when people make connections across concepts and have applied that knowledge across an array of problems.
3. Learning environments should be organized to privilege certain dispositions and to enable participants to recognize generative pat-

terns and attendant strategies for tackling configurations of problem types.
4. Learning complex knowledge requires time and consistency.
5. Because affect is a critical component of cognitive competence, the design of learning environments must address participants' developmental as well as cognitive needs (Dai and Sternberg, 2004).

Learning Knowledge in Meaningful Packages

One of the key differences between experts and novices is the ability to recognize generative patterns (Chi, Feltovich, and Glaser, 1981). For example, chess masters recognize patterns of moves that novices do not and are able to assess an array of possible moves and countermoves that may follow (DeGroot, 1965: Simon and Chase, 1973). School subject matters like mathematics and physics are far more complex than chess. Some of the recent efforts in developing content-based standards in science and mathematics articulate how topics are related, what concepts are foundational, and what kinds of problems these concepts will help students to solve. For example, in mathematics, LiPing Ma (1999) has argued that children in China are taught what she calls knowledge packets. In early reading, the teaching of phonemic families is viewed as more efficient than teaching short vowels, long vowels, and then irregular patterns. An example of a phonemic family would include the long vowel sound of "a" captured in the spelling patterns (a_e; ai, eigh, ay). The implication of this and related studies is that teaching discrete content knowledge or strategies is less likely to have a long-term impact on student learning. Vocabulary, a content that is addressed across all subject matters, is often taught in this way, as a set of terms to be memorized for the moment, tested, and then forgotten. Vocabulary is a central component of all literacies and is a major stumbling block for many students in terms of reading comprehension.

The importance of learning knowledge in meaningful patterns has significant implications for the teaching of literacy. Literacy serves as a gatekeeper for participation in virtually all subject area learning. Consequently, schools need to focus on the importance of reading for understanding across subject areas. How students learn to read literature, social studies, science, and even mathematics can determine whether they are able to learn the ways of reasoning that characterize different disciplines. Gordon and Bridglall refer to this as a critical pedagogy (see chapter 1 for a fuller discussion of this idea). In reading literature, students need to be able to recognize configurations of plots, character types, and archetypal themes, as well as typical kinds of interpretive problems they can expect to meet (e.g., irony, symbolism, satire, etc.) (Lee, 2004; Smith and Hillocks, 1988). For young children, plot configurations may include fables where animals act like human beings; character types may include tricksters like Br'er Rabbit; and archetypal themes are captured in stories like Cinderella and Little Red Riding Hood. For adolescents, plot configurations may include mysteries and the bildung roman (i.e., coming of age stories); character types may include the detective and the epic hero; and archetypal themes may include the explorations of human justice and love. If literature texts are organized randomly or organized around principles that do not privilege or highlight the kinds of plot configurations, character types, and archetypal themes discussed, it is unlikely that students will develop the particular kinds of intellective competence required to tackle complex works of literature. Lacking such competence, it is unlikely that students will develop dispositions to read such texts on their own or to exert much effort to make sense of them when assigned in school. Many children and adolescents will develop such competencies with social supports outside school. These are students who read widely, discuss what they read with others in socially meaningful contexts, and as a result develop the required knowledge and dispositions. However, this is not the case for many students, and for them, opportunities to learn to read literature, as well as expository texts in the other subjects, is important.

In reading texts from the sciences (i.e. biology, chemistry, physics), students need to learn the genres, organization, and modes of reasoning underlying arguments (Lemke, 1998; Martin and Veel, 1998). Science texts include illustrations, graphs, and mathematical data supporting the particular argument being made. These texts also include specialized uses of vocabulary that are often counterintuitive to everyday uses. If instruction is not organized to help students recognize these patterns, much of students' knowledge-building capacities will be severely limited.

With historical texts, students need experiences reading a variety of genres of primary documents. They need to learn features of these genres and how to interrogate the affordances and limitations of each. They need to learn to interpret vocabulary in historical documents in the historical contexts, as the same word may not have an equivalent meaning today. These experiences will allow students to understand a critical feature of the epistemology of historical understanding; that is, that history is a reconstruction of events of the past and as such is always partial and biased in some ways (Leinhardt and Greeno, 1994; Seixas, 1993; Wineburg, 1991). For example, the diary of a soldier who fought in the Civil War can give the reader only a particular perspective on the battle described.

As briefly illustrated, generative instruction focuses on how subject matter features of texts allow the reader to approach these texts in systematic ways that capture intellective competence. The content of the subjects themselves can also be packaged or structured in ways that privilege conceptual frameworks, relationships among concepts, and features of problem solving. Current standards for the sciences, mathematics, and social studies articulate quite clearly the big ideas, relationships among concepts, and problem-solving strategies as meaningful wholes. In reading (including literature and expository reading), the New Standards Project has developed what may be one of the best articulations of subject area standards. The case examples published by the National Council of Teachers of English also provide good examples of standards in action (Smagorinsky and Gevinson 1989).

While knowledge of subject areas needs to be coherent, the knowledge must also be meaningful to students. The higher the grade level, the more challenging it becomes to make subject areas meaningful to students. High school students routinely question what role understanding algebra or physics will play in their lives. Studies have shown that middle and upper middle class students may be motivated to achieve because they see grades, not necessarily knowledge, as the gatekeeper to college, and college as the gatekeeper to high-salaried job opportunities in the future. Students from low-income backgrounds often have fewer models in their lives to illustrate the economic advantages of academic achievement and often lack the knowledge of what is required, for example, in college admissions (Wilson, 1987). In addition, students from low-income backgrounds are more likely than not to experience low-level instruction, focusing on basic skills, and very little long-term exposure to instruction that captures the features of academic intellective competence described thus far (Darling-Hammond, 1999; Darling-Hammond and Green, 1990; Oakes, 1985, 1990). I want to make a strong and perhaps controversial claim here. Low-income students, and especially low-income students of color, are primarily the product of their socialization inside schools. The existence proofs to the contrary are the thousands of examples of schools in low-income communities where students routinely achieve at high levels (Foster, 1997; Ladson-Billings, 1994; Langer, 2001; The Education Trust, 1998, 2005).

Additionally, data clearly show that many students of color, on the whole, decline in achievement the longer they stay in school (Haycock, 1998). This ironic twist may have important implications for students' perceptions of the enterprise of schooling. To make knowledge meaningful, students must both understand and see usefulness in the knowledge. Usefulness may be construed as either extrinsic or intrinsic. Extrinsic usefulness may include how the acquisition of knowledge may lead to such ends as good grades, postsecondary opportunities, admission to selective high schools, and so on. Intrinsic usefulness relates to the goals of the subject matter. These may include an intrinsic pleasure in the tasks of the subject area (i.e., reading books in history or science or using mathematics to solve problems observed in one's environment); the ego-fulfillment of being and feeling competent; and having access to peer social networks that value academic achievement. Martin (2000) provides rich illustrations of African-American adolescents who are influenced by extrinsic and intrinsic motivation to achieve in mathematics.

Apparently, both extrinsic and intrinsic motivation can be influenced by the structure of learning environments in families, communities, classrooms, and within schools (Eccles, Wigfield, and Schiefele, 1998). Bronfenbrenner's (1989) ecological framework, referenced earlier, captures the range of contexts that impact children's and adolescent's development.

An ecological orientation suggests that we need to take the multiple contexts of students' lives into account as we design learning environments to foster the competencies Gordon and Bridglall discussed in chapter 1 (Lee, Spencer, and Harpalani, 2003). School interventions such as the Cultural Modeling Project (Lee, 1993, 1995a, 1995b, 2001), the Funds of Knowledge Project (Moll, 2000; Moll and Gonzalez, 2004; Moll and Greenberg, 1990), the Algebra Project (Moses and Cobb, 2001), and the KEEP Project (Au, 1980; Tharp and Gallimore, 1988) are examples of approaches that take an ecological orientation to subject matter learning. Across these ecological models to subject area learning, meaningfulness is approached in different ways. In some cases, meaningfulness is operationalized through the exploration of powerful analogies that help students make connections between tacit knowledge constructed from home and community experiences and target concepts and problem-solving strategies in a subject area. In high school literature classrooms, Cultural Modeling structures instruction to help students understand similarities between how they reason about symbols and satire in rap lyrics and how they will need to reason about similar problems in literature, for example. In the Algebra Project, students use scheduled trips on an urban transit system as an anchoring analogy for reasoning about problems of displacement in algebra. Older students tutor younger students in algebra. In the Funds of Knowledge Project, students collaborate with community residents in using practical skills to carry out academic projects that have community impact. In these and other efforts throughout the country, meaningfulness is operationalized through close personal relationships with adults in the school community.

The distinctions I have made are arbitrary for purposes of illustrating the varied paths that making subject matter meaningful may take. In fact, most of the interventions I have described actually incorporate all of these ways of making subject matter meaningful to students. It is likely the joint impact of these approaches incorporated together increase the likelihood of success of these projects. Fundamentally, what I am calling ecological models are very similar to culturally responsive models of instruction, which highlight the role of race and ethnicity as part of the cultural capital that students bring when they enter classrooms. The Cultural Modeling Project, the Funds of Knowledge Project, the Algebra Project, and the KEEP Project were all developed as culturally responsive models, each taking knowledge developed in community contexts (usually defined by race and ethnicity) as resources for instruction in schools. The small schools networks within and across cities, on the whole, do not explicitly address race and ethnicity, but do view relationships between teachers, students, parents, and community members as foundational to students' development, academically and socially (Ancess, 2003).

Accessing Relevant Knowledge

An important goal of academic intellective competence is the ability to tackle complex problems. What makes a problem complex is there is no single, straightforward path to solution; and it is quite possible that the problem is not yet solvable (Resnick, 1987). The as-yet-unsolvable problems are certainly the stuff of the practice of real experts in and across disciplines (e.g., world peace, AIDS, or Fermat's Last Theorem in mathematics prior to 1994). Therefore, learning how to wrestle with complexity is clearly a valued disposition. I discuss the issue of dispositions in a later section of this chapter. But if we want to understand how people are able to tackle complex problems, we must examine how they figure out how to address such problems when a straightforward, previously learned solution is not possible. This usually involves drawing in inventive but systematic ways on what they already know that may be relevant to the problem at hand. The cognitive science literature addresses this problem by investigations of learning transfer and recall of knowledge.

Two classic problems in learning are the issue of transfer and being able to access knowledge that is relevant to a given problem (Singley and Anderson, 1989; Whitehead, 1929). The problem of transfer, briefly, is relevant to our discussion when considering instruction that purports to teach general problem-solving skills, such as critical thinking, broadly conceived. The question of near transfer involves the ability to apply what one already knows to a problem that is not the same, but sufficiently similar to that with which the learner is already familiar. Virtually all school-based assessments (in the best sense) demand competence in near transfer. That is, they pose problems that students are sufficiently familiar with so that when tested, students will demonstrate something of the depth and breadth of their understanding. Related to this problem of near transfer are situations in which students have knowledge that is relevant to a given problem, but for whatever reason do not access it in the act of problem solving. For purposes of efficiency, I position near transfer and accessing relevant knowledge when appropriate as related for purposes of instruction that facilitates academic intellective competence.

The instructional implications of these two issues require deep pedagogical content knowledge on the part of teachers. It is also an arena where I believe schools are likely to have greater impact than most parents can have, precisely because of the subject area specificity required.

First, the problem of coherence in the curriculum, both within classrooms and across grades, addressed above in this chapter, is a prerequisite. Second, as problems are introduced to students, instruction must focus their attention on what features of the problem signal the kind of problem it is, what the problem is an instance of. For example, complex problems may include concepts that are explicitly linked or implicitly linked in ways that the learner must construct. Generally, these concepts will be associated with several strategies and solution paths. As such, instructors should address:

- exploring, articulating, and debating the features of a particular problem,
- what each student already knows and doesn't know about these features,
- what these features signal about concepts and problem-solving strategies that may be relevant,
- the strengths and weaknesses of what will inevitably be multiple solution paths, and
- the goodness of fit of solutions (i.e., what the solution explains or accounts for and what it does not).

In most instances, instruction should involve some form of modeling before students begin to work on problem(s). Equally important is for teachers to provide what Cazden (2000) calls "as needed" support while students are in the act of problem solving, whether individually, working in groups, or in whole class work.

Here, both the sequence of problem types and how students are socialized to engage with these problems (as described above) are important. These socialization experiences must be made public and must be articulated and evaluated individually and collectively by students. If such experiences are a routine part of instruction across subject areas and grades, students may be more likely to develop several important dispositions and competencies (Perkins, 1992): (a) a willingness to persist with difficult problems in the face of uncertainty; (b) a willingness and ability to search one's repertoire of existing knowledge to look for connections to new problems, particularly when the connections are not obvious; and (c) a sensitivity to look closely for recognizable patterns that help define the kind of problem one is addressing (known in the cognitive literature as defining and constraining the problem space). These are not dispositions or competencies that one develops in the short run, and especially not in erratic learning environments. I illustrate an example of someone developing competence in a near transfer problem, involving the need to figure out what features of the target problem must be attended and what existing prior knowledge may be relevant. The example also illustrates quite powerfully the complexities of developing expertise. This example is taken from an engaging article by Alan Schoenfeld (1998) on mathematics and pasta making.

Schoenfeld (1998) refers to the common practice (despite the many years of NCTM reforms) of teaching mathematics in a set of procedures as *cookbook mathematics*. Schoenfeld notes that this orientation can be found from elementary classrooms to advanced courses in mathematics. Schoenfeld extrapolates from this analogy to make a cogent argument for the nature of complex reasoning in mathematics. This example has implications for other domains as well. Schoenfeld notes that, over time, cooks cease to follow their recipes verbatim and begin to "work with the materials themselves." He explains his evolution over the last twenty years in learning to make fresh pasta. He began by following the recipes to the letter. Over time he developed a feel for the dough as an indicator of readiness to roll and adjusted approximations of ingredients—flour, olive oil, etc.—as needed. As he introduced new tools to help him at different points in this adventure—first a pasta machine from Italy and later a food processor—his relationship with the materials of the dough changed; that is, different features of the dough became important signals of readiness. His observations about the evolution of his expertise are intriguing:

> I no longer follow a recipe, although I have clearly internalized the recipe's main structure. More important, I have learned the features of the dough. I have learned to read its properties or perceive the affordances it offers to the point where the visual cues the dough provides tell me how to adjust the quantities of the major ingredients and when the dough is ready to go through the rollers of the pasta machine in a way that requires minimal effort on my part. With my experience has come not only skill, but a change in my relationship to the dough. (p. 302)

Schoenfeld makes another interesting observation. He was never explicitly taught the properties he came to recognize through his own process of invention and systematic trial and error. The possible implications for academic instruction are that explicit instruction in noting patterns may not be necessary. However, I would counter that Schoenfeld elected to participate in this practice, perceived from the very beginning its functionality, and therefore was highly motivated to observe and deduce patterns on his own (relatively on his own, since I'm sure he had access to the pasta cookbook that likely came with the pasta-making machine, as well as feedback from more knowledgeable others who observed him as he engaged in the practice or who were sufficiently knowledgeable to deduce his errors from the cooked pasta itself).

Schoenfeld relates the pasta analogy to problem solving in mathematics with the following example, given to a variety of groups:

> You have $7.00 in cash. Do you have enough cash to purchase all four items?
> Item #1: $2.59
> Item #2: $2.69
> Item #3: $2.19
> Item #4: $0.59.
> (Schoenfeld, 1998: 303)

He illustrates four of the variety of methods that people use to solve this problem.

1. Add each quantity in sequence: $2.59 + $2.19 + $2.69 + $.59 = $8.06
2. Adding one item at a time, starting with the most expensive, and stopping when the subtotal exceeds $7.00.
3. Approximate, first using the whole dollar amounts, equaling $6.00, and then noting through simple approximation that the change exceeds $1.00.
4. Note that two of the items cost more than $2.50 (i.e. $2.59 and $2.69), equaling more than $5.00; so that the next large item will bring the total beyond the $7.00. (p. 303)

Mathematically adept adults in his mathematics education study group did not add the numbers but used either method 3 or 4. Schoenfeld subsequently makes the following analogy to his pasta example:

> methods 3 and 4 are not taught in standard instruction. . . . Each of the mathematically sophisticated adults had, in essence, invented those procedures for him or herself. The invention came as a result of experience with the domain. . . . Hence, real expertise, even in domains as simple as that of whole number arithmetic, constitutes a progression from reliance on instructed procedures to the development of personal, flexible, and idiosyncratic methods. It also involves the development of and access to multiple methods. . . . Those who are really good at a task are not simply mechanically good. They do not do the same thing over and over the same way, but have access to a range of methods they can use and may not distinguish among those methods unless the context calls for it. . . . Second . . . features of the materials at hand may have alerted the (knowledgeable) problem solvers to ways of proceeding. This perception of features—or, more precisely, the fact that the features become salient and suggest a particular utilization for the task at hand—is, quite likely, task- and context dependent. (p. 304)

DISPOSITIONS AND DEVELOPMENTAL NEEDS

The development of dispositions bears a symbiotic relationship to the acquisition of usable academic knowledge or academic intellective competence. Disposition refers to the willingness to deploy effort. In displays of academic competence, it involves more than effort in the traditional sense. I can both desire and try hard to solve a complex algebra problem, but if I do not have the appropriate knowledge and specialized dispositions that characterize mathematical, especially algebraic thinking, I will not likely be successful, nor will I likely persist very long. Dispositions develop over time as a result of long-term socialization. From a cognitive perspective, dispositions require executive control. They are an outgrowth of metacognitive functioning, that is, thinking about one's thinking; establishing goals, evaluating one's efforts to achieve those goals, amending those efforts when they are not fruitful, and reworking goals as needed (Flavell, 1981). While each of these aspects of metacognitive functioning are related in large part to the demands of the subject area, they are also a function of processes of ego-fulfillment both within and beyond the academic task at hand, providing a sense of competence (Ericsson, Krampe, and Tesch-Romer, 1993).

Perkins (1992) and others refer to academic dispositions as habits of mind. We can conceptualize these habits of mind as both generic and subject area specific. In children's early schooling, instruction is likely to aim at generic habits of mind. As students progress, the need for specific habits of mind relative to disparate subject areas becomes more important. Perkins proposes seven generic dispositions of the thinker:

1. The disposition to be broad and adventurous;
2. The disposition toward sustained intellectual curiosity;
3. The disposition to clarify and seek understanding.
4. The disposition to be planful and strategic;
5. The disposition to be intellectually careful;
6. The disposition to seek and evaluate reasons;
7. The disposition to be metacognitive. (Perkins, 1992: 116)

Collins (Collins and Ferguson, 1993) offers another version that he calls epistemic games. These dispositions distinguish students who are very high academic achievers from others. This is not simply a distinction between very strong students and very weak students, but more importantly, between very strong students and students of average achievement. Citing a study by Bloom and Broder (1950) of college students, Perkins notes distinctions observed between "better and worse students . . . [:] impulsive responses to problems on the basis of superficial cues, little effort to understand a problem thoroughly, indifference to gaps in their knowledge, and a general 'either you get it or you don't' attitude" (p. 121). Of particular concern to the contributors to this volume are the economic, racial, and ethnic correlates to this issue. As Sarah Lawrence Lightfoot (1983) notes in *The Good High School:*

> To the working class student who has strived mightily to gain a loftier place, the intellectual play may seem threatening and absurd. With such high stakes, how can he dare to test out alternative propositions? He must search out the right answer. How can he spin out fantasies of adventurous projects? He must take the sure and straight path. (quoted in Perkins, 1992: 111)

Although I know of no empirical data to support this claim, it seems to me that one is more likely to observe such problem-solving dispositions described by Bloom and Broder in classrooms serving students from low-income backgrounds, students of color, and English language learners. While many would cite the enduring achievement gap among SES, racial and ethnic groups as evidence, there are few high stakes assessments that actually evaluate students' abilities to engage the dispositions of good thinking that Perkins describes. This is evident in NAEP findings that less than 10 percent of seventeen-year-olds, regardless of ethnicity or SES, are able to comprehend highly rigorous texts (Campbell, Hombo, and Mazzeo, 2000); yet there are many examples where state and NAEP results do not align (RAND Corporation, 2005). Thus developing the academic intellective dispositions I describe becomes difficult because schools serving students of color and from low-income communities typically are not organized to support such learning, and large-scale assessments do not typically measure such learning. These challenges are made more complex by the additional sources of risk that such youngsters face (Spencer, 1999):

- neighborhoods with poor housing;
- limited health care resources;
- mediocre jobs;
- inadequate or absent social service supports
- higher levels of neighborhood violence;
- and schools with fewer certified teachers, with more teachers teaching outside fields of their training, with mandates for scripted lessons and high stakes basic skills tests.

These students are further handicapped by teachers with low expectations and with a community, embodied in district, state, and federal policy makers, who fundamentally believe in innate intelligence that circumscribes ability, in the force of ability over effort, and in stereotypes regarding the abilities and social functioning of children, adolescents, and families who are not *both* white and middle class. Learning to develop these dispositions in academic subject areas is no easy task for anyone; learning to develop these dispositions in academic subject areas while simultaneously wrestling with both the school and neighborhood based challenges I have described is extraordinarily more difficult. At the same time, I demonstrate above that the same students who fare poorly in our schools often display these same dispositions in other domains of their lives. Thus, I am situating the problem not in the capacity of students, but rather in the capacity of public schools as instruments of public will. These broad dispositions (either Perkins's habits of mind or Collins's epistemic games) are teachable.

As described above, these dispositions can be taught through the general routines of classroom instruction. Because they take time and are context dependent, students should not learn them erratically but through sustained experience across subject areas, within classrooms, and across grade levels. Further, such dispositions must be a focus of academic socialization across urban school systems where student mobility rates are high. This has profound implications for teacher preparation and continuous professional development of teachers, administrative staff, and those who set educational policy at district, state, and federal levels. While this may seem like an overwhelming task, countries around the world have proven much more effective at it than the United States, in the face of ethnic diversity and high levels of poverty within their borders (Hampden-Thompson and Johnston, 2006; Wossmann, 2003).

Instructional practices that support the socialization of these intellective dispositions need to include:

1. *The selection of a few generative topics* and concepts in a subject area;
2. *Sequencing the introduction of problems* in ways that invite the careful exploration of important problem types and that build on one another so that connections between related concepts can be made;
3. *Modeling problem-solving strategies* relevant to the problem at hand, with particular emphasis on multiple solution paths and relationships to students' prior knowledge;
4. *Focusing attention on key features* of the problem that signal what concepts may be relevant;
5. *Distributing responsibility for efforts to make sense* of the problem so that teachers and knowledgeable others provide in-time assistance as needed, individual students exert effort to make sense of the problem, and that students in collaboration (in small and whole groups) exert such efforts;
6. Requiring that students *create, explain, and evaluate representations* of how they solve the problem at hand; introducing tools of representation that can be useful to students;
7. Engaging students in constantly *evaluating the goodness of fit* of their explanations, the limitations of their explanations, and in weighing

alternative explanations; including feedback to students that helps them understand the affordances and limitations of their thinking;

8. *Fostering positive collegial relationships* among all students and nurturing relationships with high expectations between teachers and their students;

9. *Connecting* the target of learning to students' prior knowledge, personal goals, other subjects, and to the real world functions of the knowledge (especially as it relates to the proximal communities in which students live).

The myriad ways that these precepts can be taken up in the idioculture of daily classroom practice is the purview of the skillful teacher who must negotiate how these precepts play out in different subject areas (Grossman and Stodolsky, 1995) and with different students (Ball, 2000; Foster, 1997; Irvine, 1990; Ladson-Billings, 1994,). In this enterprise of developing academic intellective competence, the joint work of students and teachers together requires what Hatano and Inagaki (1986) call adaptive expertise. The development of adaptive expertise among teachers and among students takes time and requires sustained intellectual, practical, and social support.

Having described generic dispositions, I would like to briefly illustrate what such dispositions look like in terms of subject area differences, using response to literature as an example. In response to literature, there are important differences between those who read complex and canonical literature and those who do not. Canonical literature is here defined as works whose value persists over long periods of time and is in no way limited to selections from any particular national tradition. Such readers display the following dispositions while making sense of literary texts; these students:

(1) attend to language play as an aesthetically pleasing end in itself;

(2) suspend disbelief in order to enter the subjective world of an imaginative text;

(3) impose coherence even when on the surface there appears to be no coherence (even if from a deconstructionist position, the coherence is in fact a lack of coherence or unity);

(4) hold conclusions in abeyance while reading;

(5) are playful and fanciful;

(6) make connections between the subjunctive world of the text and the world or social order outside the text;

(7) look for patterns within and across texts and impose meaning on those patterns; and

(8) position one's interests or dispositions as a reader as valuable and important to the process of making sense of literary works.

Several observations are relevant here. First, these dispositions bear some relationship to the generic ones described by Perkins (1992) and by Collins and Ferguson (1993), but they are also fundamentally different in their specificity. Second, as literary works are narratives, these dispositions can be applied to any sustained and serious efforts to understand narratives in other contexts, such as soap operas on television and gangster tales on both TV and in the movies (just as Schoenfeld explores unique, amusing, yet revealing analogies between qualities of reasoning in mathematics and the art of making pasta). Because of these strategic connections among everyday experience and many concepts in academic domains, useful analogies, anchors, and models can help students see connections between their prior knowledge and the target knowledge being taught. This is one reason why such dispositions are teachable. Making such connections is precisely the foundation for the Cultural Modeling Framework. Third, for these dispositions to be useful in interpreting complex and canonical works of literature, they must be linked to the reader's understanding of concepts, problem types, strategies, topics, and interrelationships among these.

My own work (Lee, 1993, 1995a, 1995b, 2001) and that of others (Booth, 1974; Rabinowitz, 1987; Smagorinsky and Gevinson, 1989; Smith, 1989; Smith and Hillocks, 1988) have sought to define what these concepts and problem types may include. In my work in cultural modeling, I have identified problem types as irony, satire, symbolism, and use of unreliable narration; and typical configurations of plots (i.e., genres, such as detective stories, science fiction, or fables) and character types as key features of texts that allow the reader to make hypotheses about the unfolding of the story, and to test against the text itself. In the act of reading, both disposition and knowledge of content, concepts, types of problems, relevant problem-solving strategies (both procedural knowledge—i.e., how to do—and conditional knowledge—i.e., when to use) are necessary to work in dynamic relation to one another. Because all are necessary, curriculum approaches that aim to teach "critical thinking" in isolation rarely have long-term impact and rarely help students become academically competent across subject matters.

THE ROLE OF DEVELOPMENT IN LEARNING ACADEMIC INTELLECTUAL COMPETENCE

In order for the human organism to grow, our multiple needs for physical sustenance, attachment to other human beings, and the ability to participate in the social practices that are valued by our community (including those that support our physical and social/emotional development) have to be met. We are born with both genetic and cultural resources that we inherit from our ancestors. Neither our genetic material nor our cultural resources acts as an arbitrary determinant of our individual development across the life span (Quartz and Sejnowski, 2002). Most of our genetic resources are common across the species, but it is likely that we also inherit genes that may predispose particular strengths. These potential strengths, however, cannot be actualized except in the garden that human culture provides (Cole, 1996a). It is likely that even with the best of practice, most basketball players will not become Michael Jordans; it is equally likely that if Michael Jordan had not been introduced to the intense cultural socialization of high school and college basketball (as well as likely intense playing as a young child in his neighborhood), his strengths in, say, spatial orientation, in and of themselves would not have led him to basketball. The debate over genes and social context are heated and remain (Gould, 1981). However, no one can argue that both likely play a role, and that genes are rarely (even with populations with special mental or physical disabilities) the final arbiter of development. The weight of evidence currently suggests that human intelligence is highly malleable and teachable.

I want in this final section to discuss the role of attachment and cultural socialization in the development of academic intellective competence. Broadly speaking, cultural socialization refers to the processes through which people are socialized to participate in cultural life; how they learn tasks, roles, ways of using language appropriate to the situation; how they learn to be children of particular families, caretakers, siblings, friends; how they learn to make sense of experiences in the world; how they learn to perceive, understand, and respond to risks, challenges, and threats. Processes of cultural socialization are complex because across the life course, people learn to participate in many different cultural communities (especially in highly technical and urban societies) (Super and Harkness, 1986; Weisner, 2002). These cultural communities may include routine institutional practices within ethnic and/or national communities.[1] These cultural communities may also include religious groups, professional groups, or other groups that form around shared interests. For our purposes, they may also include intellectual communities such as those defined by the academic subject areas. One purpose of schooling in the twenty-first century is to apprentice students into peripheral participation in the work of the disciplines. In K–8 schooling (and probably K–16 schooling), even in the most intense project or inquiry-based classrooms, students do not participate in the work of the disciplines in the ways that experts do. Even so, our attempts at socializing academic intellective competence is about helping young people learn about the cultural practices of the disciplines so that (1) these practices are not foreign to them; (2) they can use the knowledge embedded in those practices to do meaningful work in the world; and (3) they are in a position to participate in the civic debate knowledgeably (Gutmann, 1987; Paulos, 1995). These are among the many reasons that the development of academic intellective competence is important (Dewey, 1963; DuBois, 1973; Woodson, 1969).

As people move across cultural communities of practice, they will always face a variety of challenges in adapting to the different demands of participation in each. For young people, one question is where and how they learn to make such transitions. In some cases, parents, family social networks, and familial institutions such as the church actively facilitate such transitions. In other cases, the organization of the cultural communities of practice provides structures and supports for such transitions. This is generally the case when people self-select into a community that has high prestige (at least within the group) and lots of internal supports. For example, many young people, across SES, ethnic, racial, and language groups participate actively in communities defined by computer games (Alvermann and Hagood, 2000; Gee, 2000). These are often communities that do not meet face to face and they communicate using imaginary personae over the Internet. On the whole, few adults are involved in supporting how young people learn in these environments. Because young people self-select and because among their peers this community is viewed as a social good, young people expend tremendous effort to advance their deep understanding of the games.

K–12 students, however, do not elect to go to school. In most industrialized societies, they are forced to attend. That fact alone places special burdens on schools to motivate students to make concerted efforts to learn. At the same time, because schools are not the only sphere of students' lives, there is always competition for their interests and time. For a lot of students, the challenges with which they must grapple are many. The kinds of cultural socialization they experience at different points in their development will influence how they perceive these challenges and how they respond to them (Graham and Golan, 1991; Nasir and Saxe, 2003).

Margaret Beale Spencer of the University of Pennsylvania has developed a framework for understanding identity processes in the course of life development, PVEST (Phenomenological Variant of Ecological Systems Theory) (Spencer, 1995, 1999; Spencer, Dupree, and Hartmann, 1997). Spencer emphasizes the importance of people's perceptions of experience. In this case, we are focusing on the perception of students of color and students from low-income backgrounds about their experiences in school over time (as young children, as pre-adolescents, and as adolescents or young adults), and how their perceptions of school experiences map on to their perceptions of other experiences in their lives. Spencer argues that how we experience risk is determined by the balance between the nature of the risks themselves and the quality of social supports we have. From this interaction of real risk and social supports, we learn patterned ways of responding to the threats. These patterned ways of responding may be adaptive or maladaptive, leading to either resiliency or lack thereof. Over time, these patterned ways of responding become an integral part of our identity and help to structure how we respond to perceptions of risk or threat as a way of maintaining and protecting the ego or sense of selfhood. Figure 8.2 captures the PVEST model.

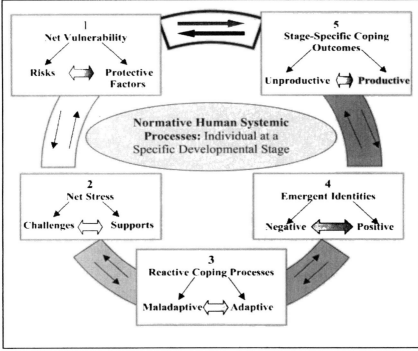

Source: Spencer 1995

Figure 8.2. Spencer's Phenomenological Variant of Ecological Systems Theory

Students of color and students from low-income backgrounds face numerous risks, including stereotypes regarding ability (Steele, 1997), low expectations, greater exposure to violence, greater likelihood of classroom instruction that is low in intellectual rigor, and greater responsibility for adultlike roles at earlier ages (Burton, Allison, and Obeidallah, 1995). An African-American adolescent male can expect to be negatively disciplined in school, to face peer violence in the process of coming to and from school, to be harassed by police (both in his neighborhood and if in high school inside the school as well). He must learn how to make sense of these challenges in addition to the other normative psychosocial tasks of adolescent male development that other male teenagers (in societies such as the United States) face (Bowman, 1989; Bowman and Howard, 1985). Also, when a student does not understand what he is being taught and does not see the relevance of what he is being taught (and unless he experiences a set of socialization processes that can help him learn how to frame these challenges and how to respond to them), it is no surprise that he will make maladaptive choices that will lead him to negative life course outcomes. Considering the rates for low academic achievement, high school drop out, incarceration, illness, and early death for African-American males, there can be no question that cultural socialization is necessary (Boykin, 1994, 2000; Boykin and Bailey, 2000; Cross, 1991; Nobles, 1974, 1985). For such students, school is not a protective bubble that allows them to get away from many challenges in their lives but is rather a clear part of the challenges in their lives. Maladaptive responses such as not completing class work, skipping classes, and getting into verbal and physical altercations actually make a lot of sense from the naïve perspective of a young person who may not be aware of alternative ways of responding nor see their potential payoff.

We can certainly talk about the important role of parents, family networks, and community-based institutions in providing cultural socialization for youth who are placed at particular risk because of their race, ethnicity, class, or language use. There are many efforts underway in this regard, although clearly not enough. My concern, however, is equally for the role of schools in providing such cultural socialization, understanding that to socialize students in academic intellective competence is not merely a cognitive task. It involves a realistic understanding of the nature of the risks students face both in and outside of school. For example, many African-American and Latino males, from all ages, must take on a macho orientation to navigate difficult streets. In many instances, certainly not all, such a macho orientation serves as a protective factor on the streets. Learning to switch off the macho when he enters the school building is not easy or intuitive (Spencer, 1999). The work of the Comer Project (Comer, 1993) in helping elementary school teachers to understand the developmental needs of children to avoid discipline problems and to encourage academic learning is an example of one kind of cultural socialization process in which schools can engage.

CONCLUSION

I argue in this chapter that intellective competence is a feature of the human species. Across the varied contexts of human cultural communities, people demonstrate systematic ways of reasoning, of inferring generative patterns from their environments and using them to maintain practices and to invent new ones. Neither poverty, nor language variation, nor ethnicity or race impede people's ability to reason and engage in meaningful problem solving. This claim needs to be emphasized because a common but not often articulated folk theory in the United States is that young people and families living in poverty, speaking other languages or language varieties than an academic or presumed middle class dialect of English, who are largely black and brown, are not achieving in schools because of some inherent deficits (Lee and Slaughter-Defoe, 1995). Having said that, academic intellective competence is a highly specialized set of abilities that are a direct result of particular kinds of experiences over long periods of time in Western schooling. I attempt here to capture meaningful features of these competencies, including knowledge, skills, and dispositions, particularly as they relate to various subject areas. I have linked my argument to the nature of such expertise within school subject matters because these domains are, on the whole, only accessible to people through formal schooling. I acknowledge here the range of debates about the nature of expertise within each of the disciplines and the important distinctions in how the disciplines are practiced in the professional communities.

I do not wish to imply that any single approach to instruction is the linchpin to success, particularly for black and brown students and students from low-income backgrounds (Gutierrez and Rogoff, 2003; Lee, 2000a, 2000b). Humans, even young children, are very flexible and adaptable. Depending on their perceptions of their own needs, different kinds of supports may be more important than others. Depending on the risks and social supports in the various cultural communities in which they participate, and on the relationships among those various cultural communities, different targeted interventions may be more or less salient (Sizemore, 1987).

In making this case that academic intellective competence can be taught, I call on the wisdom embodied in the old African-American proverb: "Every shut eye ain't sleep."

REFERENCES

Alvermann, D. E., and Hagood, M. 2000. Critical media literacy: Research, theory, and practice in "New Times." *Journal of Educational Research,* 93, 193–205.

Ancess, J. 2003. *Beating the odds: High schools as communities of commitment.* New York: Teachers College Press.

Au, K. H. 1980. Participation structures in a reading lesson with Hawaiian children: Analysis of a culturally appropriate instructional event. *Anthropology and Education,* 11(2), 91–115.

Ball, A. F. 2000. Empowering pedagogies that enhance the learning of multicultural students. The Teachers College Record 102(6), 1006–34

Bandura, A. 2001. Social cognitive theory: An agentic perspective. *Annual Review of Psychology, 52,* 1–26.

Baron, R., Tom, D., and Cooper, H. 1985. Social class, race and teacher expectations. In Jerome B. Dusek (Ed.), *Teacher expectations.* Hillsdale, NJ: Erlbaum.

Bereiter, C., and Engelmann, S. 1966. *Teaching disadvantaged children in pre-school.* Englewood Cliffs, NJ: Prentice Hall.

Bloom, B. S., and Broder, L. 1950. *Problem-solving process of college students.* Chicago: University of Chicago Press.

Booth, W. 1974. *A rhetoric of irony.* Chicago: University of Chicago Press.

Bowman, P. 1989. Research perspectives on black men: Role strain and adaptation across the adult life cycle. In R. L. Jones (Ed.), *Black adult development and aging* (pp. 117–50). Berkeley, CA: Cobbs and Henry.

Bowman, P., and Howard, C. 1985. Race-related socialization, motivation, and academic achievement: A study of black youth in three-generation families. *Journal of the American Academy of Child Psychiatry,* 24(2), 134–41.

Boykin, A. W. 1994. Harvesting culture and talent: African American children and educational reform. In R. Rossi (Ed.), *Educational reform and at risk students.* New York: Teachers College Press.

———. 2000. Talent development, cultural deep structure, and school reform: Implications for African immersion initiatives. D. Pollard and C. Ajirotutu (Eds.), *African centered schooling in theory and practice.* Westport, CT: Greenwood.

Boykin, A. W., and Bailey, C. T. 2000. *The role of cultural factors in school relevant cognitive functioning: Synthesis of findings on cultural contexts, cultural orientations, and individual differences* (Research Report No. 42). Washington, D.C.: Center for Research on the Education of Students Placed at Risk.

Bransford, J. D., Brown, A. L., and Cocking, R. R. 1999. How people learn: Brain mind, experience, and school. Committee on Developments in the Science of Learning, National Research Council. National Academy Press, Washington, D.C.

Bransford, J. D., and Jhonson, M. K. (1972). Contextual prerequisites for understanding: Some investigations of comprehension and recall. *Journal of Verbal Learning and Verbal Behavior,* 11, 717–26.

Bronfenbrenner, U. 1989. Ecological systems theory. In R. Vasta (Ed.), *Annals of child development* (pp. 187–248). Greenwich, CT: JAI Press Inc.

Burton, L., Allison, K., and Obeidallah, D. 1995. Social context and adolescents: Perspectives on development among inner-city African-American teens. In L. Crockett and A. Crouter (Eds.), *Pathways through adolescence: Individual development in social contexts* (pp. 119–38). Mahwah, NJ: Lawrence Erlbaum.

Campbell, J. R., Hombo, C. M., and Mazzeo. 2000. *NAEP 1999 trends in academic progress: Three decades of student performance.* Washington, D.C.: National Center for Educational Statistics.

Cazden, C. 2000. *Classroom discourse: The language of teaching and learning.* Portsmouth, NH: Heinemann.

Ceci, S. J., and Ruiz, A. I. 1993. Inserting context into our thinking about thinking: Implications for a theory of everyday intelligent behavior. In M. Rabinowitz (Ed.), *Cognitive science foundations of instruction* (pp. 173–88). Hillsdale, NJ: Lawrence Erlbaum Associates.

Chi, M. T. H. 1978. Knowledge structures and memory development. In R. Siegler (Ed.), *Children's thinking: What develops* (pp. 73–96). Hillsdale, NJ: Erlbaum.

Chi, M. T. H., Feltovich, P. J., and Glaser, R. 1981. Categorization and representation of physics problems by experts and novices. *Cognitive Science,* 5, 121–52.

Cole, M. 1996a. *Cultural psychology: A once and future discipline.* Cambridge, MA: The Belknap Press of Harvard University Press.

———. 1996b. Putting culture in the middle. In M. Cole (Ed.), *Cultural psychology* (pp. 116–45). Cambridge, MA.: The Belknap Press of Harvard University Press.

Collins, A., and Ferguson, W. 1993. Epistemic forms and epistemic games: Structures and strategies to guide inquiry. *Educational Psychologist,* 28(1), 25–42.

Comer, J. 1993. *School power: Implications of an intervention project.* New York: Free Press.

Cross, W. 1991. *Shades of Black: Diversity in African-American Identity.* Philadelphia: Temple University Press.

Dai, D. Y., and Sternberg, R. 2004. *Motivation, emotion, and cognition: Integrative perspectives on intellectual functioning and development.* Mahwah, NJ: Lawrence Erlbaum.

Darling-Hammond, L. 1999. *State teaching policies and student achievement (Teaching Quality Policy Briefs).* Seattle, WA: Center for the Study of Teaching and Policy (University of Washington).

Darling-Hammond, L., and Green, J. 1990. Teacher quality and equality. In J. Goodlad and P. Keating (Eds.), *Access to knowledge: An agenda for our nation's schools* (pp. 237–58). New York: College Entrance Examination Board.

DeGroot, A. D. 1965. *Thought and choice in chess.* The Hague, The Netherlands: Mouton.

Dewey, J. 1963. *Experience and education.* New York: Collier.

DuBois, W. E. B. 1973. *The education of Black people: Ten critiques 1906–1960.* New York: Monthly Review Press.

Eccles, J. S., Wigfield, A., and Schiefele, U. 1998. Motivation to succeed. In W. Damon and N. Eisenberg (Eds.), *Handbook of child psychology* (5th ed., vol. 3). New York: Wiley.

Education Trust. 1998. *Good teaching matters: How well qualified teachers can close the achievement gap* (vol. 3).

———. 1999. *Ticket to nowhere* (vol. 3, issue 2). Washington, D.C.: The Education Trust.

———. 2005. *Gaining traction, gaining ground: How some high schools accelerate learning for struggling students.* Washington, D.C.: The Education Trust.

Ericsson, K., Krampe, R. T., and Tesch-Romer, C. 1993. The role of deliberate practice in the acquisition of expert performance. *Psychological Review,* 100, 363–406.

Feuerstein, R. 1980. *The dynamic assessment of retarded performers: The learning potential assessment, device, theory, instrument, and techniques.* Baltimore, MD: University Park Press.

Flavell, J. H. 1981. *The development of comprehension monitoring and knowledge about communication.* Chicago: University of Chicago Press.

Foster, M. 1997. *Black teachers on teaching.* New York: The New Press.

Garcia, G. E. 1998. Mexican-American bilingual students' metacognitive reading strategies: What's transferred, unique, problematic? *National Reading Conference Yearbook,* 47, 253–63.

Gee, J. P. 2000. Teenagers in new times: A new literacy studies perspective. *Journal of Adolescent and Adult Literacy,* 43, 412–20.

Goslee, S. 1998. *Losing ground bit by bit: Low-income communities in the information age.* Benton Foundation.

Gould, S. J. 1981. *The mismeasure of man.* New York: W. W. Norton.

Graham, S., and Golan, S. 1991. Motivational influences on cognition; Task involvement, ego involvement, and depth of information processing. *Journal of Educational Psychology,* 83(2), 187–94.

Griffin, S. A., Case, R., and Capodilupo, A. 1995. Teaching for understanding: The importance of the central conceptual structures in the elementary mathematics curriculum. In A. McKeough, J. Lupart, and A. Marini (Eds.), *Teaching for transfer: Fostering generalization in learning.* Hillsdale, NJ: Erlbaum.

Grossman, P. L., and Stodolsky, S. S. 1995. Content as context: The role of school subjects in secondary school teaching. *Educational Researcher,* 24(8), 5–11.23.

Gutierrez, K. D., and Rogoff, B. 2003. Cultural ways of knowing: Individual traits or repertoires of practice. *Educational Researcher,* 32(5), 19–25.

Gutmann, A. 1987. *Democratic education.* Princeton, NJ: Princeton University Press.

Hall, W. S., and Guthrie, L. 1980. On the dialect question and reading. In R. Spiro, B. Bruce, and W. Brewer (Eds.), *Theoretical issues in reading comprehension* (pp. 439–52). Hillsdale, NJ: Erlbaum.

Hall, W. S., Reder, S., and Cole, M. 1975. Story recall in young black and white children: Effects of racial group membership, race of experimenter, and dialect. *Developmental Psychology,* 11, 828–34.

Hampden-Thompson, G., and Johnston, J. 2006. *Variation in the relationship between nonschool factors and student achievement on international assessments.* Statistics in brief. Washington, D.C.: U.S. Department of Education, Institute of Education Sciences.

Hatano, G., and Inagaki, K. 1986. Two courses of expertise. In H. Stevenson, H. Azuma, and K. Hakuta (Eds.), *Child development and education in Japan* (pp. 262–72). New York: Freeman.

Haycock, K. 1998. Good teaching matters . . . a lot. *Thinking K–16: A Publication of the Education Trust,* 3(2), 3–14.

Hernstein, Richard J., and Murray, C. 1994. *The bell curve: Intelligence and class structure in American life.* Free Press.

Holland, J. 1995. *Hidden order: How adaptation builds complexity.* Cambridge, MA: Perseus.

House, E., Glass, G. V., and McLean, L. D. 1978. No simple answer: Critique of the follow through evaluation. *Harvard Educational Review,* 48, 128–60.

Irvine, J. 1990. *Black students and school failure.* New York: Praeger.

Klausmeier, H. J. 1985. *Educational psychology.* 5th ed. New York: Harper and Row.

Ladson-Billings, G. 1994. *The dreamkeepers.* San Francisco: Jossey-Bass.

Langer, J. A. 2001. Beating the odds: Teaching middle and high school students to read and write well. *American Educational Research Journal,* 38(4), 837–80.

Lave, J. 1977. Cognitive consequences of traditional apprenticeship training in West Africa. *Anthropology and Education Quarterly,* 8, 177–80.

Lave, J., Murtaugh, M., and de la Rocha, O. 1984. The dialectics of arithmetic in grocery shopping. In B. Rogoff and J. Lave (Eds.), *Everyday cognition: Its development in social context.* Cambridge, MA: Harvard University Press.

Lee, C. D. 1993. *Signifying as a scaffold for literary interpretation: The pedagogical implications of an African American discourse genre* (Research Report Series). Urbana, IL: National Council of Teachers of English.

————. 1995a. A culturally based cognitive apprenticeship: Teaching African American high school students' skills in literary interpretation. *Reading Research Quarterly*, 30(4), 608–631.

————. 1995b. Signifying as a scaffold for literary interpretation. *Journal of Black Psychology*, 21(4), 357–81.

————. 2000a. The state of research on black education. Invited Paper. Commission on Black Education. American Educational Research Association.

————. 2000b. Signifying in the zone of proximal development. In C. D. Lee and P. Smagorinsky (Eds.), *Vygotskian perspectives on literacy research: Constructing meaning through collabative inquiry* (pp. 191–225). New York: Cambridge University Press.

————. 2001. Is October Brown Chinese: A cultural modeling activity system for underachieving students. *American Educational Research Journal*, 38(1), 97–142.

————. 2004. Literacy in the Academic Disciplines and the Needs of Adolescent Struggling Readers. *Voices in Urban Education, 3*.

Lee, C. D., and Slaughter-Defoe, D. 1995. Historical and sociocultural influences on African American education. In J. Banks and C. Banks (Eds.), *Handbook of research on multicultural education* (pp. 348–71). New York: Macmillan.

Lee, C. D., Spencer, M. B., and Harpalani, V. 2003. Every shut eye ain't sleep: Studying how people live culturally. *Educational Researcher* (Carol Lee, guest editor) June/July, 32(5), 6–13.

Leinhardt, G., and Greeno, J. G. 1994. History: A time to be mindful. In G. Leinhardt, I. L. Beck, and C. Stainton (Eds.), *Teaching and learning in history* (pp. 209–225). Hillsdale, NJ.: Erlbaum.

Lemke, J. 1998. Multiplying meaning: Visual and verbal semiotics in scientific text. In J. R. Martin and R. Veel (Eds.), *Reading science: Critical and functional perspectives on discourse of science* (pp. 87–113). New York: Routledge.

Lightfoot, S. 1983. *The good high school: Portraits of character and culture.* New York: Basic Books.

Luchins, A. S., and Luchins, E. H. 1970. *Wertheimer's Seminar revisited: Problem solving and thinking* (vol. 1). Albany, NY: State University of New York.

Ma, L. 1999. *Knowing and teaching elementary mathematics.* Mahwah, NJ: Erlbaum.

Martin, D. 2000. *Mathematics success and failure of African-American students.* Mahwah, NJ: Erlbaum.

Martin, J. R., and Veel, R. 1998. *Reading science: Critical and functional perspectives on discourse of science.* New York: Routledge.

Moll, L. (2000). Inspired by Vygotsky: Ethnographic Experiments in Education. In C. Lee and P. Smagorinsky (Eds), *Vygotskian Perspective on Literacy Research.*

Moll, L. C., and González, N. 2004. Engaging life: A funds of knowledge approach to multicultural education. In J. Banks and C. McGee Banks (Eds.), *Handbook of research on multicultural education* (2nd ed). New York: Jossey-Bass.

Moll, L., and Greenberg, J. B. 1990. Creating zones of possibilities: Combining social contexts for instruction. In L. Moll (Ed.), *Vygotsky and education: Instructional implications and applications of sociohistorical psychology* (pp. 319–48). New York: Cambridge University Press.

Moses, R., and Cobb, C. 2001. *Radical equations: Math literacy and civil rights.* Boston: Beacon Press.

Mullis, I. V., Dossey, J. A., Foertsch, M. A., Jones, L. R., and Gentile, C. A. 1991. *Trends in academic progress: Achievement of U.S. students in science, 1969–70 to 1990, mathematics, 1973 to 1990, reading, 1971 to 1990, writing, 1984 to 1990* (Prepared by Educational Testing Service). Washington, D.C.: Office of Educational Research and Improvement, U.S. Department of Education.

Nasir, N., and Saxe, G. 2003. Ethnic and academic identities: A cultural practice perspective on emerging tensions and their management in the lives of minority students. *Educational Researcher* (32)5.

Nasir, N., Rosebery, A. S., Warren, B., and Lee, C. D. 2006. Learning as a cultural process: Achieving equity through diversity. In K. Sawyer (Ed.), *Handbook of the learning sciences*. New York: Cambridge University Press.

Nobles, W. 1974. African root and American fruit: The black family. *Journal of Social and Behavioral Sciences*, 20, 66–77

———. 1985. *Africanity and the black family: The development of a theoretical model*. Oakland: Black Family Institute Publication.

Nunes, T., Schliemann, A. D., and Carraher, D. W. 1993. *Street mathematics and school mathematics*. New York: Cambridge University Press.

Oakes, J. 1990. *Multiplying inequalities: The effects of race, social class and tracking on opportunities to learn mathematics and science*. Santa Monica, CA: Rand Corporation.

———. 1985. *Keeping track: How schools structure inequality*. New Haven, CT: Yale University Press.

Paulos, J. A. 1995. *A mathematician reads the newspaper*. New York: Doubleday.

Perkins, D. 1992. *Smart schools: Better thinking and learning for every child*. New York: The Free Press.

Piller, C. 1992. Separate realities: The creation of the technological underclass in America's public schools. *Macworld*, 218–30.

Quartz, S., and Sejnowski, T. 2002. *Liars, lovers and heroes: What the new brain science reveals about how we become who we are*. New York: Harper Collins.

Rabinowitz, P. 1987. *Before narrative: Narrative conventions and the politics of interpretation*. Ithaca, NY: Cornell University Press.

RAND Corporation. 2005. *Meeting literacy goals set by No Child Left Behind: A long uphill road*. Santa Monica, CA: RAND Corporation.

Resnick, L. B. 1987. Learning in and out of school. *Educational Researcher*, 16(9), 13–20.

Ritchhart, R. 2002. *Intellectual character: What it is, why it matters and how to get it*. San Francisco, CA: Jossey-Bass.

Rogoff, B. 1990. *Apprenticeship in thinking: Cognitive development in social context*. New York: Oxford University Press.

———. 2003. *The cultural nature of human development*. New York: Oxford University Press.

Rogoff, B., and Chavajay, P. 1995. What's become of research on the cultural basis of cognitive development. *American Psychologist*, 50(10), 859–77.

Rumelhart, D. 1978. Schemata: The building blocks of cognition. In R. Spiro, B. Bruce, and W. Brewer (Eds.), *Theoretical Issues in Reading Comprehension*. Hillsdale, NJ: Erlbaum.

Saxe, G. 1991. *Culture and cognitive development*. Hillsdale, NJ: Erlbaum.

Scribner S., and Cole, M. 1981. *The psychology of literacy.* Cambridge, MA: Harvard University Press.

Schoenfeld, A. 1998. Issues in Education 4, no. 1. The issue presents and critiques Schoenfeld's theory of teaching-in-context.

Seixas, P. 1993. The community of inquiry as a basis for knowledge and learning: The case of history. *American Educational Research Journal,* 30(2), 305–326.

Simon, H.A., and Chase, W.G. 1973. Skills in chess. *American Scientist,* 61, 394–403.

Singley, K., and Anderson, J. R. 1989. The transfer of cognitive skill. Cambridge, MA: Harvard University Press.

Sizemore, B. A. 1987. The effective African American elementary school. In G. W. Noblit and W. T. Pink (Eds.), *Schooling in social context: Qualitative studies* (pp. 175–202). Norwood, NJ: Ablex.

Smagorinsky, P., and Gevinson, S. 1989. *Fostering the reader's imagination: Rethinking the literature curriculum, grades 7–12.* Palo Alto, CA: Seymour Publications.

Smith, M. 1989. Teaching the interpretation of irony in poetry. *Research in the Teaching of English,* 23(3), 254–72.

Smith, M., and Hillocks, G. 1988. Sensible sequencing: Developing knowledge about literature text by text. *English Journal,* October, 44–49.

Spencer, M. B. 1995. Old issues and new theorizing about African American youth: A phenomenological variant of ecological systems theory. In R. L. Taylor (Ed.), *Black youth: Perspectives on their status in the United States* (pp. 37–70). Westport, CT: Praeger.

———. 1999. Social and cultural influences on school adjustment: The application of an identity-focused cultural ecological perspective. *Educational Psychologist,* 34(1), 43–57.

Spencer, M. B., Dupree, D., and Hartmann, T. 1997. A phenomenological variant of ecological systems theory (PVEST): A self-organization perspective in context. *Development and Psychopathology,* 9(4), 817–33.

Steele, C. 1997. A threat in the air: How stereotypes shape intellectual identity and performance. *American Psychologist,* 52, 613–29.

Super, C. M., and Harkness, S. 1986. The developmental niche: A conceptualization at the interface of child and culture. *International Journal of Behavioral Development,* 9, 545–69.

Tharp, R., and Gallimore, R. 1988. *Rousing minds to life: Teaching, learning, and schooling in social context.* New York: Cambridge University Press.

Varenne, H., and McDermott. 1998. *Successful failure: The school America builds.* Boulder, CO: Westview Press.

Vygotsky, L. 1978. *Mind in society: The Development of higher psychological processes.* M. Cole, V. John-Steiner, S. Scribner, and E. Souberman (Eds.). Cambridge, MA: Harvard University Press.

Weisner, T. 2002. Ecocultural understanding of children's developmental pathways. *Human Development* 45(4), 275–82.

Whitehead, A. N. 1929. *The aims of education.* New York: MacMillan.

Wilson, W. 1987. *The Declining Significance of Race.* Chicago: University of Chicago Press.

Wineburg, S. 1991. Historical problem solving: A study of the cognitive processes used in the evauation of documentary and pictorial evidence. *Journal of Educational Psychology,* 83(1), 73–87.

Woodson, C. G. 1969. *The mis-education of the Negro.* Washington, D.C.: The Associated Publisher. Original work published 1933.

Wossmann, L. 2003. Schooling resources, educational institutions and student performance: The international evidence. *Oxford Bulletin of Economics and Statistics,* 65(2), 117–70.

NOTE

1. Most national communities include multiple ethnic groups (Basques in France and Spain; the Scots, Welsh, and Irish in Great Britain; the Kurds and Arabs in Iraq). The United States has one of the most diverse arrays of ethnic groups, most of whom move back and forth between national, ethnic, and pan-ethnic identities according to the nature of practices in which they engage at any point in time. I am arguing here that racial groups are ethnic groups for whom particular physical features (usually skin color) have been highlighted as indicative of social status within the national society. This is the case of the untouchables in India, the coloreds in South Africa (even today), and the array of people of African descent in the United States. The great irony is that some evolutionary biologists have argued that all humans are of African descent. Equally ironic is that in order to claim African heritage on the basis of physiognomy, persons of lighter skin tones need to argue either for or against where in their ancestry a person of undeniable African ancestry appears (note the heated debate among descendants of Thomas Jefferson regarding the meaning of Sally Hemmings in their genetic ancestry). In a different but related vein, Jews argue over the rule that one's mother must be Jewish in order for an individual to be considered Jewish, and some Native American kinship groups debate over who is a member when legal issues arise around collective inheritance.

9

Psychosocial Processes in the Cultivation of Intellective Competence

The Interpenetration of Affective, Cognitive, and Situative Processes in Intellective Behavior

Rodolfo Mendoza-Denton and Joshua A. Aronson

In their seminal book *The Shape of the River*, Bowen and Bok (1998) tracked and followed a group of high-achieving minority students entering the nation's top colleges and universities. The authors found that similarly qualified minority students tended to receive lower grades relative to their majority peers—even when they have similar qualifications. Similarly, the National Task Force on Minority Achievement (College Board, 1999) reports a startling pattern in the 1994 National Assessment of Educational Progress (NAEP) reading test for twelfth grade, such that higher parental education was associated with *greater* gaps in reading scores between white students and minority students. A related, and well-documented, phenomenon arises from what has been termed *overprediction*—the fact that minority students do not achieve relative to what might be expected of them based on their prior grades or their standardized achievement test scores (College Board, 1999; Young, 1994).

The College Board's task force identified several components necessary for the affirmative development of minority high achievement. One such component is the *expansion of access* to good schools, colleges, and universities—and the resources they offer—to these students (College Board, 1999). Nevertheless, the above trends suggest that gaining access, while a necessary factor, may not be a sufficient one for the full realization of intellective competence and the maintenance of high achievement. These data, rather, hint at the possibility that there may be specific challenges that high-achieving minority students face, particularly as they come closer and closer to "reaching the top."

This chapter is concerned with understanding some of those special challenges, marshaling research in social psychology over the past decade to help uncover some of the psychological processes that play a role in the phenomenology and experience of minority students as they strive for the pinnacle (see also Aronson, 2002). In particular, we argue, along with Michelle Fine and colleagues (1997), that the achievement of *numerical diversity* through equal access to good schools, programs, and support systems lays the groundwork for something even more critical. We argue that, for intellective competence to fully blossom, numerical diversity needs to be complemented by systematic and institutional policies that ensure *relational diversity*—namely, the type of diversity where individuals feel—and have a legitimate basis for feeling—a sense of trust, acceptance, and inclusion in the institutions that open their doors to them.

In the pages that follow, we summarize recent social psychological research in support of this view, with a special emphasis on the psychological processes and meaning systems that are associated with being a member of a historically stigmatized group in institutions and practices that have been historically dominated by the majority. Our journey will take us through three related but distinct psychological processes—attributional ambiguity, stereotype threat, and prejudice apprehension—that shed light on the phenomenology of being a member of a stigmatized group in historically homogenous institutions, where high-achieving students are increasingly likely to be exposed to these processes as their success grows. In addition, we examine the role that theories of intelligence can play in undermining—or in boosting—the performance of minority students in the face of debilitating ability stereotypes. Based on this review, we make the case that the social psychological literature points to a clear message that *feelings of trust* in the institution, and in those who are seen to represent the interests of those institutions (e.g., teachers, professors, administrators), are a fundamental building block in the affirmative development of high minority achievement. We argue that these psychological processes are most pronounced precisely among those students reaching the top—those high-achieving students who are most identified with and center their sense of self around the endeavor of academic achievement. Finally, we conclude this chapter with specific policy recommendations that these social psychological findings imply, which complement and supplement those already outlined by the National Task Force on Minority Achievement (College Board, 1999).

In what follows, we present data from within a social psychological tradition. The types of studies in this tradition differ from larger-scale studies in education in certain important respects. These different traditions and methodologies complement each other in important ways. Large-scale survey studies have the advantage of being applicable to a broad group of students but are often correlational in nature and descriptive in their approach. Social psychological studies, by contrast, focus on smaller samples of students and may thus be of limited applicability, but they often employ methodologies that help establish causality between variables and address the psychological processes that underlie the relationships observed in the larger studies. In this chapter, we try to marshal studies in social psychology to shed light on some of the psychological processes associated with being a high-achieving minority student. In this way, we hope to complement findings from larger-scale studies and establish a link of communication between two disciplines.

PSYCHOLOGICAL SEQUELAE OF MINORITY HIGH ACHIEVEMENT

Over the past decade, there have been significant advances in research on stereotyping, prejudice, and bias from the perspective of its targets, which directly impact and inform our present discussion. Whereas research in this area has traditionally focused on the cognitive and motivational mechanisms that allow us to understand stereotyping and prejudice from the perceiver's perspective, yielding important insights into, for example, how teachers' expectations can play an adverse role in schooling (e.g., Weinstein, 2003), not until recently have we begun to deeply understand the experience and psychological legacy of stigmatized group membership. This research is particularly pertinent for the present discussion because successful minority students are increasingly likely, as they move up the achievement ladder, to encounter contexts and situations in which their group has been historically excluded and underrepresented (e.g., gaining access as a participant to the science fair, or gaining admission to a historically homogenous Ivy League college), and their group membership is more likely to be a salient characteristic (Higgins, 1996).

The past decade in particular has witnessed an explosion of research on the experience of being stigmatized, attributable in large part to seminal work in two areas: one is attributional ambiguity (e.g., Crocker and Major, 1989), and the other is stereotype threat (e.g., Steele and Aronson, 1995). We begin by reviewing these two phenomena, then move on to more recent research on the implications of theories of intelligence (Aronson, Fried, and Good, 2002) and prejudice apprehension (Mendoza-Denton, Purdie, Downey, Davis, and Pietrzak, 2002) in education.

Attributional Ambiguity

In their now classic doll preference study, Clark and Clark (1947) asked African-American youngsters to choose which of two dolls they would prefer to play with. A simple choice, but with important psychological and policy implications: one doll had light skin, and the other doll had dark skin. Across various studies, the researchers found that a large percentage of the children preferred the white doll over the black doll. When asked about the reasons for their preference, the researchers reported that many of the children cited the ugliness, and dirtiness, of the black doll. These findings were interpreted to mean that the children had internalized the negative societal stereotype of African Americans; this interpretation, moreover, was consistent with the assumption that members of minority groups should have lower self-esteem relative to members of majority groups (who enjoy societal approval of their group membership).

In the decades since, however, the data has failed to corroborate this popular assumption. African Americans and Latinos consistently show equal, and sometimes even *higher*, self-esteem relative to comparable white populations (for a review, see Twenge and Crocker, 2002). How does one make sense of this data? Crocker and Major (1989) proposed that, in a paradoxical way, stigmatized group membership can actually serve as a buffer for self-esteem. The rationale is as follows: when one is a member of a stigmatized group and receives negative feedback or evaluation (for example, a low score on a test), one can attribute such an outcome either to one's ability (and thus it is diagnostic of self), or alternatively, to discrimination on the part of the evaluator (and thus, it is not diagnostic of the self). Thus, the term *attributional ambiguity* refers to the state where the reasons for why one receives negative evaluation are not clear. It follows that when negative outcomes do occur, minority group members can selectively protect their self-esteem by making attributions to the evaluator's bias rather than to one's own ability or effort (Crocker and Major, 1994).

In one of the many elegant experiments that demonstrate this phenomenon, Crocker and colleagues (1991) invited African-American participants to take part in an experiment involving social evaluation. Participants thought that their evaluator, who was purportedly sitting in a room next door, was white. A one-way mirror separated the two rooms. The critical experimental manipulation was that in one condition, the blinds to the one-way mirror were drawn, so that participants thought that the evaluator could not see them through the one-way mirror. In the other condition, the blinds remained open, so that participants thought the evaluator could see them. When participants received negative feedback from the evaluator, those in the blinds-closed condition reported lower levels of self-esteem, but those in the blinds-open condition reported no change in self-esteem. The findings thus suggest that participants who thought the evaluator could see them (blinds-open condition) attributed the negative feedback to the evaluator's prejudice, leaving their self-esteem intact. By contrast, those who could not draw such a conclusion (because the evaluator could not see them) could only make an internal attribution, thus affecting their self-esteem.

Implications for Affirmative Development

These general findings have been replicated with a variety of methodologies and seem to indicate a robust phenomenon (see Crocker, Major, and Steele, 1998 for a review). What implications does this have for affirmative development? As one begins to think about this issue, a particular conundrum begins to take shape for the high-achieving minority student. On the one hand, an important aspect of academic achievement comes from the integration of academic success into the self-concept (Steele, 1992). Similarly, people want to achieve mastery and have at least some control over their outcomes (Bandura, 1986). Thus, when faced with negative feedback or obstacles along the way that *all* high-achieving students are bound to face, minority students *in particular* may be faced with a catch-22 with attributional ambiguity at its heart. If one receives negative feedback, should one discount it because it may be more reflective of external bias than of one's own internal ability? Or does it in fact reflect one's own internal ability? Moreover, if one chooses to see it as reflective of one's own ability, is one ignoring or being foolishly blind to systematic biases that can affect one's evaluations? Such a state of uncertainty can be distracting and intrusive, and may moreover lead to confusion when thinking about effective coping strategies for addressing the negative feedback itself. The point here is that high-achieving minority students in particular have reason to be attracted to *both* explanations for negative feedback when it is received, and as such, may have a more difficult time resolving the state of attributional ambiguity.

Stereotype Threat

A second line of research that has fueled recent interest in the experience of being stigmatized, and which impacts directly on affirmative development, is Steele, Aronson, and colleagues' work on *stereotype threat*. This research shows that when one belongs to, or can be identified as a member of, a group that has a negative stereotype associated with it, the worry or concern that one may be viewed or treated through the lens of that stereotype has pernicious effects on performance. An elderly person in the workplace, for example, may grow concerned that his younger colleagues will assume that he does not know how to operate a computer, and this preoccupation itself may lead him to work more slowly or to push the wrong button on the keyboard—thus confirming the stereotype. Stereotype threat becomes a relevant psychological process when people find themselves in contexts where a stereotype about their group is applicable. As such, Latino and African-American students may be particularly vulnerable to stereotype threat in the domain of academics, because the stereotype surrounding these students concerns a generalized suspicion about their intelligence. Importantly, stereotype threat effects can occur without the stereotyped individual him/

herself believing the stereotype—one simply has to have the knowledge of the stereotype, and that others may view one through that stereotype.

Stereotype threat research has had a major impact on thinking and theory surrounding the academic achievement gap—one of the central concerns of the National Task Force. It has had such impact in part because it provides a testable psychological account of the contextual and societal forces that can account for this gap, and provides a powerful, empirically validated alternative to biological explanations that attempt to account for achievement differences on the basis of innate ethnic ability differences. In one experiment, for example, Steele and Aronson (1995) presented African-American students with questions similar to those found in a standardized achievement test. A simple yet powerful experimental manipulation had a large impact on students' performance. In one condition, the students were told that the researchers were interested in the participants' verbal ability, and they were thus being tested with items diagnostic of that ability. In the other condition, the students were told that the (same) questions were being used to understand the psychological processes associated with problem solving, but that the researchers would not be evaluating the participants' ability. The researchers intended this latter manipulation to relieve the students' possible concern that, as members of a negatively stereotyped group, their ability was under suspicion or scrutiny. The data confirmed the researchers' expectations: whereas white students performed comparably regardless of which condition they were in, the African-American students underperformed relative to white students in the "ability-diagnostic" condition—yet performed just as well as the white students in the "non-diagnostic" condition. In other words, African-American participants' performance on the same set of questions was significantly affected by a small, but psychologically critical, framing of the test. More recent studies have shown that stereotype-relevant intrusive ideation and concerns about fulfilling the stereotype help explain this underperformance effect. To the degree that schooling in general, and standardized testing in particular, place particular emphasis on diagnosis of ability as a gateway for tracking, or college admissions, or other future opportunities, the implications of stereotype threat in relation to minority student achievement are profound.

Implications for Affirmative Development

How does stereotype threat impact our discussion of affirmative development? As reformers and educators continue to make headway into the affirmative development of academic achievement—and increasing numbers of minority students grow to self-identify with the academic endeavor—increasing research and policy attention will have to be paid to stereotype threat effects. Various studies have found that the students who are most vulnerable to intrusive ideation about being reduced to a stereotype are precisely those students who are most domain-identified. In one study reported by Steele (1997), for example, minority students were divided into academically identified and nonidentified students. The results revealed that stereotype threat manipulations (i.e., those that made the possibility of confirming or being evaluated on the basis of a stereotype most salient) negatively impacted the performance of the identified students most strongly. Theoretically, this makes sense, as it is those who are identified in a given domain, and are committed to their own achievement within that domain, who should be most concerned about factors that may negatively impact on that achievement. In sum, then, the effects of stereotype threat are potentially more pronounced the higher one comes to reaching the top—almost as if the air were getting thinner. As The College Board's National Task Force (1999) notes, "the negative impacts of these beliefs do not seem to be confined to the most disadvantaged underrepresented minority students" (p. 16). Indeed, when combined with the possibility that the state of attributional ambiguity may be more pronounced, and more difficult to dispel, for students who succeed at succeeding, a picture of the psychological weight of being a high-achieving minority student in this country comes increasingly into focus.

The Role of Theories of Intelligence

A key component of the stereotypes that minority students must contend with are their deterministic nature: the implication that one's group membership dictates one's intelligence or abilities. Thus, such stereotypes carry the message that one's intelligence or abilities, being determined by one's race, cannot be changed. The idea that intelligence is fixed is reiterated in the schooling system itself: from intelligence assessments to tracking procedures within schools, students can quickly learn and adopt an implicit model of intelligence as a fixed entity.

Such notions of intelligence may be particularly damaging to students as they strive toward the top. Psychological research has shown that people's implicit *theories of intelligence* can have a significant impact on motivation, performance, and responses to academic setbacks. In particular, Carol Dweck and her colleagues (see Dweck, 1999; Dweck and Leggett, 1988; Hong, Chiu, and Dweck, 1995; Kamins and Dweck, 1999) have found evidence that people differ in how they think about intelligence: whereas some people view intelligence as a fixed entity that cannot be changed or altered ("entity theorists"), others see it as a malleable quality that can change with practice and training ("incremental theorists").

Research has shown that entity theorists view examinations as diagnostic of ability, and use performance information as a diagnostic tool of their global intellectual ability. Incremental theorists, by contrast, use the same performance information as informative about their effort, task strategies, and where they could be doing better (Dweck and Leggett, 1988). In the face of challenging tasks, entity theorists adopt a "performance orientation," opting for easier tasks that will guarantee success. Incremental theorists, by contrast, are more likely to adopt a "learning orientation" and opt for more challenging tasks that offer greater opportunities for learning without the same guarantee of success. Negative feedback can also be particularly debilitating for entity theorists, who respond with increased negative affect, reduced task motivation, and disengagement (Dweck, 1999).

Implicit Theories and Stereotype Threat

As Aronson, Fried, and Good (2002) have argued, minority students—being targets of stereotypes that imply low, fixed ability—may adopt a similar performance orientation as entity theorists in academic settings, leading them to choose easier, less challenging tasks, and to disengage from domains in which their abilities are continuously in question. Further, as they move up the educational ladder, minority students may be most likely to adopt a performance orientation, given that academic challenges are likely to become more commonplace the closer one gets to the pinnacle.

Aronson and colleagues (Aronson, Fried, and Good, 2002; Good, Aronson, and Inzlicht, in press) have reasoned that one way to help students cope effectively with stereotype threat is by shaping students' beliefs about the malleability of intelligence. In an empirical investigation of this reasoning, Aronson and colleagues (2002) manipulated African-American and white students' theories about the malleability of intelligence and subsequently examined these students' end-of-year academic performance and attitudes relative to two relevant control groups. Those African-American students who had been taught about the malleability of intelligence reported greater academic engagement and enjoyment, and also obtained significantly better grades (assessed independently from the registrar's records) relative to students who had not received the manipulation. Similar trends, although not as strong, were observed for the white students. Attitude change with regard to theories of intelligence, moreover, seemed to prove more long-lasting for the African-American students: over the course of several weeks, African-American participants' endorsement of the incremental view grew stronger, whereas white participants' endorsement tended to dissipate.

Nevertheless, the results from this study also showed a direct effect between race and GPA that was left unaccounted for, even when controlling for prior academic preparation and for stereotype threat. In the words of the authors, "some other factor not captured by SAT or our measures of stereotype threat were operating to depress African Americans' grades relative to those of Whites" (p. 121). Below, we argue that one such factor (although not the only one) might be anxious expectations of race-based rejection, which beyond capturing the threat associated with confirming stereotypes, taps students' apprehension about being discriminated or rejected on the basis of one's race, regardless of one's own behavior.

Race-based Rejection Sensitivity (RS-race)

As the College Board's National Task Force on Minority High Achievement (1999) points out, quite independently of negative stereotypes, another critical dimension of the experience of being stigmatized is that "most racial and ethnic groups simply hold a *general dislike* for some other groups" (p. 16). Within social psychology, a similar distinction has been made between *stereotypes*, the cognitively based belief systems associated with particular groups, and *prejudice*, the affectively based attitudes that people hold against other groups. As the task force anticipates, "because White students are still a large majority on most campuses, the negative views of some Whites can contribute to a perception that minorities are 'unwelcome' [and] appears to undermine the academic performance of many minority students" (p. 16).

But if not through stereotype threat, how can one quantify and psychologically assess the impact of such a "lack of hospitality"? Recent research on African-American students' apprehensive anticipation of prejudice (Mendoza-Denton et al., 2002) yields some insight into this issue. According to the researchers, direct or vicarious experiences of exclusion, discrimination, and prejudice can lead people to anxiously anticipate that they will be similarly treated in *new* contexts where the possibility of such treatment exists. Mendoza-Denton and colleagues have referred to this processing dynamic (expectations, perceptions, intense reactions) as *race-based rejection sensitivity* (RS-race). As several researchers have noted, minority students in particular are likely to experience doubts about their acceptance in educational institutions, and such concerns are likely to be accentuated in academic environments and institutions that high-achieving minority students strive for.

By tracking the progress of two successive cohorts of high-achieving African-American students at an Ivy League university from the first day of their freshman year up until their graduation, the researchers were able to shed light on the psychological sequelae of RS-race. The researchers reasoned that, when making the transition to the university, anticipatory apprehension of prejudice might play a formative role in students' overall college experience by influencing the quality of the relationships they form with professors and peers and the sense of belonging they feel during the first weeks of college. The participants in this longitudinal study completed a structured daily diary for the first three weeks of classes of their freshman year. The results revealed that individual differences in RS-race independently predicted a heightened sense of alienation and of personal failure on the typical day of the diary period. Such apprehension was also associated with feeling less welcome at the university, greater difficulties with roommates, and as predicted, less positive views of professors.

Longitudinally, students who entered the university with concerns about how welcome they would be experienced less diverse friendships and felt less trust and obligation toward the university at the end of their first year in college. As sophomores and juniors, they also reported decreased attendance at academic review sessions, as well as increased anxiety about approaching professors and TAs with academic problems. Unsurprisingly, then, RS-race was predictive of students' change in GPA over the first five semesters of college, such that students who experienced prejudice apprehension were particularly likely to experience a decrease in their grades over time (Mendoza-Denton et al., 2002).

Implications for Affirmative Development

Mary McPherson, former president of Bryn Mawr college, quoted in *The Shape of the River* (Bowen and Bok, 1998), summarized how insecurity about whether one belongs and can feel comfortable in college might undermine academic success as follows: "Since students have only a limited amount of time and emotional energy, those able to concentrate on their academic tasks, without constant concern about their place on the campus and their relationships to others, are most likely to do well academically" (p. 82).

The research reviewed above suggests that high-achieving minority students who gain access to elite, but likely historically homogenous, educational institutions may face a unique challenge in the pursuit of their personal and academic goals: that of assessing how much *trust* they can place on the institution and its representatives. In addition to channeling resources from academic pursuits into worrying about belonging, race-based rejection concerns may impede achievement by inhibiting students from seeking assistance for academic and personal needs, given that in predominantly white colleges the source of assistance probably comes from a person of a different race. At a physiological level, such apprehension may function like other stressors to undermine immune functioning and thus increase susceptibility to common infectious illnesses like colds and influenza that may affect students' academic performance (Clark et al., 1999).

IMPLICATIONS

The National Task Force on Minority High Achievement's (College Board, 1999) central mission was to promote the affirmative development of minority students' intellective competence. The task force outlined a set of specific recommendations to achieve that goal. As these recommendations begin to be followed, and minority students increasingly gain access to the resources, institutions, and opportunities that they did not avail themselves of before, the question raised at the introduction of this chapter becomes even more relevant: how do we successfully navigate the transition from mere numerical diversity to relational diversity?

So far, we have attempted to provide a picture of some of the social psychological mechanisms that may be particularly relevant for high-achieving minority students. By understanding how the experience of reaching the top changes along the journey, it may be possible to further tailor our recommendations for affirmative development to suit students' needs—and to make the pinnacle possible.

Affirmative development is based on the notion that academic abilities are nurtured and developed through pedagogical, social, and interpersonal supports—a type of developmental "scaffolding" around and within which students can grow and find support. What should the nature of that scaffolding be? The above research suggests that beyond the opening of doors and beyond the achievement of numerical diversity, educators—and the institutions that they represent—must work together toward the achievement of relational diversity (Fine et al., 1997). By relational diversity, we mean a type of diversity where institutions are not merely filling numerical quotas but are instead actively working to secure the trust and confidence of those students whom they have opened their doors to. As the research summarized above implies, such trust and confidence is a critical component of minority students' achievement on several levels.

When high-achieving minority students succeed, many times they will be faced with situations and environments where their group membership becomes particularly salient. Whether this is an opportunity to attend an academic summer camp, present a stellar project at a conference, or attend an elite university, these contexts can strengthen suspicions about one's belonging and acceptance. As research on prejudice apprehension shows, concerns about one's belonging can directly impact one's achievement by leading people to not take advantage of the various resources that the institution may offer. Although this self-protective strategy minimizes the possibility of rejection and future prejudice, it also reduces the number of resources and support systems one can count on when faced with the difficulties that all students face.

Similarly, high achievement—particularly in our current culture—often becomes equated with performance, such that the attainment of high grades often takes precedence over learning (see Covington, 2000). While this differential emphasis is detrimental for all students (e.g., Dweck, 1999), the research reviewed here suggests that it may be particularly pernicious for students whose group is associated with low ability (Aronson et al., 2002). In addition, intrusive ideation associated with both stereotype threat and with attributional ambiguity may be more pronounced among high achievers, precisely because they are identified within the domain and their sense of self is likely to be wrapped up within it.

How does one build a bridge to the pinnacle for high achieving minority students? Are there measures that educators can take to alleviate some of the pressures faced by such students? In the next section, we outline two such mechanisms—one at the interpersonal level, and the other at the institutional level—that may help us address these issues.

Interpersonal Level: "Wise" Feedback across the Racial Divide

Cohen, Steele, and Ross (1999) have shown the influence of different types of feedback on minority students' motivation and impressions of bias. Although there is often a premium placed on emotion-free critical analysis in our culture (Cosmides, Tooby, and Barkow, 1992), Cohen and colleagues' research suggests that when it comes to mentoring across the racial divide, minority students' discomfort and apprehension must be actively addressed. How does one best achieve this? Does one, for example, provide critical feedback that is as straightforward as possible, so as to eliminate lack of objectivity? Or, does one address potential anxiety and mistrust by providing clear signals across the racial divide precisely of trust and caring?

To test these possibilities, the researchers invited African-American and white students at Stanford University to write an essay for possible publication in a university magazine. All students were given feedback on their essay one week later and were led to believe that a white university professor (the purported editor of the magazine) was the one to provide such feedback. Unbeknown to the students, the experimenters manipulated the way in which the feedback was given. Participants received one of three different feedback types. In the "criticism only" condition, students received critical feedback on their essay in the form of red markings along the margins (e.g., "unclear," "awkward"), two checkmarks for good points, plus specific suggestions. In the "criticism plus high standards" condition, students received the critical feedback, but the professor also wrote, "remember, I wouldn't go through the trouble of giving you this feedback if I weren't committed to the quality of this journal—I want to uphold the highest standards for what I consider a suitable entry." Finally, in a "criticism plus high standards plus *assurance*" condition, the professor provided critical feedback but additionally wrote: "Remember, I wouldn't go through the trouble of giving you this feedback if I didn't think, based on what I've read in your letter, that you are capable of meeting the higher standard I mentioned."

The results from this study clearly showed that African-American students' motivation to revise the essay, based on the professor's feedback, was the greatest in the "wise" criticism condition—that is, criticism plus high standards plus assurance. By contrast, unbuffered criticism led to the lowest task motivation, identification with the writing task—and the greatest ratings of bias (for most of these dependent variables, criticism plus high standards only fell squarely between the two other conditions). What these results suggest is that there may be negative motivational consequences, particularly for black students, in the face of pointed, unmitigated criticism. Such negative effects were not observed among the white students, who were less sensitive to the experimental manipulations. Consistent with the arguments presented here, those students most likely to have doubts about their professors' attitudes toward them benefited the most from the "wise" feedback.

Institutional Level: Allowing for Positive Race-related Experiences

How can the institution itself move from mere numerical diversity, toward earning the trust of all its members? One suggestive finding comes from Mendoza-Denton et al. (2002), who found that students who anxiously expected rejection at the university felt an increased sense of belonging at the university following days in which they had had a positive race-related experience. Examples of positive race-related experiences included speaking with another student about the experience of being black at the university, as well as attending a meeting of the Black Student Organization at the university. This finding provides initial evidence for the beneficial effect of having institutionally-sanctioned events and organizations that foster positive race-related experiences. When universities explicitly value and support such organizations and events, they may defy negative expectations about the institution's lack of support and instead foster a sense that the institution is attentive to the needs of all its members. Thus, in contrast to the perception that student groups organized around ethnicity lead to balkanization, these findings suggest instead that such organizations may lead to greater institutional belonging. These findings await replication and expansion, however: a task for future research is to identify institutional arrangements that can lead to—and those that can hinder—the realization of true relational diversity (Fine et al., 1997).

RECOMMENDATIONS

A common thread that runs through the psychological accounts summarized above is that of *trust*. Consistent with the notion that affirmative development centers around pedagogical and social interventions that foster intellective competence, the research outlined here underlines the essential nature of a trusting relationship between students and their educators. More broadly, it also suggests working toward the development of institutional policies that signal to those climbing to the top that their needs are being met, and their voices heard. Policy implications that derive from this perspective are:

- Increased focus on the part of educational institutions to support minority students *after* access to the institution has been secured. Efforts by many traditionally homogenous educational institutions to achieve numerical diversity are commendable, and these have translated into a concentrated effort to recruit minority applicants and convince them to join the institution. Upon arrival, however, students are often left to explore the new opportunities available to them on their own. While such treatment can be justified as equitable treatment for all new students, minority students often report feeling abandoned or brought in only to fill a quota, especially when compared to intense attention received during the recruitment phase.
- Having granted equal access to the resources and opportunities that are conducive to success (including use of libraries, extra help sessions, tutoring, and after-school activities) there needs to be an increasing awareness that a sense of mistrust—fears about confirming a stereotype or of being stigmatized on the basis of one's group membership—can hinder high-achieving minority students' utilization of such resources. Making the resources available is only the first step: winning students' trust to be able to utilize the resources must follow.
- Enactment of publicly sanctioned practices and procedures, endorsed at an institutional level, communicates a commitment to relational diversity on the part of the institution. These are likely to be institution-specific but may include one-time events such as diversity forums, calendar events such as the observance of important holidays associated with specific groups, or public endorsement of student-run organizations centered around race or ethnicity. The latter in particular may provide "safe spaces" (Crocker, Major, and Steele, 1998) for minority students and provide a context for the sharing of group-specific coping resources and strategies (Cross and Strauss, 1998). Endorsement of such organizations by the institution can communicate that the institution does not "turn a blind eye" toward the special challenges of minority students.

CONCLUSION

Despite the removal of legal and institutional barriers to achieving diversity, clear disparities remain in educational achievement outcomes between minority and white students (College Board, 1999). Not only is this academic achievement gap present at all levels of schooling, but it seems to grow increasingly pronounced over the course of schooling.

Thus, while it is important to address these challenges early on, since presumably these disparities originate at early levels of schooling, it is also imperative to recognize that special challenges may face minority students the more successful they are in reaching the top. In this chapter, we argue that minority students may experience the psychological impact of being a member of a stigmatized group more acutely as they become more academically successful. The reasons for this are twofold: first, such success implies developing an academic identity, which for minority students is a threatened identity. Second, as minority students become more successful, the likelihood increases that educational opportunities and institutions will continue being overrepresented by majority group members—thereby increasing suspicions about one's belonging and acceptance. It is argued that the development of trust, both of the institution and its representatives, is a central and necessary psychological factor—a basic need—for the development of intellective competence. The notion of trust development is consistent with the tenets of affirmative development, which stresses pedagogic, social, and interpersonal support systems in the healthy development of all students.

In this chapter we have covered some of the psychological processes that high-achieving minority students may be particularly likely to face as they approach the pinnacle. We have covered how attributional ambiguity, stereotype threat, and sensitivity to race-based rejection can all contribute to a lack of trust and belonging within the academic setting. What have traditionally been known as the three R's of education—reading, 'riting, and 'rithmetic—do not occur in a social vacuum, but rather take place within the context of social relationships. We argue that the traditional three R's must stand alongside three complementary R's that invoke trust: respect, relationships, and reciprocity.

REFERENCES

Aronson, J. 2002. *Improving academic achievement: Impact of psychological factors on education.* San Diego: Academic Press.

Aronson, J., Fried, C. B., and Good, C. 2002. Reducing the effects of stereotype threat on African American college students by shaping theories of intelligence. *Journal of Experimental Social Psychology,* 38, 113–25.

Bandura, A. 1986. *Social foundations of thought and action: A social cognitive theory.* Englewood Cliffs, NJ: Prentice-Hall.

Bowen, W. G., and Bok, D. 1998. *The shape of the river: Long-term consequences of considering race in college and university admissions.* Princeton, NJ: Princeton University Press.

Clark, K. B., and Clark, M. P. 1947. Racial identification and preference in Negro children. In H. Proshansky and B. Seidenberg (Eds.), *Basic studies in social psychology.* New York: Holt, Rinehart, and Winston.

Clark, R., Anderson, N. B., Clark, V. R., and Williams, D. R. 1999. Racism as a stressor for African Americans: A biopsychosocial model. *American Psychologist,* 54, 805–816.

Cohen, G. L., Steele, C. M., and Ross, L. D. 1999. The mentor's dilemma: Providing critical feedback across the racial divide. *Personality and Social Psychology Bulletin,* 25, 1302–18.

College Board. 1999. *Reaching the top: A report of the National Task Force on Minority High Achievement.* New York: The College Board.

Cosmides, L., Tooby, J., and Barkow, J. H. 1992. The psychological foundations of culture. In Barkow, Cosmides, and Tooby (Eds.), *The adapted mind.* Oxford: University Press.

Covington, M. V. 2000. Goal theory, motivation, and school achievement: an integrative review. *Annual Review of Psychology,* 51, 171–200.

Crocker, J., and Major, B. 1989. Social stigma and self-esteem: The self-protective properties of stigma. *Psychological Review,* 96, 608–630.

———. 1994. Reactions to stigma: The moderating role of justifications. In M. P. Zanna and J. M. Olson (Eds.), *The psychology of prejudice: The Ontario symposium* (vol. 7, pp. 289–314). Hillsdale, NJ: Erlbaum.

Crocker, J., Major, B., and Steele, C. 1998. Social stigma. In D. Gilbert, S. Fiske, and G. Lindzey (Eds.), *Handbook of social psychology* (4th ed., pp. 504–53). Boston, MA: McGraw-Hill.

Crocker, J., Voelkl, K., Testa, M., and Major, B. 1991. Social stigma: the affective consequences of attributional ambiguity. *Journal of Personality and Social Psychology,* 60, 218–28.

Cross, W. E., and Strauss, L. 1998. The everyday functions of African American identity. In J. K. Swim and C. Stangor (Eds.), *Prejudice: The target's perspective* (pp. 267–79). San Diego: Academic Press.

Dweck, C. 1999. Self-theories: Their role in motivation, personality, and development. *Essays in social psychology.* Philadelphia, PA: Psychology Press.

Dweck, C., and Leggett, E. L. 1988. A social-cognitive approach to motivation and personality. *Psychological Review,* 25, 109–116.

Fine, M., Weis, L., and Powell, L. C. 1997. Communities of difference: A critical look at desegregated spaces created for and by youth. *Harvard Educational Review,* 67, 247–84.

Good, C., Aronson, J., and Inzlicht, M. In press. Improving adolescents' standardized test performance: An intervention to reduce the effects of stereotype threat. *Journal of Applied Developmental Psychology.*

Higgins, E. T. 1996. Knowledge activation: Accessibility, applicability, and salience. In E. T. Higgins and A. W. Kruglanski (Eds.), *Social psychology: Handbook of basic principles* (pp. 133–68). New York: Guilford Press.

Hong, Y., Chiu, C., and Dweck, C. S. 1995. Implicit theories of intelligence: Reconsidering the role of confidence in achievement motivation. In M. Kernis (Ed.), *Efficacy, agency, and self-esteem* (pp. 197–216). New York: Plenum.

Kamins, M., and Dweck, C. S. 1999. Person versus process praise and criticism: Implications for contingent self-worth and coping. *Developmental Psychology,* 35, 835–47.

Mendoza-Denton, R., Purdie, V., Downey, G., and Davis, A. 2002. Sensitivity to race-based rejection: Implications for African-American students' college experience. *Journal of Personality and Social Psychology*, 83, 896–918.

Steele, C. M. 1992. Race and the schooling of black Americans. *Atlantic Monthly*, April, 68–78.

———. 1997. A threat in the air: How stereotypes shape the intellectual identities and performance of women and African Americans. *American Psychologist*, 52, 613–29.

Steele, C. M., and Aronson, J. 1995. Stereotype threat and the intellectual performance of African Americans. *Journal of Personality and Social Psychology*, 69, 797–811.

Twenge, J. M., and Crocker, J. 2002. Race and self-esteem revisited: Reply to Hafdahl and Gray-Little. *Psychological Bulletin*, 128, 417–20.

Weinstein, R. 2003. *Reaching Higher: The power of expectations in schooling*. Cambridge, MA: Harvard University Press.

Young, J. W. 1994. Differential prediction of college grades by gender and by ethnicity: A replication study. *Educational and Psychological Measurement*, 54, 1022–29.

10

Politicalization

A Neglected Pedagogical Process

Edmund W. Gordon

In a society that has alternately pushed ethnic separation or ethnic amalgamation and that has never truly accepted cultural and ethnic pluralism as its model, African Americans, Hispanic Americans, and Native Americans are insisting that the traditional public school is guilty not only of the intellectual and social but of the cultural genocide of their children. For many members of these groups, the problem in education is that their children have been subjected to white education, which they see as destructive to people of color. When one views this argument in the context of the current stage in the development of craft unionism in education, the position cannot be ignored. The conditions and status of professional workers in education are justly the concern of their unions, but blacks increasingly view the union concern as being in conflict with their concern for their children's development. That in New York City the workers are predominantly white makes it easy for the conflict to be viewed as ethnic in origin unless one looks at the situation in Washington D.C., where the origin of the conflict can be viewed as class. In D.C., despite blacks being heavily represented in the educational staff, some of the problems between professionals and clients are just as apparent.

There are class and caste conflicts to which insufficient attention has been given in the organization and delivery of educational services. If cultural and ethnic identification are important components of the learning experience, to ignore or demean them is poor education. If curriculum and delivery systems do not take these factors into account, inefficient learning may be the result. One would hope that black education by black educators is not the only solution, yet we are being pressed to no longer ignore it as a possible solution.

Would that the problems ended even there. It may well be that what has surfaced as cultural nationalism may be only the wave crest of a more important issue. Public schools as social institutions have never been required to assume responsibility for their failures. They, nonetheless, eagerly accept credit for the successes of their students. This may be related in part to the functions that schools serve in modern societies. The noted anthropologist, Anthony Wallace (1968), has discussed the differential attention given to training in technique (or skills education) for morality, and the development of intellect in societies that are revolutionary, conservative, or reactionary. For more than one hundred years the United States has been a conservative society—liberal in its traditions but essentially conservative in its functions. Some of us fear that this conservatism has given way to a reactionary stance. According to Wallace, the conservative society places highest emphasis on training in techniques and skills, with secondary attention to morality (correct behavior), and least attention to the development of the intellect. Societies in the reactionary phase place greatest emphasis on morality (now defined as law and order), second emphasis on techniques and skills, and only slight or no attention to the development of intellect. Wallace sees society in its revolutionary phase as placing greatest emphasis on morality (humanistic concerns), with second-level interest on the development of intellect, and the least attention given to training in technique and skills. Schools may not have developed a tradition of accountability because techniques and skills may be the least difficult of the learning tasks to master, if the conditions for learning are right. For large numbers of children who have progressed in the mastery of technique, their status in the society has facilitated technique mastery. Our society has been able to absorb those who have not mastered the skills into low-skill work and nondemanding life situations. But by the middle of the twentieth century, entry into the labor force and participation in the affairs of the society increasingly required mastery of skills and techniques. Those who would move today toward meaningful participation and the assertion of power are increasingly demanding that the schools be accountable not only for pupils' mastery of skills, but also for the nurturance of morality and the development of intellectuality. In fact, with the rapidly increasing demand for adaptability and trainability in those who are to advance in the labor force, Du Bois's (1968) concern with the liberating arts and sciences (the development of intellect) moves to the fore. Yet we must remember that the schools are presently instruments of a conservative (possibly reactionary) society; but blacks, other minority groups, and poor people increasingly see revolution (radical change) as the only ultimate solution to the problems and conditions in which their lives are maintained. As such, their concern with schooling may more sharply focus on issues related to morality and intellectual development, broadly defined, concerns that the schools have never been competent to meet. If circumstance has converted these concerns to educational needs, the schools then, in their present form, are ill-prepared to educate these young people whose ideals and goals should be revolutionary, not conservative, and certainly not reactionary.

Does this mean that schooling cannot be effective in the development of young people? No! To insure that our schools effectively educate is one of our tasks. To reduce or eliminate economic inequality is a related but separate task. It is from the accidental or deliberate confusing of these tasks, along with the distortion of the meaning of possible genetically based differences in the intellectual functioning of ethnic groups, that the threat to adequate support for educational and other human welfare programs is perceived. We do not equalize income by making schooling equally available or equally effective for all people. We equalize income, if that is our goal, by redistributing income and by eliminating the opportunity to exploit the wealth-producing labor of others and to hoard capital. But that does not mean that there are not good reasons for a democratic and humane society to make schooling equally available and optimally effective for all people. Similarly, people do differ individually and by groups. It is quite likely that assertions that groups of people differ by race with respect to qualitative aspects of intellectual function will find further support. Researchers have been reporting data and advancing postulates indicating ethnic group and social class differences in the character of intellectual function (see Jensen; Lesser, 1965; Zigler, 1966, and others). That genetic factors influence mental function and in part account for individual and group differences does not mean that schooling and other environmental conditions have no effect, nor does it mean that these differences are not useful. Rather, the fact of difference, no matter what the source, in the interest of human development requires diversity of facilitative treatments and sufficiency of the resources to deliver them. This, then, is where the problem lies, rather than in the fact of diversity in human characteristics.

EDUCATION AND SOCIAL JUSTICE

Education is, perhaps, the quintessential human enterprise. Unlike other forms of animal life that train their younger members to recognize signs and signals and to execute the techniques by which they adapt to environments and communicate with each other, human beings educate each other. That is, we teach each other to learn how to learn. Of even greater importance, we teach each other how to think—how to use signs and symbols, how to develop and use techniques and technologies, how to generate and apply concepts, numbers, and information in other forms to address problems and situations that are real, as well as those that are abstract, even those that are only imagined. Human beings, as animals capable of transforming conceptual and material phenomena, use education deliberately to enable the development of human intellective competence. Humans do, of course, use training to transfer knowledge and skill from more experienced learners to novice learners. However, it is the intentional involvement of learners in the following intellective processes that is unique to education as a human developmental enterprise. These processes include:

1. engagement in the discovery of relationships and the generation and recognition of meanings;
2. engagement in the construction of knowledge, in its critical understanding, and in its appreciation; and
3. engagement in the adaptation, application, and internalization of knowledge, values, and techniques.

Education so conceived, while training is done for and to others, is a process in which persons are enabled to engage, and, in its essence, a process learners must experience for themselves. We who teach can only guide and mediate those experiences.

Education then, is both a social and a very personal process. To the extent that it is initiated, guided, and mediated by others, the process is necessarily social. To the extent that education cannot be fully experienced without the complicity and engagement of the learner, it is a very personal phenomenon. If the process is one that requires social interaction and engagement by teaching and learning persons, then the social context must be one that enables and supports such human transactions. Thus the reciprocal social and personal nature of the process makes the social context in which it is experienced potentially as important to the achievement of the purposes of education as are the processes by which they are experienced.

There may be some education context/process relationships that are so symbiotic as to defy separation. It appears that education and social justice are so symbiotically related. In modern societies the achievement of universally effective education may not be possible in the absence of contexts in which social justice is valued and practiced. Similarly, the achievement of social justice may not be possible in the absence of the achievement of universally effective education.

The failure to achieve universally effective education in our society is known to be a correlate of our failure to achieve social justice. By almost any measure, there continue to be serious differences between the level and quality of educational achievement for children coming from rich and poor families and from ethnic majority and some ethnic minority group families. Low-status ethnic minority groups continue to be overrepresented in the low-achievement groups in our schools and are correspondingly underrepresented in high academic achievement groups. Most disturbing is the fact that non-Asian minority group students from middle class families are grossly underrepresented, in proportion to the number of such students, in the high achievement student pool. This suggests that poor academic achievement among low-status groups may be a castelike phenomenon—relatively independent of family income and class status. If you are black, high income and social position may not lift your children as high in achievement as similar status does for white children. The camouflaged absence of social justice is indicated by differentials in such intergenerational factors as conditions of life, income and wealth, participation in political and social intercourse, quality of the institutions to which students have access, quality of health and health care, sustained employment, and sense of membership in the social order.

We have tended to think of social justice as a value that we are morally committed to pursue for the underprivileged, for ethnic minorities, or for any low-status group. However, I argue that the absence of justice is more than a moral problem, it is incompatible with the purposes of education. It is a threat to the economic and political stability of the society. With respect to education, I argue that full engagement in the pedagogical process and optimal educational outcomes are impossible without it. I assert that once the issue of human diversity is permitted to enter the calculus of human affairs (and it must), the question of social justice becomes critical. I argue that education, then, is emerging as the most unique and essential of human endeavors; that concern for social justice is a necessary condition for education; and that our nation cannot continue to function as a democracy in the absence of social justice. I argue further that social justice is a necessary condition for the production of the knowledge and understanding by which pedagogical theory, policy, and practice are informed.

Several issues concerning the relationship between education and social justice support the positions advanced above. I begin with the moral and philosophical issues related to the construct *social justice*. In *A Theory of Justice*, Rawls has developed a conceptual framework for the examination and explication of a system of justice in which a concern for fairness as an expression of equitable treatment is a central feature. His effort at explication of such a theory rests upon two principles of justice. The first is:

- Each person is to have an equal right to the most extensive total system of equal basic liberties compatible with a similar system of liberty for all. (Rawls, 1971: 302)

His second principle holds that:

- Social and economic inequalities are to be arranged so that they both (a) are to the greatest benefit to the least advantaged, consistent with the just savings principle and (reasonable reserve for future generations), and; (b) attached to offices and positions open to all under conditions of fair equality and opportunity. (Rawls, 1971: 302)

Rawls's principles rest on the dual notions that justice not only requires equality in the treatment of all members of the society but also the protection of the least advantaged members of the society. It is the concern for equal treatment that has dominated much of our nation's efforts toward the achievement of democracy. Through constitutional provisions, court decision, legislative actions, and administrative mandates we have affirmed the nation's official commitment to equal access and equal justice. Although we recognize that these goals have not been achieved, and debate continues as to how best to achieve them, there is almost no open debate as to the validity of the commitment to equality as opposed to equity as a national value. Equity requires that treatments be appropriate and sufficient to characteristics and needs of those treated. In the pursuit of a just society, our nation has tended to hold equal treatment as its criterion. Yet for educational equity to be served, treatment must be specific to one's functional characteristics and sufficient to one's condition. To address the problems of appropriateness and sufficiency, we seek to go beyond the status labels that apply to individuals and groups and examine their functional characteristics, which in concert with their status, may handicap them in their school experience. Rawls's concern for the least favored has not gained wide acceptance as a guiding principle in our society, yet it may be that with respect to equalizing educational opportunity, it is the sensitive protection of the least advantaged that may be at the heart of this problem. Foundational to concern with justice and pedagogy is a concern for the human resource capital available to the society and its members for investment in education. While such resource capital is in good supply in the United States, there are critical problems in the distribution of these resources and access to them by most low-status persons. In the absence of access to essential human resource capital, there well may be limits to what any within-school educational reform can achieve.

AFRICAN-AMERICAN MALE PROBLEMATIQUE

In making the case for affirmatively developing academic ability, it is appropriate to invoke the conceptions related to the study of subaltern cultures as introduced by my son, Professor Edmund T. Gordon (1995). Gordon sees black male culture as a subaltern culture in the sense that it appears to be a distinct culture that is both alternative and resistant to the hegemonic culture but that is infused with hegemonic ideology. While it is produced and reproduced within the context of critically informed struggle against subordination/oppression, resistant and accommodative aspects of subaltern cultures are only parts of cultural production and reproduction. Subaltern cultures "have their own internal dynamic. They are not just or even predominantly reactive." E. T. Gordon sees subaltern cultures "as circumscribed and infused by past meaning and practice," but also "invented, emergent, and highly variable" adaptive responses to the life conditions of dominant groups. (Gordon 2005: 95)

Gordon, now an associate professor at the University of Texas at Austin, has provided what I think is probably the best conceptualization of the African-American male. He calls it the "African-American male problematique." He argues that black males are more appropriately thought of as a subaltern cultural group. When he uses that term *subaltern* he is suggesting at least three characteristics or conditions. A subaltern group is a group that is characterized by its subordinated cultural position. Young black males are being acculturated to an alien hegemonic culture, an alien dominant culture, that subordinates them, but because they live in that culture, acculturation does occur. Acculturation is what happens as a result of constantly being exposed to some particular set of cultural experiences. Acculturation can be positive or negative in its impact. When one is in a subordinated position and is acculturated to a dominating culture, one is likely to internalize aspects of the dominant culture, even as one holds on to alternate cultural forms and develops some attitudes and behaviors that are resistant to the hegemonic culture. This condition has been referred to as subaltern status. Once when I was using this language at a faculty meeting, someone heard me as saying that this was a subcultural and inferior position, a gross misunderstanding of this construct and what it is all about. Gordon has used *subaltern* to characterize the African American male who is living in the hegemonic culture, adopting and adapting to that culture under conditions of subordination. He also sees these males as developing and maintaining alternative cultural creations and retentions from their indigenous culture. These are alternative ways of doing things. Some of them may be African cultural retentions, others are new creations born of the group's experience in America. They are different from the hegemonic cultural elements and they are expressed as alternative to them. The third manifestation of subaltern status, the one that E. T. Gordon concentrates on most, is the resistant alternative or adaptation. Those behaviors, those cultural forms are adopted as open acts of rebellion, open acts of resistance. The interesting feature of these three characteristics, however, is that they are not just peculiar to black men; they are part of the hegemonic society. However, in the subordinated form, in their alternative expression, and in their resistant expression they come to be viewed as disruptive and disturbing to the society.

An interesting and critically important aspect of the study of subaltern cultures is the fact of the cultural continuum. "Subaltern cultures range between 'deeper' (basilect) and 'standard' (acrolect) nodes." Stated differently, they range from "resistant (different, oppositional) to accommodative (similar, assimilationist, [acculturated]) relative to the dominant or hegemonic culture." This phenomenon is represented in the interesting continuum in black male culture and identity with respect to reputation and respectability. To understand the production of black male culture from the perspective of a continuum from reputation to respectability, one must note that black male culture is "underpinned by a patriarchal ideological grammar which it shares with [w]hite male culture."[Au: source of quotes?] For example, in relation to respectability, there are several basic ideological notions defining successful, high-status males: these males have (a) control of women and children over whom they have proprietary rights within domestic units for whose material needs they provide; and, in general, success with women, (b) recognized leadership/dominance over other men, and (c) demonstrable material success. Respectability is less threatening than is reputation to whites because it shares many of the core values of Anglo middle-class male culture. By contrast, reputation is almost a substitute for respectability in that it is self-constructed, often from pretense, pose, and idealized image.

Given this range of issues, it is not surprising that some observers have seized upon alienation and hopelessness, not only as characteristics of African-American males, but as causal factors in their development. To the extent that alienation and hopelessness are high in this population, it is reasonable to assume that it is in response to the circumstances of their lives. Current efforts at the treatment of substance abuse in this population include medication designed to control depression. The logic of this treatment flows from the observation that there is a high incidence of situational depression in the histories of these patients. Alienation, situational depression, and hopelessness are thought to be reactive disorders, that is, behavior disorders that develop in response to chronic dissonance in person-environment transactions. It may well be that professional treatment is indicated by the time such reactive disorders become fixed, but the classic treatment for mild reactive disorders is the reduction of the sources of dissonance in the life of the suffering person.

The press will have us think of "them" as disturbed, that there is something wrong with "those people." Back in my early days of work with the New York City Public Schools, I had the good fortune of working with a chap named Louis Haye. Lou Haye founded the elementary schools for emotionally disturbed kids. He used to distinguish between the disturbed kids, that is the kids who are truly mentally ill, and the disturbing kids, those who simply were disturbing to the authorities. Gordon is making that same distinction here; a lot of these adaptations from the hegemonic society are simply disturbing to the social order, so we label them as pathological. We label them as negative and begin to find strategies to deal with them. It looks like our major current strategy is a strategy of containment or incarceration.

E. T. Gordon suggests that if we look at this group that we see as being so problematic, we will see some of all of these subaltern cultural elements present. He suggests that what is important about these elements is their potential as the basis for a new political force. The resistant activity of the subaltern group is in its nature political activity that has the seeds of leverage for changing the status of black males through political action. I return later to this concern with political action.

The notion E. T. Gordon is advancing suggests that in this black male subaltern group, you have three phenomena operating. One is a value that privileges patriarchy. Gordon is not arguing in favor of patriarchy, he is simply calling attention to the fact that black men have borrowed it from the dominant society, a characteristic that is present in a number of cultures, that is, the assignment to the male of a superior position. Even more important than its hierarchical position is the assignment of responsibility to the male for the protection of children and the females in the group. Gordon reminds us that black males have endorsed it, that they have embraced it and in some instances, are taking it too far, but it is a part of both the hegemonic and the subaltern cultures.

The second construct, reputation, and a third category, respectability, I discuss in more detail here. Gordon refers to reputation as being at one end of the continuum, with respectability at the other. This is the radically different countercultural alternative to respectability for African-American males, especially the young. It has historical roots in the rebellious slaves, the trickster figures like B'rer Rabbit, and the legendary badman like Stafford Lee. In its public form, reputational practices are often identified with some black entertainers, black athletes, politicians, and participants in the alternative economies. These practices were epitomized in the 1960s and 1970s by hustlers and pimps. Reputation today is characterized by a complex of cultural practices. One of the leading practices is being successful with women and producing offspring. Gordon is not endorsing these practices, but as an anthropologist he is simply describing them. These cultural practices include elements of those patriarchal attitudes that establish reproductive prowess, heterosexuality, fertility, masculinity, and so on. Reputation is also established through one-on-one competition and dominance over other male peers as in fighting and other forms of physical violence, athletic contests, verbal bouts, drinking bouts, even music and dance contests. These are some of the manifestations of this concern with reputation in the subaltern black male population.

Respectability has to do with the capacity to command respect. It has to do with accord and acclaim, and the accommodation shown by the people around you. Black men achieved this as a group with its peak toward the end of the eighteenth century as blacks began to recover from both the period of enslavement and the period of the betrayal of the reconstruction.

It was a time when blacks enjoyed reasonably intact communities that had stable institutions, successful black businesses, effective black schools, and the black church was riding high. Gordon argues that in that context there were many opportunities for the demonstration and experience of respectability. You might define respectability as reputations that are earned on the basis of solid achievement, as opposed to reputations earned on the basis of symbols of achievement. During this period there were many respectable black people who developed extensive kinship and social networks, people who were turned to as moral authorities, people who were economically viable, economically stable, people with technical expertise, even people with political acumen. In their segregated communities, these people exercised authority and responsibility. We were getting there in the nineteen-sixties and seventies; just about the time when the United States began to export the type of jobs that enabled black men in Detroit and similar cities to build middle class homes and to own automobiles and send their kids to college. With the exportation of those jobs and with the automation, actually the cybernation, of the jobs that remain, this period of economic viability ended all too soon. However, these were sources of respectability for these black males.

With many of the natural and historic sources of opportunities for asserting and experiencing respectability greatly reduced for black males, the alternative that replaced respectability was the assertion of reputation. E. T. Gordon simply reminds us that in the lives of many African-American males, the tension between respectability and reputation is very real. One of the ways he argues that we as a society might deal with this tension is to recognize it as a potential political force, which when guided into the proper channels can be a positive force for African-American male development. How can this be channeled in affirmatively developing the intellect? I find this conceptualization of the issue especially relevant for the political implications in asserting our responsibility for political action and the reassertion of respectability.

CONCLUSION

It is tempting to anticipate that the current outbreak of enthusiasm for equality in education will produce results consistent with the quantity of time, energy, money, and concern being expended. However, in dealing with problems for which solutions are based upon significant social and scientific advances, popularity and productivity do not necessarily go hand in hand. In the present situation there is grave danger that work with the unfortunate may, unfortunately, become a fad. This threat is so great that those truly committed to the long-range goal to significantly improve the life chances of disadvantaged populations need to adopt an attitude of restraint and considered action. It is not the quantity of effort that will solve the complex problems of disadvantaged populations, but rather "high quality" approaches—those that reflect scientific and social reality.

Having recently reviewed some of the research and a few of the current programs concerned with the disadvantaged, I am impressed by the pitifully small although growing body of knowledge available as a guide to work in this area. The paucity of serious research attention to these problems has left us with little hard data, many impressions, and a few firm leads. Equally distressing is the slight representation of even this research in the rapidly proliferating programs. Much of what is being done for and to the disadvantaged seems to be guided by the conviction that what is needed is more of those things we feel we know how to do. Despite the fact that much of our knowledge and techniques of behavioral change have proved to be of dubious value in our work with more advantaged populations, these same procedures and services now are being poured into the new programs. Although service to the disadvantaged has become popular, there remains a serious lack of basic research on the developmental needs of such children as well as on the applicability of specific techniques of behavioral change to their directed development.

It is not intended to suggest that the extension of known techniques to these previously neglected populations is entirely negative. Humanitarian concern calls for the use of all possible resources to relieve human suffering. However, there may be vast differences between what we feel we know how to do and that which must be done. Unfortunately, our society has permitted us to place the burden of proof of the worth of our services on the beneficiaries of these services rather than on the professional worker or the system in which he or she functions. This has permitted us to ignore or rationalize our failures. If real progress is to be made, we as professionals must assume greater responsibility for the success of our work, recognizing that it is our role to better understand these problems and to design techniques and measures more appropriate to their solution. It must be clear to all of us that more counseling is not going to solve the problems of a population we have defined as nonverbal. Reading texts in technicolor is not going to solve the reading problems of youngsters whom we claim are deficient in symbolic representational skills. Reduced demand curricula and work study programs are not going to advance the conceptual development of youth whose conditions of life may have produced differential patterns of intellectual function so frequently interpreted as evidence of mental retardation rather than as challenges to improved teaching. Occupational information and aspirational exhortation are not going to provide motivation for youth who have yet to see employment opportunities, employed models with whom they can identify, and accessible routes to achievement.

Intensive psychotherapy is going to have little impact on a neurotic mother whose energies are consumed by the struggle to meet the minimum physical needs of herself and her children. Similarly, preschool programs that capture the form but not the content of some of the more advanced models are doomed to failure. Nor will good pre-school programs that are not followed by greatly strengthened primary, elementary, and secondary school programs make a major difference in the lives of these children. Improved and expanded mental health services will mean little unless our nation comes to grips with the problems of economic, political, and social opportunities for masses of disenfranchised and alienated persons.

To honor our traditional concern and for the sake of the disadvantaged, it is essential to recognize the limitations of the current effort. If the products of serious research were as well represented in this effort as the good intentions, the enthusiasm, the "bandwagon hopping," and the grant hunting, we could be more hopeful that meaningful solutions would be found to the problems of the disadvantaged. Unfortunately, some of us viewing the current efforts are left with a nagging suspicion that the net result of many of these programs will be to provide (for those who choose to interpret it so) empirical evidence of fundamental inferiority in these populations we are trying so hard to help. When, five or ten years from now, the populations we now call disadvantaged are still at the bottom of the heap, those who only reluctantly acceded to the current attempts to help may revive their now dormant notions of inherent inferiority to explain why all the money and all the effort have failed to produce results. The more likely fact will be that we shall have failed to produce the desired results simply because we shall have failed to develop and apply the knowledge and the skill necessary to the task. Unless the issues are more sharply drawn, we may not even then recognize the nature of our incompetencies.

To honor our commitments to education, we must understand the limitations of our knowledge and our practice. Much of what we do is based on the hopeful assumption that all human beings with normal neurological endowment can be developed for participation in the mainstream of our society. We believe this because we have seen many people from a great variety of backgrounds participate and because we want to believe it. But we do not yet have definite evidence to support our belief. We operate out of an egalitarian faith without knowing whether our goals are really achievable. Yet it must be our aim, not only as scientists and professional workers, but as humanitarians as well, to determine the potential of human beings for equality of achievement. If in the light of our most sophisticated and subtle evaluations, we conclude that equality is not generally achievable, if in spite of the best we can do it seems likely that some of our citizens will remain differentiated by their own biology (genes), then we shall merely have answered a persistent question. As Sternberg, Grigorenko, and Bridglall discuss in chapter 3 of this volume, we still have no evidence that group differences per se imply any inability on the part of particular individuals to meet the demands of society. Hence, we should be able to turn our energies to helping individuals meet the demands of education. And if, on the other hand, as we believe, true equality of opportunity and appropriate learning experiences will result in equality of achievement, then we must organize our professional services and our society such that no person is kept from achieving that potential by our indifference to his or her condition, by the inadequacy or inappropriateness of our service, or by the impediments society deliberately or accidentally places in his or her path. It is not an unhopeful paradox that the only way we shall ever know whether equality of human achievement is possible is through providing for all our citizens, privileged and underprivileged, the kind of service and society that assumes it is possible and makes adequate provision for the same. It should be the sole pursuit of our "Great Society."

REFERENCES

Dubois, W. E. B. 1968. *The autobiography of W. E. B. Dubois.* 1st ed. New York: International Publishers.

Gordon, E. T. 1992. *Subaltern culture and assessment.* Paper presented at the African-American Adolescent Male Seminar. San Diego, CA.

Gordon, E. T. 2005. Academic Politization: Supplementary Education from Black resistance. In E. W. Gordon, B. Bridglall, and A. S. Meroe (Eds). *Supplementary Education: The Hidden Curriculum of High Academic Achievement.* Lanham, MD: Rowman & Littlefield Publishers, Inc. 88–103.

Jensen, A. R. 1969. How much can we boost IQ and scholastic achievement? *Harvard Education Review* 39, 1–123.

Lesser, G. S., Fifer, G., Clark, D. H. 1965. *Mental abilities of children from different social-class and cultural groups.* Chicago: University of Chicago Press for the Society for Research in Child Development.

Rawls, J. 1971. *A theory of justice.* London: Oxford University Press.

Wallace, A. 1968. Schools in revolutionary and conservative societies. In E. Lloyd-Jones and N. Rosenau (Eds.), *Social and cultural foundations of guidance.* New York: Holt, Rinehart, and Winston.

Zigler, E. 1966. Mental retardation: Current issues and approaches. Hoffman and Hoffman (Eds.), *Review of Child Development Research,* vol. 2. New York: Russell Sage Foundation.

11

The Problem of
Transfer and Adaptability

Applying the Learning Sciences to
the Challenge of the Achievement Gap

Howard T. Everson
Fordham University

In early Spring, I usually visit my neighborhood gardening center to buy plants, shrubs, and flowers. This past year was no different—new shrubs, more gardening tools were on the list. This time, though, as I approached the checkout counter I recognized the young cashier. It was Paul, a high school senior who lived with his family around the corner from my house. Dutifully, Paul began tallying the bill when suddenly the power failed to all the electronic cash registers in the store. The cash registers were useless, and Paul seemed not to know what to do next.

To avoid delay, I suggested to Paul he simply add up the cost of the items, calculate the sales tax, and tell me what I owed. The look on Paul's face said it all—he couldn't complete the transaction without the help of the store's computerized cash register. Encouraging him to try, I told Paul the sales tax rate was 8.25%. The young man reached for a pen and began jotting down numbers. Paul looked up anxiously, stopped, and asked "now what do I do?" Here he was, a college-bound student with three years of high school math behind him, and he was unable to solve a simple rate problem while on the job—a math problem I know he had seen time and again in his high school math classes.

Many see this scenario as evidence of the dreadful state of mathematics education in U.S. schools. This view, however, is both simplistic and incorrect. It is likely that in both middle and high school Paul's math teachers were knowledgeable and would be judged as qualified teachers. The more complex truth is that, like Paul, many students—and minority students are particularly vulnerable—are graduating from high school with little understanding of key mathematical and scientific concepts. Evidence of this lack of understanding and transfer of learning can be seen in many large-scale assessments, including the much publicized international math and science assessments. Students from across the United States score lower than those from most industrialized nations in both science and mathematics achievement (Martin et al., 2000; Mullis et al., 2000). Clearly, we are not teaching or testing for conceptual understanding, nor in ways that promote the transfer of learning to other "real world" contexts.

Applying what we learn in school to address problems in other settings is the very essence of learning. Indeed, the very reason we send our children to school is so they will acquire the knowledge, skills, and abilities that will serve them later in life, when they are in the "real world." Distressingly, the research on the problem of transfer of learning suggests we have a wholesale failure of learning from instruction (Bransford and Schwartz, 1999; Haskell, 2001; McKeough, Lupart, and Marini, 1995). This problem is even more troubling when viewed in the larger social context of the declining college-going rates in the United States and the concomitant black-white achievement gap (Mortenson, 2003).

The goal in this chapter is to situate this larger concern about the black-white achievement gap in the context of school learning with a particular focus on the problem of the transfer of learning. What we have available today is a large (and growing) body of research evidence on how people learn and what teachers can do to promote learning and transfer, and that this research ought to influence classroom practice. I make the case for designing instruction based on principles of learning derived from the learning sciences—the interdisciplinary field of researchers from psychology, neuroscience, linguistics, philosophy, computer science, anthropology, and education—to enhance the critical thinking abilities of all students. Nearly two decades of research has taught us about how to improve learning, problem solving, long-term retention, and the transfer of learning to novel situations. Research suggests that we are poised to capitalize on knowledge of how people think, learn, and remember; it offers instructional design principles to improve classroom learning and promote transfer of learning for all students (Bransford and Schwartz [1999], Halpern and Hakel [2003], and DeCorte [2003]).

This chapter briefly reviews the black-white achievement gap in the United States, highlighting what we know about differences in test scores and other indices of academic achievement. Test scores provide evidence of performance differences on academic tasks and, as such, are robust indicators of the failure of classroom learning to transfer to novel tasks (e.g., test items) and situations. Key findings from the literature on transfer of learning is described and the cognitive perspective, which stresses students' ability to learn during transfer, is emphasized. This chapter concludes by suggesting how these learning principles can be applied in the classroom to improve teaching, learning, and transfer for *all* students.

THE CHALLENGE OF THE ACHIEVEMENT GAP

In his award-winning book, *Savage Inequalities*, Jonathan Kozol admits to being startled by the "remarkable degree of racial segregation that persisted . . . and was common in the public schools" (p. 3). Research on schooling in the United States does little to counter the bleak picture painted by Kozol. The continuing educational disadvantages of many segments of the African American, Latino, and Native American communities is presented in painstaking detail by L. Scott Miller in his widely cited work, *An American Imperative: Accelerating Minority Educational Advancement* (1995). More recently, in her introduction to a special issue of the *Teachers College Record*, Michele Dabady noted that . . . "blacks, Hispanics, and American Indians—compared with whites, Asians, and Pacific Islanders—are more likely to attend lower-quality schools with fewer material and teacher resources, and are more likely to have lower test scores, drop out of high school, not graduate from college, and attend lower-ranked programs in higher education" (Dabady, 2003, p. 1048).

Long-term trends in achievement test scores from the National Assessment of Educational Progress (NAEP), for example, provide evidence of the persistent black-white achievement gap; white students outperform blacks and Latinos in reading, mathematics, and science across grade levels. Table 11.1, below, shows these achievement differences in science, mathematics, and reading scores on the NAEP scale for a national sample of eighth and twelfth grade students, and over a four-year period from 1996 to 2000.

Table 11.1. NAEP Reading, Mathematics, and Science Scores: Grades 8 and 12, 1996–2000

	Grade 8		Grade 12	
Science	**1996**	**2000**	**1996**	**2000**
Blacks	120	121	122	122
Latinos	127	127	128	126
Whites	159	160	159	153
Mathematics				
Blacks	242	246	279	273
Latinos	250	252	287	281
Whites	281	285	310	307
Reading				
Blacks	253	236	263	272
Latinos	238	239	267	276
Whites	266	266	293	296

Source: The Nation's Report Card: Science 2000 (O'Sullivan, Lanko, Grigg, Qian, and Zhang 2003); *The Nation's Report Card: Mathematics 2000* (Braswell, Lutkus, Grigg, Santapau, Tay-Lim, and Johnson 2001); *The Nation's Report Card: Reading 2002* (Grigg, Daane, Jin, and Campbell 2003).

At each grade level, the NAEP results tell us, black students perform significantly lower than white students in mathematics, reading, and science. Trends in black and white average scores on the SAT, which are taken by college-bound high school juniors and seniors, tell much the same story. Table 11.2, below, shows the average SAT verbal and mathematics reasoning scores for black and white students over the past eight years—1996 through 2003.

Table 11.2. Eight-Year Trends in SAT Verbal and Mathematics Scores for Black and White Students: 1996–2003

Year	Mean SAT Verbal Scores		Mean SAT Math Scores	
	Black	White	Black	White
1996	434	526	422	523
1997	434	526	423	526
1998	434	526	426	528
1999	434	527	422	528
2000	434	528	426	530
2001	433	529	426	531
2002	430	527	427	533
2003	431	533	426	534

Source: Digest of Education Statistics, 2000 (National Center for Education Statistis, 2001); Digest of Education Statistics, 2002 (National Center for Education Statistics, 2003); 2003 College-Bound Seniors: Tables and Related Items (College Entrance Examination Board, 2003).

The black-white SAT score gaps, which are about one standard deviation (or 100 points) in the scale score metric, are seen clearly in these trend lines. To put a finer point on these achievement differences, these achievement scores have ramifications in terms of subsequent educational attainment as measured by college enrollment rates. We see, for example, in the ten-year trends in college entrance rates for both black and white students, published recently by the Pell Institute for the Study of Opportunity in Higher Education (http://www.postsecondary.org), more reason for concern. The gap between blacks and whites has been growing wider since 1996. This trend can be seen easily in figure 11.1, below.

A host of other indicators of academic achievement show similar differences by race and ethnicity. Indeed, evidence suggests these achievement gaps appear even before disadvantaged African-American and Latino children enter kindergarten (Camara and Schmidt, 1999; Jencks and Phillips, 1998; Mickelson, 2003). Research into the factors associated with these achievement differences—looking, for example, at school-level effects, the role of learning standards, and achievement in honors and advanced courses—suggests that we may be observing differential rates of transfer of learning between black and white students, particularly in sequestered, high-stakes testing situations (Everson and Miller, 2004; Everson and Tobias, 2001; Everson and Skinner, 2003; Tobias and Everson, 2002).

Figure 11.1. Ten-Year Trends in College Entrance Rates for Black and White Students: 1992–2002

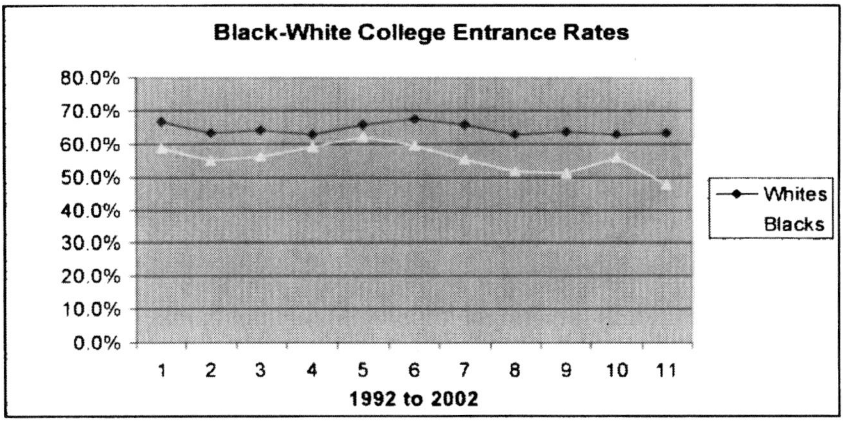

Black-White College Entrance Rates

Source: "Postsecondary Education Opportunity. College Entrance Rates by Race/Ethnicity and Gender for Recent High School Graduates 1959–2002," no.132 (June 2003), www.postsecondary.org (accessed 11/15/03).

Reducing or eliminating the black-white achievement gap would go a long way toward reducing racial inequality in the United States. Educators, generally, are perplexed when it comes to finding affordable ways of raising black students' achievement. For example, when superintendents of large urban school districts were surveyed recently they listed the issue of the achievement gap between minority and nonminority students as one of their major concerns (Huang, Reiser, Parker, Muniec, and Salvucci, 2003). Many of these educators spoke of their frustrations and said, repeatedly, that they need practical advice, research that tells them what to do in their schools and classrooms to address this challenge. We believe that contemporary research on the transfer of learning may provide the guidance educators need to help reduce the achievement gap.

THE PROBLEM OF THE TRANSFER OF LEARNING

Scientific inquiry into the question of transfer of learning has a long history, dating back more than a century to the work of E. L. Thorndike (Thorndike and Woodworth, 1901). From the very beginning, this line of research has suggested that transfer—that is, how well what we learn in one set of circumstances transfers or is adapted to other, novel situations—is both fragile and controversial. Indeed, the only clear finding we have from this long history of research is that there have been a number of failed attempts at achieving transfer, as well as a number of successes (Barnett and Ceci, 2002; Determan, 1993). In an especially clear treatment of the research on transfer, Bransford and Schwartz (1999) refer to the "agony and ecstasy" that characterizes this body of research. It would not be unfair, for example, to summarize the literature on transfer by concluding that "there is no evidence to contradict Thorndike's general conclusions: Transfer is rare" (Determan, 1993).

Despite the pessimism, a number of researchers have pointed out recently that research is uncovering a number of important learning perspectives and principles that appear to be capable of enhancing transfer (DeCorte, 2003; Halpern and Hakel, 2003). In a classic study that involved teaching subjects to throw darts while underwater, Judd (1908) demonstrated the value of promoting understanding as part of the initial learning experience. Judd's experiment demonstrates the benefits of guided practice. Two groups of boys practiced throwing darts at an underwater target. Prior to practice, the experimental group was instructed about how water refracts light and how this principle may affect the accuracy of their performance. The control group was not given this instruction, but simply practiced. Boys in the experimental group were more accurate at throwing darts at new targets at varying depths. Building on these early studies, Bransford and Stein (1993) studied how learning with understanding affects transfer. In general, these studies show that when knowledge and information is presented in a problem-solving context it is more likely to be recalled and activated in novel problem-solving situations. Rethinking the problem of transfer from a cognitive perspective may yield insights into strategic knowledge about learning, including monitoring one's learning across domains and contexts (Bransford and Schwartz, 1999; Brown, 1978; Tobias and Everson, 2002). These contemporary views of learning are discussed next.

LEARNING FROM THE LEARNING SCIENCES

Modern, research-based views of learning are beginning to reach schools and are finding their way into the classroom. We see examples of this in initiatives such as *Success for All* (Slavin and Madden, 2002), *Teaching for Successful Intelligence* (Sternberg, 2002), and *Applying the Learning Sciences* (Halpern and Hakel, 2000, 2003). A central premise of many, if not all, of these interventions is what the literature refers to as a *constructivist* view of learning. The constructivist perspective is based on a simple proposition: students (and this includes teachers as well) come to school with constructed understandings of the world, not with empty minds to be filled up through lectures, drills, and rote learning. They have prior knowledge, albeit sometimes incomplete, of the world and how things in it work. Children arrive at school with minds that are actively constructing their understanding of the world (Piaget and Inhelder, 1971).

This view of the learner stands in contrast to the more traditional, often more familiar, approaches to teaching that are rooted in a largely unworkable blend of folk psychology and early twentieth century behaviorist perspectives on learning. Recall that the behaviorists attempted to break down learning into its component parts and teach students how to put those pieces back together to create the intended behavior. Learning, in this framework, is seen simply as a demonstration or instantiation of the target behavior. More contemporary, cognitively based instructional designs suggest that most complex cognitive processes—problem solving, activating inert knowledge, reasoning, monitoring one's performance—cannot be learned by decomposing and teaching the component parts without first understanding the context for learning. Cognitive research on learning has reinforced decisively the age-old adage that the whole is greater than the sum of its parts (Resnick and Resnick, 1992). To repeat, contemporary theorists subscribe to the belief that the knowledge a learner comes to school with affects her ability to learn and acquire new knowledge. By extension, if what we are attempting to teach conflicts with the previously constructed knowledge of the student, this new knowledge will make little sense and will be ill-constructed and unavailable for future use in other settings (Anderson, 1987; Brooks and Brooks, 1999; Glasersfeld, 1989, 1992; Resnick, 1987; Schauble, 1990).

Obviously, this constructivist perspective has important implications for promoting long-term retention and transfer. Again, students do not arrive in our classrooms with minds like blank slates (Pinker, 2002). Teachers do not simply write new knowledge onto the minds of their students. On the contrary, teachers need to explore what their students already know, inquire into how they have constructed their prior knowledge, and try to determine if what they wish to teach students conflicts with their students' previously constructed understanding of the subject. To return to our earlier point, this view of learning suggests that perhaps much of the failure to transfer new learning to other contexts may stem from the buzz of confusion learners experience when previously constructed knowledge and new knowledge (and novel contexts) conflict or are not well aligned. Simply making the new knowledge clearer to students, the research suggests, will not enhance understanding or lead to adaptive forms of transfer (Cheng and Holyoak, 1985; Gick and Holyoak, 1983; Gentner, Ratterman, and Forbus, 1993). The drill and practice, as well as other direct teaching methods, found in many large, urban, and otherwise poorly funded schools may be working to mitigate against transfer. And this may be particularly damaging to minority students attending these schools.

More to the point, the achievement gaps we see between white and black children as early as kindergarten suggest that, indeed, *all* students are constructing knowledge long before they enter school. Some, perhaps, have constructed understandings and acquired knowledge that may be more practicable and relevant to the classroom, others have not. Some students apparently arrive at school with richer and deeper stores of prior knowledge—stories, words, and schemas for understanding the world around them. Research indicates that the body of *private understandings* that many students have acquired before coming to school may be incomplete, inaccurate, and in conflict with the curricula demands of them (Di Sessa, 1988).

Given this brief overview of cognitive research, the question becomes, do we have the strategies and principled pedagogical approaches that reflect our best understanding of how students learn and how we can affect long-term retention and transfer? Work done recently under the auspices of the National Research Council (2000) suggests that indeed we do, and their report makes a strong case for improving how we teach. The National Research Council writes:

> Modern theories of learning and transfer retain the emphasis on practice, but they specify the kinds of practice that are important and take learner characteristics (e.g., existing knowledge and strategies) into account (e.g., Singley and Anderson, 1989). In the discussion below we explore key characteristics of learning and transfer that have important implications for education:
> - Initial learning is necessary for transfer, and a considerable amount is known about the kinds of learning experiences that support transfer.
> - Knowledge that is overly contextualized can reduce transfer; abstract representations of knowledge can help promote transfer.
> - Transfer is best viewed as an active, dynamic process rather than a passive end-product of a particular set of learning experiences.
> - All new learning involves transfer based on previous learning, and this fact has important implications for the design of instruction that helps students learn. (p. 53)

Building on this work, Bransford and Schwartz (1999), DeCorte (2003), de Groot (1965), Halpern (1998), Halpern and Hakel (2000; 2003), Sternberg, (2002), and Willingham (2002, 2003), among others, provide specific guidance by applying the sciences of learning to the challenge of teaching for transfer, preparing students for future learning. Through a variety of collaborative efforts, these researchers have developed theories and extracted basic principles that, we suspect, can be applied broadly in schools and classrooms. Below, we describe a representative set of these principles and offer examples of possible educational applications.

DeCorte (2003) recently articulated five principles for the design of powerful and productive teaching and learning environments. These include:

- Environments that facilitate the productive use of knowledge, skills, and motivations provide support within a constructive teaching and learning process;
- Teaching and learning environments should enhance students' cognitive and motivational self-regulation to promote productive uses of knowledge and skills;

- To broaden students' cognitive and motivational skills and tools, teachers should support collaboration and interaction in their classrooms;
- The power of situated learning suggests that teachers need to prepare their students for future learning by challenging them with problems that have personal meaning and that are representative of the novel tasks they will encounter in the future; and
- Powerful learning environments include pedagogical strategies that promote reflection during learning and problem solving, raising students' awareness of their use(s) of productive knowledge and self-regulated learning strategies.

In sum, these guidelines are rooted in a constructivist view of learning, promote the use of self-regulated learning strategies, foster collaboration both inside and outside the classroom, require teachers to develop challenging and meaningful learning tasks, and foster a metacognitive awareness in students. DeCorte (2003), like others, calls for a reconceptualization of transfer based on preparing students for future learning and stressing the productivity of learning results.

In a similar vein, Halpern and her colleagues provide more specific guidance by applying the sciences of learning to teaching (see Halpern and Hakel, 2000; 2003). Through this collaborative effort, these researchers have extracted a set of basic principles that we suspect can be applied broadly in schools and classrooms. Below, we describe these principles and offer examples of possible educational applications.

Practice at Retrieval.

Research tells us that a powerful way to promote long-term retention and transfer is to allow students to practice retrieving previously taught material from long-term memory. Practice at retrieval is more effective than having students spend more and more time studying academic subjects without actively engaging in memory retrieval. Opportunities to practice can occur during either review for tests or in actual testing sessions (Cull, 2000; Dempster and Perkins, 1993; Glover, 1989; Wheeler and Roediger, 1992). Teachers are encouraged to work with students as they retrieve information and knowledge from both short-term and long-term memories. Doing so repeatedly, in varied contexts, strengthens students' abilities to access these knowledge bases, and solidifies their ability to recall previously learned material from long-term memory, thus promoting transfer across contexts. Halpern and Hakel (2000; 2003) also tell us that repeated testing helps in the recall of information. These researchers suggest that teachers, at the start of instruction, assess students' knowledge and probe for underlying assumptions and beliefs. Teachers are encouraged to align classroom discussions, homework assignments, and tests, so that important information will have to be remembered at different times and distributed throughout the academic year or course, enhancing long-term retention. Test questions, too, offer another opportunity for "practice at retrieval" and deepen students' knowledge of the material being tested. Ideally, tests should be cumulative and test items should probe for understanding of the material. The key idea is to cue students' prior knowledge in ways that are relevant to the learning context.

Vary the Conditions of Learning.

When learning takes place under a variety of conditions and contexts, conceptual understanding becomes more rounded and multiple retrieval cues are activated. Research from the learning sciences provides insights into the benefits of providing differing types of problems and alternative solution strategies. Although we are warned that learning may take longer, and be somewhat less enjoyable to students, research suggests that students and teachers will see significant gains in long-term retention and transfer.

Represent Knowledge Using Alternate Forms.

Learning is more powerful when students are prompted to take information presented in one format and "represent" it in an alternative way. Cognitive research tells us that we process information in multiple ways—visually and through auditory-verbal channels. Students' learning and recall can be improved by integrating information from both the verbal and visual-spatial forms of representation. Teachers are encouraged, therefore, to use both modes of representation in all their learning tasks, explicitly and consciously incorporating multiple forms of representation into their instructional designs.

Build on Students' Prior Knowledge and Experience.

Research comparing experts to novices reveals that experts have a larger knowledge base, compared to novices, and can compile information into more meaningful chunks, which further facilitates learning. For example, relative to novices, chess experts have a better memory for positions of chess pieces on a game board (Chi et al., 1981). When chess pieces are placed randomly on the board, however, this advantage disappears, suggesting that chess experts do not have superior general memory but, rather, they are able to draw upon their knowledge of common chess positions when useful for remembering and developing game strategies. As we note above, students arrive in our classrooms with sets of assumptions and beliefs that serve as a mental framework for learning. As they construct knowledge students build on their prior knowledge to infuse meaning into newly learned material. In this way, prior knowledge influences how students interpret new information and decide what aspects of this information are relevant and irrelevant. They can be misled, however. In 1929, Alfred Whitehead coined the term *inert knowledge* to reflect the fact that relevant knowledge is not always applied in the right situations. Thus, it is important for teachers to cue students' knowledge, making it active and helping to ensure transfer of learning across situations and contexts.

Theories about Learning Matter.

Learning new concepts and developing understanding is often difficult and uncomfortable. Students' views of the world are challenged, and long-held beliefs are questioned in the teaching and learning process. Students and teachers often complain that some subjects, like math and science, are just too difficult for them to learn. All of us want learning to be easy. Thus, when students are faced with some school subjects they become discouraged by the difficulty they encounter during the learning process. Halpern and Hakel (2003) remind teachers that optimizing learning depends on what it is we want students to learn, and what they already know about that subject. Teachers can help students by discussing ways of learning, infusing their lessons with strategies for learning to learn, and by surfacing students' own beliefs about learning.

Experience Alone Is Insufficient for Learning.

Not surprisingly, and as we discuss above, students come to school with preconceived ideas about the subjects we teach them in the classroom. Even if these notions are wrong, belief in them can solidify based on ordinary, everyday experiences, especially when objective, corrective feedback is not provided. This has serious implications for learning and performance. For instance, students may come to believe incorrectly in causation by attributing an effect to a salient possible causal agent without considering plausible alternative causes, engaging in spurious causal reasoning. Similarly, students may often rely on a heuristic device to judge or interpret events and outcomes. These mental shortcuts may not always lead to correct solutions, or to the resolution of complex problems. We also know that students, typically, have poor metacognition; that is, they are poor judges of what they know and do not know (Tobias and Everson, 2002). These misguided notions and feelings of confidence about what they know may also develop in the course of learning. Learners may be fooled into believing that they are learning by the apparent ease of their performance; whereas optimal learning is usually derived from moderately difficult learning situations. A dramatic example of where experience alone is a poor teacher is illustrated by situations in which errors are highly costly, such as piloting an airplane or performing surgery.

Of course, the costs of incorrectly answering a test question are not as consequential as, say, a pilot's error. However, when physicians base their medical diagnoses on a faulty knowledge or limited experience, there are arguably more serious consequences. Teachers can become more aware of students' common misconceptions and present lectures and lead discussions in class that address them. Teachers can provide systematic feedback on homework assignments, tests, and projects throughout the course of instruction to combat the persistence of erroneous thinking.

DYNAMIC CLASSROOM ASSESSMENT

Research is emerging, largely from a psychometric perspective, that indicates that some standardized test items and tasks are more difficult for black than white students, even when the two groups are equal with respect to their ability levels and have been taught by the same teachers in the very same classes. From a cognitive perspective, it has been suggested that the test items may have features or characteristics that are more or less salient with respect to classroom learning, and that these saliency characteristics differ for black and white students. These test items, which are often considered the final transfer task, particularly in high stakes testing situations, have been viewed as presenting "sequestered problem solving" (Bransford and Schwartz, 1999). In such situations students rarely have the opportunity to seek help from other resources such as other students, teachers, or texts. They rarely have the opportunity to engage in trial and error forms of learning, get feedback, or even revise their work.

By shifting to a perspective that looks at transfer in terms of preparing students for future learning, as DeCorte (2003) and Bransford and Schwartz (1999) suggest, we are then free to look at assessments as opportunities to gauge students' abilities to learn in knowledge-rich environments. The key idea is that assessments serve as opportunities to measure students' abilities to learn new information and relate this new learning to previous experiences. According to Bransford and Schwartz, "assessments can be improved by moving from static, one-shot measures of 'test taking' to environments that provide opportunities for new learning" (p. 88). These dynamic forms of assessment hold promise for promoting transfer and reducing the achievement gap. For example, teachers who direct their instruction to forms of "teaching to the test" often find that their students have difficulty engaging in metacognitive knowledge monitoring. By treating the testing situation as external to the learning environment, as a hurdle to be leaped, a one-shot, maximal performance event, they are depriving students of the opportunity to assess their own learning, to monitor and regulate their learning strategies, and to capitalize on corrective feedback and engage in new learning. By incorporating dynamic forms of assessment in the classroom, teachers have a tool that will allow them to better measure how prior learning and experience has prepared their students for future learning, knowledge that in itself promotes transfer of learning.

CONCLUSION

The principles presented in this chapter, which derive from research in the learning sciences, are intended to provide teachers with a set of techniques and strategies for developing students' critical thinking skills. By design, they are aimed at promoting long-term retention and transfer of learning across subject matter domains. As Halpern (1998) reminds us, this is hard work for both students and teachers. "Beliefs that have been constructed over many years and the habits of mind that developed along with them will take multiple learning experiences, distributed over time and settings, before they will be successfully replaced with new ways of thinking and knowing about the world" (p. 454).

Following up on the policy recommendations of the College Board's National Task Force on Minority High Achievement (College Board, 1999), our colleague Edmund W. Gordon has called for a national effort at affirmative development to parallel our continuing efforts at affirmative action (Gordon, 2001). Gordon's notion of affirmative development creates a social justice framework for the cognitive research we present in this chapter. In his brief treatise outlining his views on affirmative development, Gordon asserts, for example, that

> the purpose of learning, and the teaching by which it is enabled, is to acquire knowledge and technique in the service of the development of adaptive human intellect. . . . These developed abilities are not so much reflected in the specific discipline-based knowledge a student may have, but in the student's ability and disposition to adaptively and efficiently use knowledge, technique, and values in mental processes to engage and solve both common and novel problems. (p. 3)

In keeping with this theme, we identified the question of transfer and adaptive intellective competence as a critical pedagogical issue; one that, if addressed squarely in teacher professional development and with well-developed pedagogical strategies, can help mitigate the black-white achievement gap. In this chapter we have been concerned with how well (and whether) what is learned in the classroom transfers to performance on tests and other, novel performances outside the classroom for *all* students. We have been concerned, too, that the ability to transfer between what students learn in the classroom and the larger, real world contexts—what some have termed *near* and *far* transfer—may differ for high- and low-status students. Those differences, we suspect, may be attenuated by applying what we have learned from the learning sciences to classroom practice. It remains to be seen whether the strategic application of these learning principles can effectively serve the goal of developing adaptive intellective competence for all students and thus help reduce the achievement gap. We remain optimistic.

REFERENCES

Anderson, C. W. 1987. Strategic teaching in science. In B. F. Jones, A. S. Palincsar, D. S. Ogle, and E. G. Carr (Eds.), *Strategic teaching and learning: Cognitive instruction in the content areas* (pp. 73–91). Alexandria, VA: Association for Supervision and Curriculum Development.

Applying the science of learning to the university and beyond: Cognitive, motivational, and social factors. Online at www.berger.claremontmckenna.edu/asl.

Barnett, S. M., and Ceci, S. J. 2002. When and where do we apply what we learn? A taxonomy for far transfer. *Psychological Bulletin, 128*(4), 612–37.

Bransford, J. D., and Schwartz, D. L. 1999. Rethinking transfer: A simple proposal with multiple implications. In A. Iran-Nejad and P. D. Pearson (Eds.), *Review of research in education* (pp. 61–100). Washington, D.C.: American Education Research Association.

Bransford, J. D., and Stein, B. S. 1993. *The IDEAL problem solver.* 2nd ed. New York: Freeman.

Brooks, J. G., and Brooks, M. G. 1999. *In search of understanding: The case for constructivist classrooms.* Alexandria, VA: Association for Supervision and Curriculum Development.

Brown, A. L. 1978. Knowing when, where, and how to remember: A problem of metacognition. In R. Glasser (Ed.), *Advances in instructional psychology*, vol. 1, pp. 77–165. Hillsdale, NJ: Erlbaum.

Camara, W. J., and Schmidt, A. E. 1999. Group differences in standardized testing and social stratification. *College Board Report* No. 99–5. New York: College Board.

Champagne, A. B., Klopfer, L. E., and Gunstone, R. F. 1982. Cognitive research and the design of science instruction. *Educational Psychologist, 17*, 31–53.

Cheng, P. W., and Holyoak, K. J. 1985. Pragmatic reasoning schema. *Cognitive Psychology, 17*(4), 391–416.

Chi, M. T. H., Feltovich, P. J., and Glaser, R. 1981. Categorization and representation of physics problems by experts and novices. *Cognitive Science, 5*, 121–52.

Cohen, M. R., Cooney, T. M., Hawthorne, C. M., McCormack, A. J., Pasachoff, J. M., Pasachoff, N., Rhines, K. L., and Slesnick, I. L. 1989. *Discover science—third grade.* Glenview, IL: Scott-Foresman.

College Board. 1999. *Reaching the top: A report of the National Task Force on Minority High Achievement.* New York: The College Board.

———. 2003. *College Bound Seniors, 2003*. New York: The College Board.

Cull, W. 2000. Untangling the benefits of multiple study opportunities and repeated testing for cued recall. *Applied Cognitive Psychology,* 14, 215–35.

Dabady, M. 2003. Measuring racial disparities and discrimination in elementary and secondary education: An introduction. *Teachers College Record,* 105(6), 1048–51.

DeCorte, E. 2003. Transfer as the productive use of acquired knowledge, skills, and motivations. *Current Directions in Psychological Science,* 12(4), 142–46.

de Groot, A. 1965. *Thought and choice in chess.* The Hague: Mouton.

Dempster, F. N., and Perkins, P. G. 1993. Revitalizing classroom assessment: Using tests to promote learning. *Journal of Instructional Psychology,* 20, 197–203.

Determan, D. L. 1993. The case for the prosecution: Transfer as epiphenomenon. In D. K. Determan and R. J. Sternberg (Eds.), *Transfer on trial: Intelligence, cognition, and instruction.* Norwood, NJ: Ablex.

Di Sessa, A. 1988. Knowledge in pieces. In G. Forman and P. Pufall (Eds.), *Constructivism in the Computer Age* (pp. 49–70). Hillsdale, NJ: Lawrence Erlbaum Associates.

Everson, H., and Millsap, R. (2004), Beyond individual differences: Explaining school effects on SAT scores. *Educational Psychologist,* 39(3), 157–72.

Everson, H. T., and Skinner, P. 2003. The influence of state science standards on AP Biology test scores. Paper presented at the Advanced Placement National Conference, July. Los Angeles, CA: The College Board.

Everson, H. T. and Tobias, S. (2001). The ability to estimate knowledge and performance in college: A metacognitive analysis. In H. Hartman (Ed.), *Metacognition in Learning and Instruction.* Boston: Kluwer Academic Publishers.

Gentner, D., Rattermann, M. J., and Forbus, K. D. 1993. The roles of similarity in transfer: Separating retrievability from inferential soundness. *Cognitive Psychology,* 25(4), 431–67.

Gick, M. L., and Holyoak, K. J. 1983. Schema induction and analogical transfer. *Cognitive Psychology,* 15(1), 1–38.

Glaser, R. 1992. Expert knowledge and processes of thinking. In D. Halpern (Ed.), *Enhancing Thinking Skills in the Sciences and Mathematics* (pp. 63–75). Hillsdale, NJ: Lawrence Erlbaum Associates.

Glasersfeld, E. von. 1992. A constructivist's view of learning and teaching. In R. Duit, F. Goldberg, and H. Niedderer (Eds.), *The Proceedings of the International Workshop on Research in Physics Education: Theoretical Issues and Empirical Studies* (Bremen, Germany, March 5–8, 1991). Kiel, Germany: IPN.

———. 1989. Cognition, Construction of Knowledge, and Teaching. *Synthese, 80,* 121–40.

Glover, J. A. 1989. The "testing" phenomenon: Not gone but nearly forgotten. *Journal of Educational Psychology,* 81, 392–99.

Gordon, E. W. 2001. The affirmative development of academic ability. *Pedagogical Inquiry and Praxis,* no. 2, September. New York: Teachers College, Columbia University.

Halpern, D. F. 1998. Teaching critical thinking for transfer across domains: Dispositions, skills, structure training, and metacognitive monitoring. *American Psychologist,* 33, 4, 449–55.

Halpern, D. F., and Hakel, M. D. (Eds.) 2000. *Applying the science of learning to university teaching and learning*, No. 89. San Francisco, CA: Jossey-Bass.

———. 2003. Applying the science of learning to the university and beyond: Teaching for long-term retention and transfer. *Change*, 35, 4, 37–41.

Haskell, R. E. 2001. *Transfer of learning: Cognition, instruction and reasoning.* New York: Academic Press.

Huang, G., Reiser, M., Parker, A., Muniec, J., and Salvucci, S. 2003. *Institute of Education Sciences findings from interviews with education policymakers.* Arlington, VA: Synectics.

Jencks, C., and Phillips, M. 1998. *The black-white test score gap.* Washington, D.C.: The Brookings Institute Press.

Judd, C. H. 1908. The relation of special training to general intelligence. *Educational Review*, 36, 28–42.

Kozol, J. 1991. *Savage inequalities: Children in America's schools.* New York: Crown Publishers.

Lockhart, R. S., Lamon, M., and Gick, M. I. 1988. Conceptual transfer in simple insight problems. *Memory and Cognition*, 16, 36–44.

Martin, M. O., Mullis, I. V. S., Gonzalez, E. J., Gregory, K. D., Garden, R. A., O'Connor, K. M., Chrostowski, S. J., and Smith, T. A. 2000. *TIMMS 1999 international science report, findings from IEA's repeat of the Third International Mathematics and Science Study at the Eighth Grade.* Chestnut Hill, MA: Boston College.

McKeough, A., Lupart, J., and Marini, A. (Eds.) 1995. *Teaching for transfer: Fostering generalization in learning.* Hillsdale, NJ: Erlbaum.

Mickelson, R. A. 2003. When are racial disparities in education the result of racial discrimination? A social science perspective. *Teachers College Record*, 105, 6, 1052–86.

Miller, L. S. 1995. *An American imperative: Accelerating minority educational achievement.* New Haven, CT: Yale University Press.

Mortenson, T. G. 2003. A nation at risk, again. *Postsecondary Education OPPORTUNITY.* No. 131. Oskaloosa, IA.

Mullis, I. V. S., Martin, M. O., Gonzalez, E. J., Gregory, K. D., Smith, T. A., Chrostowski, S. J., Garden, R. A., and O'Connor, K. M. 2000. *TIMSS 1999 international mathematics report, findings from IEA's repeat of the Third International Mathematics and Science Study at the Eighth Grade.* Chestnut Hill, MA: Boston College.

National Research Council. 2000. *How people learn: Brain, mind, experience and school.* Washington, D.C.: National Academy Press.

Piaget, J., and Inhelder, B. 1971. *Psychology of the child.* New York: Basic Books.

Pinker, S. 2002. *The blank slate: The modern denial of human nature.* New York: Viking Penguin.

Resnick, L. B. 1987. *Education and learning to think.* Washington, D.C.: National Academy Press.

Resnick, L. B., and Resnick, D. P. 1992. Assessing the thinking curriculum: New tools for educational reform. In B. R. Gifford and M. C. O'Connor (Eds.), *Changing assessments: Alternative views of aptitude achievement and instruction* (pp. 37–75). Boston, MA: Kluwer.

Schauble, L. 1990. Belief revision in children: The role of prior knowledge and strategies for generating evidence. *Journal of Experimental Child Psychology*, 49, 31–57.

Schoenfeld, A. H., and Herrmann, D. J. 1982. Problem perception and knowledge structure in expert and novice mathematical problem solvers. *Journal of Experimental Psychology: Learning, Memory and Cognition, 8,* 484–94.

Shymansky, J. A., Kyle, W. C., and Alport, J. 1983. The effects of new science curricula on student performance. *Journal of Research in Science Teaching, 20,* 387–404.

Singley, K., and Anderson, J. R. 1989. *The transfer of cognitive skill.* Cambridge, MA: Harvard University Press.

Slavin, R. E., and Madden, N. A. 2002. *Success for all/roots and wings: 2002 summary of research on achievement outcomes.* Baltimore: Johns Hopkins University, Center for Research on the Education of Students Placed at Risk.

Smith, D. C., and Neale, D. C. 1989. The construction of subject matter knowledge in primary science teaching. *Teaching and Teacher Education, 5,* 1–20.

Sternberg, R. J. 2002. Raising the achievement of all students: Teaching for successful intelligence. *Educational Psychology Review.*

Thorndike, E. L., and Woodworth, R. S. 1901. The influence of improvement in one mental function upon the efficiency of other functions. *Psychological Review, 8,* 237–61.

Tobias, S., and Everson, H. T. 2002. *Knowing what you know, and what you don't know.* College Board Report (02-04). New York: College Board.

Weiss, I. 1987. Report of the 1985–1986 national survey on science and mathematics education. Washington, D.C.: U.S. Government Printing Office (1SPE8317070).

West, L. H. T , and Pines, A. L. 1985. *Cognitive structure and conceptual change.* Orlando, FL: Academic Press.

Wheeler, M. A., and Roediger, H. L. 1992. Disparate effects of repeated testing: Reconciling Ballard's (1913) and Bartlett's (1932) results. *Psychological Science, 3,* 240–45.

Willingham, D. T. 2002. Inflexible knowledge. *American Educator,* winter. Washington, D.C.: American Federation of Teachers.

———. 2003. Students remember what they think about. *American Educator,* spring. Washington, D.C.: American Federation of Teachers.

12

Task Force Report on the Affirmative Development of Academic Ability

All Students Reaching the Top: Strategies for Closing Academic Achievement Gaps

Albert Bennett, Beatrice L. Bridglall, Ana Marie Cauce, Howard T. Everson, Edmund W. Gordon, Carol D. Lee, Rudolfo Mendoza-Denton, Joseph S. Renzulli, and Judy K. Stewart

TOWARD THE AFFIRMATIVE DEVELOPMENT
OF ACADEMIC ABILITY

With support from the College Board and Learning Points, Incorporated, Edmund W. Gordon convened the National Study Group on the Affirmative Development of Academic Ability. This group of scholars met in five working sessions to plan, review, progress, and approve a report on that subject. Additional work of the study group consisted of synthesis and position papers written by members of the group. Some of these papers have been included as chapters in this book. The use of the term *affirmative development* appears to have been first used by Gordon in an exchange between Gordon and Scott Miller at the 1987 annual meeting of the National Action Council on Minorities in Engineering. In a plenary session at the NACME meeting, Gordon, Miller, and others were debating the pros and cons of affirmative action, and a finding from a report prepared for the Exxon Education Foundation (Gordon 1986), which suggested that despite considerable effort directed at special admission and specialized programming, the production and position of black and Latino engineers was problematic. Gordon observed that it may be that in addition to programs of affirmative action targeted at the admission of underrepresented populations to study for this profession, what is needed is a national program of affirmative development. We find little reference to the term until 1999, when it appeared in the recommendations of the National Task Force on Minority High Achievement (College Board 1999). This is not surprising given that the Task Force Report was written by Scott Miller.

The construct initially appeared in print in the report, *Reaching the Top* (College Board 1999) as the implicit, overarching recommendation of the task force. The continued educational underdevelopment of so many segments of the African-American, Latino, and Native American communities makes a very strong case for expanding their access to good schools and to high quality colleges and universities, the latter of which has been a primary focus of affirmative action. But expanded access does not necessarily translate directly into higher academic achievement. Thus, the task force recommends that an extensive array of public and private policies, actions, and investments be pursued, which would collectively provide many more opportunities for the academic development for underrepresented minority students through the schools, colleges, and universities that they attend, through their homes, and through their communities. We summarize this as a commitment to affirmative development.

Affirmative development is proposed as a complement to affirmative action, which we enthusiastically endorse as being in the best interest of our nation. But if affirmative action is to function well in a diverse society with inequitable opportunities to learn, attention must be given to the deliberate development of competence in those populations least likely to develop it under usual circumstances. Affirmative development places emphasis on the creation and enhancement of competence in targeted populations, in addition to the more traditional emphasis in affirmative action on the equitable reward of competence across the social divisions by which persons are classified.

In the summer of 1958, in a talk at a public hall on 125th Street and Lenox Avenue in Harlem, W. E. B. DuBois mused about his 1903 claim that the "problem of the twentieth century is the problem of the color line." In 1958 he was beginning to consider the possibility that the line between the haves and the have-nots, greatly confounded by color, could emerge as a more critical problem. Gordon believes that DuBois was correct in 1903 and in 1958. The century between 1900 and 2000 was marked by considerable turmoil associated with racist values and DuBois's "color line," but, equally significant, it was also marked by a monumental decline in significance of the "color line." Wilson's book, *Declining Significance of Race* (1978), documented this radical change in our society and validated the Duboisian prediction that inequalities in the distribution of income and wealth would emerge as more critical.

The study group's recommendations place greater emphasis on schooling than may be justified. Schools will continue to be the democratic society's major vehicle for the delivery of formal academic instruction, as well as one of the society's powerful instruments of socialization to citizenship, but as Cremin (1989) has so effectively argued, schools are simply *one* of the society's educative institutions, and as John Dewey (1931) constantly reminded us, education involves more than academic learning. Consequently, the excellent ideas and recommendations of the study group are endorsed and seconded by our inclusion of that report in this book. We argue that the affirmative development of academic ability also includes:

1. The opportunity to grow up in conditions that are supportive of wholesome physical, psychological, and social development;
2. Access to a reasonable measure of the education-relevant forms of capital, especially human, polity, and social forms of capital;
3. The opportunity for meaningful participation in the social intercourse of the society and the expectation that one will be justly compensated for one's participation in the work force;
4. The expectation that one will not be arbitrarily judged negatively or penalized because of one's self-selected or assigned biological or cultural identity;
5. Ubiquitous and redundant opportunities to learn the formal and tacit dispositions, knowledge, and skills that are rapidly becoming the universal currency of modern, technologically advanced societies.
6. Respected participation in varieties of "high" and folk cultures and artistic genre.
   (All Children Reaching the Top, the report of the National Study Group on the Affirmative Development of Academic Ability)

ALL CHILDREN REACHING THE TOP, THE REPORT OF THE NATIONAL STUDY GROUP ON THE AFFIRMATIVE DEVELOPMENT OF ACADEMIC ABILITY

This report is presented below.

Affirmative Development of Academic Ability and Intellective Competence

The National Task Force on Minority High Achievement (1999) concluded that these problems require a national effort at the affirmative development of academic ability. Academic ability is one expression of human intellective competence that, increasingly, is recognized as the universal currency of societies that are technologically advanced. Academic ability references capabilities such as the following:

- Critical literacy and numeracy
- Mathematical and verbal reasoning
- Skill in creating, recognizing, and resolving relationships
- Problem solving from both abstract and concrete situations, as in deductive and inductive reasoning
- Sensitivity to multiple contexts and perspectives
- Skill in accessing and managing disparate bodies and chunks of information
- Resource recognition and utilization (help seeking)
- Self-regulation (including metacognitive competence and metacomponential strategies)

Such capabilities appear to be the products of exposure to the demands of specialized cultural experiences—schooling being the most common—that interact with a wide variety of human potentials (Cole, Gay, Glick, and Sharp, 1971; Cole and Scribner, 1974; Hunt, 1966; Martinez, 2000; Sternberg, 1994). We therefore conclude that academic ability is a developed ability—the quality of which is not primarily a function of one's biological endowment or fixed aptitudes. With the recognition of academic ability as a developed ability, the National Study Group for the Affirmative Development of Academic Ability begins with the assumption that closing the gaps in academic achievement between groups of students from different social divisions (class, ethnicity, gender, and language) will require the affirmative development of such ability in a wide range of individuals through certain interventions in our homes, communities, and schools.

Affirmative development of academic ability is based on the notion that such abilities are nurtured and developed through (1) high-quality teaching and instructions in the classroom, (2) trusting relationships in school, and (3) environmental supports for pro-academic behavior in the school and community. These pedagogical and social activities and environmental supports should reflect a type of developmental "scaffolding" around and within which students can find support for growth in the development of abilities and dispositions to:

- Perceive critically;
- Explore widely;
- Bring rational order to chaos;

- Bring knowledge and techniques to bear on the solution of problems;
- Test ideas against explicit and considered moral values and empirical data;
- Recognize and create relationships between concrete and abstract phenomena.

According to Gordon (2001), the mastery of academic learning is instrumental to the development of intellective competence. In Gordon's vision of teaching, learning, and assessment, academic outcome standards are central. However, it is the explication of what we want learners to know about specific disciplines and be able to do that must be considered as instrumental to what we want learners to become. There is no question about the importance of what students learn and are taught. Most of us would agree that teaching and learning independent of content (subject matter) is problematic. However, just as teaching and learning without subject matter are vacuous, teaching and learning should not be so constrained by content that the purpose of engagement with these pedagogical endeavors is precluded.

Gordon (2001) also argues that the purpose of learning, and teaching by which it is enabled, is to acquire knowledge and technique to develop adaptive human intellect. Developed abilities are not so much reflected in the specific discipline-based knowledge a student may have, but in the student's ability and disposition to adaptively and efficiently use knowledge, technique, and values in mental processes to engage and solve both common and novel problems.

In summary, intellective competence is more than what advanced societies understand and measure as "intelligence." Intellective competence reflects the integration of academic content with mental processes such as reasoning and critical thinking applied within an ever-changing but highly relevant social context, which results in the mental activity that is necessary to make sense of experiences to solve problems. This end goal is less focused on what we want learners to know and know how to do, and is more sharply focused on what we want learners to be and become—compassionate and independent critically thinking members of humane communities. From this perspective, intellective competence may be a reflection of intellective character.

The next three sections of this chapter describe the research base as well as educational applications at the classroom, school, and community levels that—if appropriately integrated and implemented—should lead to high academic achievement and the development of intellective competence in all students.

HIGH-QUALITY TEACHING AND INSTRUCTION
IN THE CLASSROOM

Modern constructivist views of learning and cognition emphasize that the child is an active learner who engages the world in trying to make sense of it. In the ideal world, the home, school, and neighborhood serve as the child's laboratory; there are books at home, museums in the neighborhood, and adequate facilities in the school. The child has peers to serve as companions in exploration and adult guidance to structure interactions that are maximally conducive to learning. Support for learning continues and becomes more formalized in the classroom, with school serving as an extension of the learning environment in the home and community.

Although the above description may approximate the learning environments of affluent children in this country, it is a far cry from the settings in which too many others reside. Poor children—who are disproportionately African American, Hispanic, and Native American—often grow up in high-crime, inner-city neighborhoods. Parents often need to protect their children from these neighborhoods instead of letting them explore. In these same neighborhoods, adult authority figures often are lacking and peer interactions are as apt to result in harm as in good. (See Cauce et al. 2003 for a recent review of this literature.)

Nurturing Intellective Competence

The constructivist perspective of learning is based on a simple proposition: Students come to school with constructed understandings of the world—not with empty minds to be filled up through lectures, drills, and rote learning. They have prior knowledge, albeit sometimes incomplete, of their world and how things in it work. Contemporary theorists subscribe to the belief that the knowledge with which a learner comes to school affects his or her ability to learn and acquire new knowledge. By extension, if what teachers are attempting to teach conflicts with the previously constructed knowledge of the students, this new knowledge will make little sense and will be ill-constructed and unavailable for future use in other settings (Anderson, 1987; Brooks and Brooks, 1999; von Glasersfeld, 1989; Resnick, 1987; Schauble, 1990).

Obviously, this constructivist perspective has important implications for promoting long-term retention and transfer. Much of the failure to transfer new learning to other contexts may stem from the buzz of confusion that learners experience when previously constructed knowledge and new knowledge (and novel contexts) conflict or are not well aligned (Everson, 2006). Simply making the new knowledge clearer to students, the research suggests, will not enhance understanding to lead to adaptive forms of transfer (Cheng and Holyoak, 1985; Gentner, Ratterman, and Forbus, 1993; Gick and Holyoak, 1983). The drill and practice—as well as other direct teaching methods—found in many large, urban, and otherwise poorly funded schools might be working to mitigate against transfer. This type of instruction may be particularly damaging to minority students attending these schools.

More to the point, the achievement gaps between white and black children as early as kindergarten suggest that, indeed, all students are constructing knowledge long before they enter school. Some students, perhaps, have constructed understandings and acquired knowledge that may be more feasible and relevant to the classroom; others have not. Some students apparently arrive at school with richer and deeper stores of prior knowledge—stories, words, and schemas for understanding the world around them (Lee, 2006). Research indicates that the body of private understandings that many students have acquired before coming to school may be incomplete, inaccurate, and in conflict with what the curricula demands of them (Di Sessa, 1988).

With this caveat in mind, a handful of teaching and learning strategies can provide teachers and students respectively with a framework to refocus the learning process. These strategies include knowledge acquisition, improved comprehension through consolidation and automaticity, deep understanding, and learning for transfer. It is important to note that these strategies are defined in a somewhat arbitrary manner and do not represent clear demarcations in the learning process or distinct teaching techniques. They are merely an organizational device to ensure that our treatment of teaching is comprehensive and that we do not gloss over aspects of learning (such as automaticity and deep understanding) that typically get little treatment in the literature.

Teaching for Knowledge Acquisition

Knowledge acquisition remains a critical stage in the learning process; it is the building block for all other processes. The more that is learned about higher-order thought processes, the clearer it becomes that such processes do not occur independently of the information a child already possesses. All aspects of learning build upon the knowledge base that exists. Current understanding of pedagogical research strongly suggests that the first step in teaching for knowledge acquisition involves taking the time to find out what knowledge children already bring to the situation (Lee, 2006).

During the acquisition stage, using conventional teaching techniques, new information is combined with these existing theories or preconceptions. This combination determines whether the resulting construction is accurate. Vosniadou and Brewer's (1992) work on the child's model of the world illustrates this point beautifully. They found that if children have a mental model of the world as flat (a model perfectly in tune with their experience of it), when they "learn" that it is round, their resulting model may be that of the world as a pancake. In other words, children take their original flat model of the world and superimpose roundness on it. This example nicely illustrates why it is the teacher's job to figure out what the student's mental model is and then teach from that as a starting point.

Inquiry-based instructional techniques do an exceptionally good job of drawing out a student's assumptions and using them as the building blocks for the construction of the new knowledge. Such inquiry-based approaches begin with the learner's previous knowledge. They then actively engage him or her to search not only for answers but also for explanations. Inquiry-based approaches also involve the student in gathering new information, analyzing it, and—in the process—discarding some explanations that may have appeared to make sense. A growing body of research suggests that inquiry-based approaches lead to a broader and more robust acquisition of knowledge than a student obtains from a more conventional, didactic teaching approach.

Most of the research on inquiry-based techniques has been conducted on learning science and mathematics because inquiry-based approaches have been primarily used in these fields. A similar technique, reciprocal teaching (Palincsar and Brown, 1984), has been used to improve reading comprehension. This interactive teaching approach is based on questioning, clarification, summarization, and prediction. Each of these elements is aimed at understanding the meaning of the text. Not only do students actively participate in these activities (e.g., questioning, clarification) that are necessary for comprehension, but they watch the teacher model these behaviors. This relatively simple teaching technique has shown some dramatic and durable improvements in student learning (Brown and Campione, 1994; Browne, Campione, Webber, and McGilly, 1992).

Because of the essential role of knowledge acquisition in all other aspects of learning, focusing on improving African-American and Hispanic children's knowledge acquisition, whether it be in terms of information or actual learning skills, is the first step in bridging the achievement gaps. As Resnik and Hall (1998) put it, "What we know now is that just as facts alone do not constitute true knowledge and thinking power, so thinking processes cannot proceed without something to think about" (p. 101). Or, to put it even more simply, how much one knows affects how well one thinks.

Teaching for Improved Comprehension through Consolidation and Automaticity

After children acquire basic facts, they need to make this new information theirs, assimilating it into their existing network of ideas. The notion of improved comprehension primarily includes two key concepts: consolidation and automaticity. Both concepts are described in detail in this section.

The process of consolidation is essential for new information to stick, or to stay with an individual for a prolonged period, becoming part of long-term memory. Consolidation happens best when learning is "deep" and goes beyond the simple ability to parrot information or to explain concepts at a surface level. It is likewise essential that basic skills become automated before they can be built upon effectively. Automaticity is the ability to perform a complex task without conscious awareness or effort. Through repeated practice, the task itself becomes an automatic process.

Information-processing models of knowledge acquisition distinguish between effortful and automatic processes. Effortful processes require the use of mental resources, including consciousness and intentionality, in addition to effort. The consolidation of knowledge and learning for automaticity are important because they free up energy for other activities that require mental effort. Indeed, younger, as opposed to older, children are less likely to use even basic memory and/or metacognitive strategies, or to benefit from such strategies when used, precisely because they are effortful (see Bjorklund, 1995: 116). It is only when cognitive processing becomes more efficient with age that children begin to effectively use more sophisticated learning strategies. For example, somewhere between fourth and eighth grade there is a shift from learning to read to reading to learn. But, this shift only occurs after—and if—reading becomes a practiced, automated skill. Until this happens, limitations in working memory capacity are too great to permit the interaction between syntactic, semantic, and pragmatic information that is necessary for comprehension. It is only after reading becomes more automatic and there is excess working memory capacity that comprehension becomes the primary task of reading.

Practice is the best strategy for developing improved comprehension. With practice, comprehending complex processes becomes less effortful and more automatic. Practice can be formal or not. For example, some parents may sit down very purposely with their children and go over the day's school lessons or listen to their child read aloud. Or, they may pay for tutors to do such activities. Others may simply provide an opportunity for practicing some skills during routine activities, such as bedtime reading. Some children, however, may not get any opportunities for practice outside the classroom.

Most children develop the underlying skills that make reading relatively automatic from the combination of what they get at school and at home. However, a small proportion of children, who may represent as many as 40 percent in some urban schools, benefit from having skills such as phonemic awareness and phonic word attack taught much more systematically (Hook and Jones, 2002; Sanders, 2001). Some evidence suggests that early preventive intervention of this type can help students develop greater comprehension and fluency (Torgesen, Rashotte, and Alexander, 2001). This research suggests that children who do not get ready support for, or opportunities to practice, reading skills may benefit from more direct and explicit classroom support and instruction. The importance of developing comprehension, especially for children in environments that do not support learning, cannot be emphasized enough. What might readily appear to be deficits in higher-order processing might more accurately be attributed to a failure to develop fluency and comprehension of much simpler skills. Without the latter, the former may simply not be attainable.

Teaching for Deep Understanding

As Brown, Collins, and Duguid (1989) note, teaching of abstract concepts in the absence of authentic, naturalistic situations overlooks the fact that "understanding is developed through continued, situated use" (p. 2). The importance of this type of learning also places emphasis on the home environment or supplementary educational settings, where learning and practice may occur in more naturalistic settings (Bridglall and Gordon, 2002; Steinberg, 1996). The cognitive apprenticeship approach emphasizes the role of collaborative learning and social interaction. In this sense, it is worth noting that while most school situations emphasize individual learning, most authentic learning situations involve collaboration, including social discourse (Resnick, 1988; Resnick, Saljo, Pontecorvo, and Burge, 1997).

Two key approaches have been associated with learning that emphasizes understanding: active learning and problem-based learning (also called concept-based learning). Key to these approaches is the recognition that learning takes place through a dialectical process of active participation, and not just within an individual's mind. It is this type of participation that leads to what has been called engaged learning. Problem-based or engaged learning illustrates that to really understand what is learned, it is essential to place learning within an appropriate and authentic activity context. From the perspective of situated cognition, problem-based learning, and learning communities, learning is as much an act of socialization to "habits and skills of interpretation and meaning construction" (Resnick, 1989: 39) as it is a purely cognitive act.

This richer way of looking at learning and teaching is especially important for nonmainstream children because it highlights the fact that many important skills are learned implicitly, through the course of everyday or authentic interactions. If children already are engaged with their parents or other adults in planting a garden at home (or building a birdhouse, or raising a gerbil), they may not need to get this type of learning in the school context. But, to the degree that some youth are not exposed to environments in which such learning takes place and is encouraged, they will be at a disadvantage (Hung, 2002) unless such lessons are provided at school.

Teaching for Transferability

School learning is important only if one believes that what is learned in one context can be transferred to others. Transferability is the ability to make connections to skills learned in one context and transfer those skills to another context. Because of the importance of transferability, a great deal has been written about the learning conditions that enhance this process. Key points to emphasize are the following:

- Strategies used to enhance deep understanding and automaticity also lead to transferability. For example, one of the most important factors influencing transfer is mastery. Students who learn specific subject material well find it easier to transfer that knowledge to other subjects or material (Bransford, Brown, and Cocking, 2000, Klahr and Carver, 1988).
- Comprehension enhances transfer (Bransford and Stein, 1993). Without an understanding of the deeper concepts and/or their connections to other information, problem-solving transfer may fail because students cannot see beyond superficial content-relevant aspects of a problem. In one study, Bassok and Holyoak (1989) showed that 90 percent of students who used a distance equation to successfully solve a physics problem could not use the same equation to answer a question about salary increases, although it was an analogous problem. When learning is overly contextualized or occurs only in the context of solving a very specific problem, transferability may be compromised (Cognition and Technology Group at Vanderbilt, 1997).
- Transferability can be greatly increased when issues of transferability (e.g., the implications of one task for another) are highlighted during instruction (Anderson, Reder, and Simon, 1996). For example, after students have learned to solve the distance equation mentioned above, the teacher could provide them with the additional example of salary increases to promote further transfer of knowledge. But, even more indirect strategies for transferability have been found to enhance it. For example, strategies similar to reciprocal teaching, which is used to improve comprehension, also have been found to benefit transferability (Scardamalia, Bereiter, and Steinbach, 1984). In addition, problem-based learning and lessons acquired in a situated learning environment are more likely to lead to the transfer of knowledge to real-life problems (Im and Hannafin, 1999). Thus, while there are unique issues involved in transferability, teaching for knowledge acquisition, teaching for consolidation and automaticity, and especially teaching for deep understanding also enhance the transferability of knowledge.

In most instances, instruction should involve some preparation in the form of modeling before students begin to work on a complex new problem.

Equally important is for teachers to provide what Cazden (2001) calls "as needed" support while students are in the act of problem solving—whether individually, working in groups, or through whole-class work. Here, both the sequence of problem types and the manner in which students are socialized to engage with these problems are important. Key socialization strategies include exploring, articulating, and debating the following.

- The features of the problem to which the learner should pay attention and why
- What each student already knows and doesn't know about these features
- What these features signal about concepts and problem-solving strategies that may be relevant
- The strengths and weaknesses of what will inevitably be multiple solution paths
- The goodness of fit of solutions (i.e., what the solution explains or accounts for and what it does not)

If such socialization experiences are a routine part of instruction across subject matters and grades, students are more likely to develop several important dispositions and competencies: (1) a willingness to persist with difficult problems in the face of uncertainty; (2) a willingness and ability to search one's repertoire of existing knowledge to look for connections to new problems, particularly when the connections are not obvious; and (3) a sensitivity to look closely for recognizable patterns that help define the kind of problem one is tackling (known in the cognitive literature as defining and constraining the problem space). These dispositions or competencies are not developed in the short run, and especially not in erratic learning environments.

Transfer of Knowledge: Challenges and Educational Applications

Applying what is learned in school to address problems in other settings is the very essence of the product of effective learning. Indeed, the very reason children are sent to school is so they will acquire the knowledge, skills, and abilities that will serve them later in life, when they are in the "real world." Distressingly, the research on the problem of transfer of learning suggests that there is a wholesale failure of learning from instruction (Bransford and Schwartz, 1999; Haskell, 2001; McKeough, Lupart, and Marini, 1995). This problem is even more troubling when viewed in the larger social context of the black-white achievement gap (Mortenson, 2003).

A large (and growing) body of research evidence is available on how people learn and what teachers can do to promote learning for transfer, and this research ought to influence classroom practice. In this section, we make the case for designing instruction based on principles of learning derived from the learning sciences—the interdisciplinary field of research from psychology, neuroscience, linguistics, philosophy, computer science, anthropology, and education—to enhance the critical thinking abilities of all students. We aim to transfer what nearly two decades of research has taught us about how to improve learning, problem solving, long-term retention, and the transfer of learning to novel situations. The research we review suggests we are poised to capitalize on knowledge of how people think, learn, and remember; it offers instructional design principles to improve classroom learning and promote transfer of learning for all students. Obviously, these views are not entirely our own but derive from our reading of a number of researchers and scholars, including Bransford and Schwartz (1999), Halpern and Hakel (2003), and DeCorte (2003). We then describe the key findings from the literature on transfer of learning and emphasize the cognitive perspective, which stresses students' ability to learn during transfer. We conclude by suggesting how these learning principles can be applied in the classroom to improve teaching, learning, and transfer for all students.

Scientific inquiry into the question of transfer of learning has a long history, dating back more than a century to the work of E. L. Thorndike (Thorndike and Woodworth, 1901). From the very beginning, this line of research has suggested that transfer—that is, how well what a person learns in one set of circumstances transfers or is adapted to other, novel situations—is both fragile and controversial. Indeed, the only clear finding from this long history of research is that there have been a number of failed attempts at achieving transfer, as well as a number of successes (Barnett and Ceci, 2002; Detterman and Sternberg, 1993). In an especially clear treatment of the research on transfer, Bransford and Schwartz (1999: 62) refer to the "agonies and ecstasies" that characterize this body of research. It would not be unfair, for example, to summarize the literature on transfer by concluding that "there is no evidence to contradict Thorndike's general conclusions: Transfer is rare" (Detterman, 1993: 15).

Despite the pessimism, a number of researchers have pointed out recently that research is uncovering a number of important learning perspectives and principles that appear to be capable of enhancing transfer (DeCorte, 2003; Halpern and Hakel, 2003). In a classic study that involved teaching subjects to throw darts while underwater, Judd (1908) demonstrated the value of promoting understanding as part of the initial learning experience. Judd's experiment demonstrates the benefits of guided practice. Two groups of boys practiced throwing darts at an underwater target. Prior to practice, the experimental group was instructed about how water refracts light and how this principle may affect the accuracy of their performance. The control group was not given this instruction, but simply practiced. Boys in the experimental group were more accurate at throwing darts at new targets at varying depths.

Building on these early studies, Bransford and Stein (1993) studied how learning with understanding affects transfer. In general, these studies show that when presented in a problem-solving context, knowledge and information are more likely to be recalled and activated in novel problem-solving situations. Rethinking the problem of transfer from a cognitive perspective may yield insights into how strategic knowledge about learning, including monitoring one's learning across domains and contexts (Bransford and Schwartz, 1999; Brown, 1978; Tobias and Everson, 2002), enhances performance in novel settings.

The question before us is: Do we have the strategies and principled pedagogical approaches that reflect our best understanding of how students learn? Work done under the auspices of the National Research Council (Bransford, Brown, and Cocking, 2000) suggests that indeed we do, and the report makes a strong case for affecting students' long-term retention and transfer by improving how we teach. The authors write:

> Modern theories of learning and transfer retain the emphasis on practice, but they specify the kinds of practice that are important and take learner characteristics (e.g., existing knowledge and strategies) into account (e.g., Singley and Anderson, 1989). In the discussion below, we explore key characteristics of learning and transfer that have important implications for education:
> - Initial learning is necessary for transfer, and a considerable amount is known about the kinds of learning experiences that support transfer.
> - Knowledge that is overly contextualized can reduce transfer; abstract representations of knowledge can help promote transfer.
> - Transfer is best viewed as an active, dynamic process rather than a passive end-product of a particular set of learning experiences.
> - All new learning involves transfer based on previous learning, and this fact has important implications for the design of instruction that helps students learn. (p. 53)

Building on this work, Bransford and Schwartz (1999), DeCorte (2003), Halpern (1998), Halpern and Hakel (2002, 2003), Sternberg, (2002), and D. T. Willingham (2002, 2003), among others, provide specific guidance by applying the sciences of learning to the challenge of teaching for transfer and preparing students for future learning. Through a variety of collaborative efforts, these researchers have developed theories and extracted basic principles that, we suspect, can be applied broadly in schools and classrooms. On the following pages, we describe a representative set of these principles and offer examples of possible educational applications.

Provide Opportunities for Students to Practice at Retrieval

Research tells us that a powerful way to promote long-term retention and transfer is to allow students to practice retrieving previously taught material from long-term memory. Opportunities to practice can occur either during review for tests or in actual testing sessions (Cull, 2000; Dempster and Perkins, 1993; Glover, 1989; Wheeler and Roediger, 1992). Teachers are encouraged to work with students as they retrieve information and knowledge from both short-term and long-term memories. Doing so repeatedly, in varied contexts, strengthens students' ability to access these knowledge bases and solidifies their ability to recall previously learned material from long-term memory, thus promoting transfer across contexts. Halpern and Hakel (2002, 2003) also tell us that repeated testing helps in the recall of information. Teachers are encouraged to align classroom discussions, homework assignments, and tests so that important information will have to be remembered at different times throughout the academic year or course, enhancing long-term retention. Test questions also offer an opportunity for "practice at retrieval" and deepen students' knowledge of the material being tested. Ideally, tests should be cumulative; test items should probe for understanding of the material. The key idea is to cue students' prior knowledge in ways that are relevant to the learning context.

Vary the Conditions of Learning

The key idea here is that when learning takes place under a variety of conditions and contexts, conceptual understanding becomes more rounded and multiple retrieval cues are activated. Research from the learning sciences provides insights into the benefits of offering differing types of problems and alternative solution strategies. Although we are warned that learning may take longer and be somewhat less enjoyable to students, research suggests that students and teachers will see significant gains in long-term retention and transfer.

Maximize Time for Learning

Another factor to seriously consider in supporting minority-student learning is making sure that students have the time needed to learn. Research has demonstrated that when time to learn is allowed to vary, the best predictor of mastery learning is a student's prior knowledge. On the other hand, when time available for learning is held constant, a student's intelligence is the best predictor of mastery (Anderson and Block, 1977; Bloom, 1971). Regardless of what one thinks about the construct of intelligence or its validity, it is clear that when time to learn is held constant, as is typically the case in the present educational system, it leads to the outcome that ability is a better predictor than learning per se. Learning can be viewed as a result of opportunity to learn plus perseverance. But, while the perseverance is up to the student, the teacher controls the opportunity to learn. Ideally, a learner-centered environment would allow opportunities to be better matched to the student's, rather than the teacher's, needs.

Represent Knowledge Using Alternate Forms

Learning is more powerful when students are prompted to take information presented in one format and "represent" it in an alternative way. Cognitive research tells us that we process information in multiple ways—visually and through auditory-verbal channels. Students' learning and recall can be improved by integrating information from both the verbal and visual-spatial forms of representation. Teachers are encouraged, therefore, to use both modes of representation in all their learning tasks, explicitly and consciously incorporating multiple forms of representation into their instructional designs.

Build on Students' Prior Knowledge and Experience

Research comparing experts to novices reveals that experts have a larger knowledge base, compared to novices, and can compile information into more meaningful chunks, which further facilitates learning. For example, relative to novices, chess experts have a better memory for positions of chess pieces on a game board (Chi, Feltovich, and Glaser, 1981). When chess pieces are placed randomly on the board, however, this advantage disappears, suggesting that chess experts do not have superior general memory; rather, they are able to draw upon their knowledge of common chess positions when useful for remembering and developing game strategies. As noted above, students arrive in the classroom with sets of assumptions and beliefs that serve as a mental framework for learning. As they construct knowledge, students build on their prior knowledge to infuse meaning into newly learned material. In this way, prior knowledge influences how students interpret new information and decide what aspects of this information are relevant and irrelevant.

Emphasize Knowledge and Skill Development

Teachers, teaching assistants, and tutors need to make explicit those concepts and processes that students need to know, understand, and internalize in order to achieve mastery. This approach is especially important if students have not had previous intensive exposure to mathematics and the sciences, for example. The research literature is replete with findings that support the idea that peer study groups create opportunities for academic and social support, which appear to contribute to higher academic achievement (Treisman, 1992). Peer study groups can serve more than the purpose of helping students master the concepts in their fields; they also enable students to regard themselves as part of an academic community. In addition, peer study groups promote conversations in which participants have to articulate their own ideas and listen to the ideas of others. Peer study group interactions also ensure that students make their work and thinking public; students are thus exposed to different perspectives and the knowledge fund of their peers. The peer study group setting exposes students to peers who also struggle with various ideas and subject content. The result is that students learn quickly that excelling in a subject does not mean being able to solve problems quickly and easily but rather working very hard and persevering.

Infuse Lessons with Strategies for Learning

For students, learning new concepts and developing understanding is often difficult and uncomfortable. Students' views of the world are challenged, and long-held beliefs are questioned in the teaching and learning process. Students and teachers often complain that some subjects, such as mathematics and science, are just too difficult for them to learn. All of us want learning to be easy. Thus, when students are faced with some school subjects, they become discouraged by the difficulty they encounter during the learning process. Halpern and Hakel (2003) remind teachers that optimizing learning depends on what we want students to learn and what students already know about that subject. Teachers can help students by discussing ways of learning, infusing their lessons with strategies for learning to learn, and surfacing students' own beliefs about learning.

Provide Systematic Feedback

Not surprisingly, and as discussed above, students come to school with preconceived ideas about the subjects they are taught in the classroom. Even if these notions are wrong, belief in them can solidify based on ordinary, everyday experiences, especially when objective, corrective feedback is not provided. This lack of feedback has serious implications for learning and performance.

For instance, students may come to believe incorrectly in causation by attributing an effect to a salient possible causal agent without considering plausible alternative causes, engaging in spurious causal reasoning. Similarly, students often may rely on self-created devices to judge or interpret events and outcomes. These mental shortcuts may not always lead to correct solutions or to the resolution of complex problems. We also know that students, typically, have poor metacognition—that is, they are poor judges of what they know and do not know (Tobias and Everson, 2002). These misguided notions and feelings of confidence about what they know may also develop in the course of learning. Learners may be fooled into believing that they are learning by the apparent ease of their performance; in contrast, optimal learning is usually derived from moderately difficult learning situations. Teachers can become more aware of students' common misconceptions and lead discussions in class that address such misconceptions. They also can provide systematic feedback on homework assignments, tests, and projects throughout the course of instruction to combat the persistence of erroneous thinking.

Use Dynamic Classroom Assessment

Research is emerging, largely from a psychometric perspective, indicating that some standardized test items and tasks are more difficult for black students than for white students, even when the two groups are equal with respect to their ability levels and have been taught by the same teachers in the very same classes. From a cognitive perspective, it has been suggested that the test items may have features or characteristics that are more or less salient with respect to classroom learning, and that these saliency characteristics differ for black and white students. These test items—which often are considered the final transfer task, particularly in high-stakes testing situations—have been viewed as presenting "sequestered problem solving" (Bransford and Schwartz, 1999: 68). In such situations, students rarely have the opportunity to seek help from other resources, such as other students, teachers, or texts. They rarely have the opportunity to engage in trial-and-error forms of learning, get feedback, or even revise their work.

By shifting to a perspective that looks at transfer in terms of preparing students for future learning, as DeCorte (2003) and Bransford and Schwartz (1999) suggest, we are then free to look at assessments as opportunities to gauge students' abilities to learn in knowledge-rich environments. The key idea is that assessments serve as opportunities to measure students' abilities to learn new information and relate this new learning to previous experiences. According to Bransford and Schwartz, "Assessments can be improved by moving from static, one-shot measures of 'test taking' to environments that provide opportunities for new learning" (p. 88). These dynamic forms of assessment hold promise for promoting transfer and reducing the achievement gaps. For example, teachers who direct their instruction to forms of "teaching to the test" often find that their students have difficulty engaging in metacognitive knowledge monitoring. By treating the testing situation as external to the learning environment, as a hurdle to be leaped, or as a one-shot maximal performance event, they are depriving students of the opportunity to assess their own learning, to monitor and regulate their learning strategies, and to capitalize on corrective feedback and engage in new learning. By incorporating dynamic forms of assessment in the classroom, teachers have a tool that will allow them to better measure how prior learning and experience have prepared their students for future learning—knowledge that in itself promotes transfer of learning.

THE IMPORTANCE OF TRUSTING RELATIONSHIPS IN SCHOOL

The social-psychological literature points to a clear message that feelings of trust in the institution, and in those who are seen to represent the interests of those institutions (e.g., teachers, professors, administrators), are a fundamental building block in the affirmative development of high minority achievement (Bryk and Schneider, 2002; Mendoza-Denton and Aronson, 2006; Steele and Aronson, 1995, 2000). Yet successful minority students are increasingly likely, as they move up the achievement ladder, to encounter contexts and situations in which their group has been historically excluded and underrepresented.

Psychosocial Processes that Hinder the Development of Academic Ability

The past decade in particular has witnessed an explosion of research on the experience of being stigmatized, attributable in large part to research on two separate but related phenomena: One is attributional ambiguity (Crocker and Major, 1989), and the other is stereotype threat (Steele and Aronson, 1995, 2000). Attributional ambiguity involves the challenge that a student of color may face when receiving feedback about his or her performance and the difficulty of determining when feedback (particularly critical feedback) is accurate or is actually reflective of racial bias on the part of the one giving the feedback. Stereotype threat is the awareness that others may judge one's performance in terms of one's racial background, rather than in terms of one's individual background.

These general findings have been replicated with a variety of methodologies and seem to indicate a robust phenomenon. What implications does this have for affirmative development? As one begins to think about this issue, a particular conundrum starts to take shape for the high-achieving minority student. On the one hand, an important aspect of academic achievement comes from the integration of academic success into the self-concept (Steele, 1992). Similarly, people want to achieve mastery and have at least some control over their outcomes (Bandura, 1986). Thus, when faced with negative feedback or obstacles along the way that all high-achieving students are bound to encounter, minority students in particular may be faced with a catch-22 with attributional ambiguity at its heart. If one receives negative feedback, should one discount it because it may be more reflective of external bias than of one's own internal ability? Or does it in fact reflect one's own internal ability? Moreover, if one chooses to see it as reflective of one's own ability, is one ignoring or being foolishly blind to systematic biases that can affect evaluations? Such a state of uncertainty can be distracting and intrusive, and may moreover lead to confusion when thinking about effective coping strategies for addressing the negative feedback itself. The point here is that high-achieving minority students in particular have reason to be attracted to both explanations for negative feedback when it is received, and as such, may have a more difficult time resolving the state of attributional ambiguity.

Stereotype threat becomes a relevant psychological process when people find themselves in contexts where a stereotype about their group is applicable. As such, Hispanic and African-American students may be particularly vulnerable to stereotypes in the domain of academics, because the stereotype surrounding these students concerns a generalized suspicion about their intelligence. Importantly, the effects of stereotypes can occur without the stereotyped individual himself or herself believing the stereotype—one simply has to have the knowledge of the stereotype and the awareness that others may view him or her through that stereotype. To the degree that schooling in general and standardized testing in particular place particular emphasis on diagnosis of ability as a gateway for tracking, or college admissions, or other future opportunities, the implications of feeling stereotyped in relation to minority student achievement are profound.

The effects of stereotyping are potentially more pronounced the higher one comes to reaching the top. As the College Board's National Task Force on Minority High Achievement (1999) notes, "The negative impacts of these beliefs do not seem to be confined to the most disadvantaged under-represented minority students; they can undermine the achievement of high SES [socioeconomic status] students as well" (p. 16). Indeed, when combined with the possibility that the state of attributional ambiguity may be more pronounced, and more difficult to dispel, for students who succeed at succeeding, a picture of the psychological weight of being a high-achieving minority student in this country comes increasingly into focus.

Direct or vicarious experiences of exclusion, discrimination, and prejudice can lead people to anxiously anticipate that they will be similarly treated in new contexts where the possibility of such treatment exists. Minority students in particular are likely to experience doubts about their acceptance in educational institutions, and such concerns are likely to be accentuated in academic environments and institutions that high-achieving minority students strive for.

Longitudinally, students who entered the university with concerns about how welcome they would be experienced less diverse friendships and felt less trust and obligation toward the university at the end of their first year in college than students who entered with fewer concerns. As sophomores and juniors, they also reported decreased attendance at academic review sessions, as well as increased anxiety about approaching professors and teacher assistants with academic problems. Unsurprisingly, prejudice apprehension was predictive of students' change in grade point average over the first five semesters of college, such that students who experienced prejudice apprehension were particularly likely to experience a decrease in their grades over time (Mendoza-Denton, Purdie, Downey, and Davis, 2002). "Since students have only a limited amount of time and emotional energy, those able to concentrate on their academic tasks, without constant concern about their place on the campus and their relationships to others, are most likely to do well academically," note Bowen and Bok (1998: 82).

Building Trust

If affirmative development is based on the notion that academic abilities are nurtured and developed through pedagogical, social, and interpersonal supports, the research cited throughout this chapter suggests that beyond the opening of doors and beyond the achievement of numerical diversity, educators—and the institutions that they represent—must work together toward the achievement of relational diversity (Fine, Weis, and Powell, 1997). By relational diversity, we mean a type of diversity in which institutions are not merely filling numerical quotas but instead are actively working to secure the trust and confidence of those students to whom they have opened their doors. As the summarized research implies, such trust and confidence is a critical component of minority students' achievement on several levels.

When high-achieving minority students succeed, many times they will be faced with situations and environments where their group membership becomes particularly salient. As research on prejudice apprehension shows, concerns about one's belonging can directly impact one's achievement by leading people to not take advantage of the various resources that the institution may offer. Although this self-protective strategy minimizes the possibility of rejection and future prejudice, it also reduces the number of resources and support systems one can count on when faced with the difficulties that all students face.

We argue that minority students may experience the psychological impact of being a member of a stigmatized group more acutely as they become more academically successful. The reasons for this are twofold: First, such success implies developing an academic identity, which for minority students is a threatened identity. Second, as minority students become more successful, the likelihood increases that educational opportunities and institutions will continue being overrepresented by majority group members—thereby increasing suspicions about one's belonging and acceptance.

SUPPORTS FOR PRO-ACADEMIC BEHAVIOR
IN THE SCHOOL AND COMMUNITY

In our collective experience, most education-related policy stems from deficits-based approaches. We purposely have taken a developmental and strengths-based approach to the conceptualization of intellective competence. A number of key environmental supports are critical to the development of intellective competence:

- Access to education-relevant capital;
- Supportive family, community, and academic environments;
- Socialization to the attitudinal and behavioral demands of high academic achievement;
- Academic and social integration;
- Exposure to various forms of supplementary education;
- Exposure to models of academic excellence and exemplars of scholarly practice.

Access to Education-Relevant Capital

For students of color, the problems of inequality of access to many of the environmental supports that undergird pro-academic behavior in schools and communities are critical factors. What is the nature of the education-relevant capital that high-achieving students more often have access to through their families and communities? According to Bourdieu (1986), Coleman et al. (1966), and Miller (1995), there are several types of capital, as illustrated in table 12.1.

Obviously, wealth is more than money. It is the accessibility and control of resources. If we are correct in assuming that the effectiveness of schools and other institutions that serve students is in part a function of the availability of such wealth-derived capital for investment in human development, we may have in this relationship a catalyst for pedagogical, political, and social intervention.

Supportive Family, Community, and Academic Environments

Family Environments

In 1966, Coleman et al. concluded that differences in the family backgrounds of students, as opposed to school characteristics, accounted for the greatest amount of variance in their academic achievement. This finding was later found to be less so for low-income and ethnic minority children than for the general population (Gordon, 1999), but typically, family back-

Table 12.1.   Education-Relevant Capital

Type of Capital	Definition
CULTURAL	Collected knowledge, techniques, and beliefs of a people.
FINANCIAL	Income; wealth; family, community, and societal economic resources available for education.
HEALTH	Physical developmental integrity, health, nutritional condition.
HUMAN	Social competence, tacit knowledge, and other education-derived abilities as personal or family assets.
INSTITUTIONAL	Quality of and access to educational and socializing institutions.
PEDAGOGICAL	Supports for appropriate educational treatment in family, school, and community.
PERSONAL	Disposition, attitudes, aspirations, efficacy, sense of power.
POLITY	Societal membership, social concern, public commitment, political economy.
SOCIAL	Social network relationships, social norms, cultural styles and values.

ground and income stand as strong predictors of achievement in school (Gordon, 1999; Jaynes and Williams, 1989; Sexton, 1961). In related works, Mercer (1973) and Wolf (1966, 1995) posited that the presence of family environmental supports for academic development may explain this association between family status and student achievement. They made the now obvious point that books, positive models, help with homework, and a place to study in the home are associated with school achievement.

Community Environments

Because learning is influenced in fundamental ways by its context, promoting student achievement via the community requires the development of norms for the classroom, schools, and the community that both support and inform core learning values. In some schools, the norms may require that students build their own information base; other norms may encourage academic risk taking and provide opportunities for students to make mistakes, obtain feedback, and revise their thinking. School norms also must support students' comfort in revealing their preconceptions about a subject, their questions, and their progress toward understanding new conceptual constructs related to the subject. Teachers need to design classroom activities and promote students' intellectual camaraderie and attitudes toward learning that build a sense of community and responsibility for each other. These activities may take the form of students solving problems together by building on each other's knowledge, asking questions to clarify explanations, and suggesting differing solutions (Brown and Campione, 1994). In this way, cooperation and argumentation in problem solving enhance cognitive development (Evans, 1989; Goldman, 1994; Habermas, 1990; Kuhn, 1991; Moshman, 1995a, 1995b; Newstead and Evans, 1995; Salmon and Zeitz, 1995; Youniss and Damon, 1992) and are factors in enabling student achievement.

Lave and Wegner (1991) found that a community-centered approach also supports teachers in establishing a community of learners among themselves. Such a community fosters comfort with questioning (not just with knowing the answer) and is a model for creating new ideas that build on the contributions of individual members. Community membership also can promote in teachers a sense of ownership of new ideas that they can transfer to their classroom. Ultimately, teachers need to develop new ways to link classroom learning to other aspects of students' lives. This strategy can be operationalized in requiring that students actively participate in community service.

For example, in some education programs, all students are encouraged or required to take part in a community service activity. This strategy can help to make concrete the value of "giving back" to the larger community and deliberately encouraging students to focus on outreach activities and service to the broader community. Community service could include volunteer work with at-risk youth, tutoring, organizing environmental projects, collecting food for homeless shelters, or participating in campus outreach activities to middle schools. Community service roles give students the status and responsibility of representing their school in the community. Although the program staff is responsible for enabling community activity, the community itself grows from the human relations and interactions among all the participants: students, former students, graduate students, teachers, program staff, and university leadership. The community is at its most vital when students take an active role in shaping their own environment (Hrabowski, 2002).

Academic Environments

In environments that are learner centered, teachers pay close attention to the knowledge, skills, and attitudes that students bring into the classroom. This strategy focuses on distilling students' preconceptions about various subjects while simultaneously promoting a better understanding of students. Teachers need to become aware of the following concepts:

- Cultural differences can affect students' comfort levels in working collaboratively instead of individually. These differences also are reflected in the background knowledge that students bring to a new learning situation (Moll, Tapia, and Whitmore, 1993).

- Students' conceptions of what it means to be intelligent can affect their performance. Students who think that intelligence is a fixed entity are more likely to be performance oriented as opposed to learning oriented; they want to look good rather than risk making mistakes while learning. These students are especially likely to give up when tasks become difficult. In contrast, students who think that intelligence is malleable are more willing to struggle with challenging tasks and are more comfortable with risk (Dweck, 1989; Dweck and Legget, 1988).

Teachers in learner-centered classrooms are attentive to each student's individual progress and develop appropriate tasks that facilitate a more sophisticated understanding of the material. For instance, teachers can present students with challenging material that they can manage; that is, the difficulties are demanding enough to maintain engagement but not so difficult as to lead to discouragement. This approach demonstrates the teacher's understanding of his or her students' knowledge, skill levels, and interests (Duckworth, 1987). The underlying principle is Vygotskian (Vygotsky, 1978), in that most of the learning is within the learner's zone of proximal development at the growing edge of mastery.

Socialization to the Attitudinal and Behavioral Demands of High Academic Achievement

Although the challenges may be greater for minority students to excel academically (given issues related to race, gender, and culture bias), continuous monitoring and advising of students should emphasize the skills, values, and habits that students need to acquire and practice in their academic lives. Students should be socialized to (1) understand the importance of reading, knowing where to seek answers, solving problems, and asking questions; (2) accept their ethical and moral responsibility not only to work hard but also to work to be among the best; and (3) set high standards, follow through, be dependable, and understand how to work well with others. Similarly, given the universal importance of advanced technologies and complex communication skills, students need to learn how to use these technologies, and how to speak and write with clarity and confidence in the standard vernaculars. Students need to be reminded that these skills and abilities are necessary in the classroom and eventually in their professional lives. On yet another level, students should be coached on the importance of interacting, working, and coexisting effectively with diverse people and remaining open to new experiences without threat to their own identities. Academic socialization is thus directed at shaping the attitudes, dispositions, and habits of mind toward pro-academic intellective pursuits.

Academic and Social Integration

Research and contemporary practice show that the academic and social integration of students leads to higher grade-point averages, persistence, and retention (Maton, Hrabowski, and Schmittt 2000; Treisman, 1992). This strategy can be operationalized in the social domain through steadfast commitment from district and school leadership, teachers, and students with respect to celebrating diversity; promotion of help-seeking from a variety of sources; peer supportiveness; high academic goals; and meaningful community service. In the academic domain, consistent emphasis on solid preparation and conceptual mastery of difficult concepts; involvement in fact research; and special faculty attention to the needs of underrepresented students collectively encourage and reinforce students' participation. These acts of inclusion are intended to ensure that all students develop academic and social competencies, have a sense of membership in the learning enterprise, and are capable of discharging the responsibilities of such membership in academic and social environments.

Exposure to Various Forms of Supplementary Education

Gordon (Gordon, Bridglall, and Meroe, 2005) define supplementary education as the formal and informal learning and developmental enrichment opportunities provided for students outside of school and beyond the regular school day or year. Some of these activities may occur inside the school building but are beyond those included in the formal curriculum of the school. After-school care is, perhaps, the most widespread form of supplementary education, but supplements to schooling also include the special efforts that parents exert in support of the intellective and personal development of their children. These efforts may range from provisions for good health and nutrition to extensive travel and deliberate exposure to life in multiple cultures.

Many activities, considered routine in the settings in which they occur, are nonetheless thought to be implicitly and deliberately engaged in to ensure adequate intellective and academic development of young people. These routines include reading to and with one's children; dinner table talk and inclusion in other family discussions of important issues; exposure to adult models of behaviors supportive of academic learning; active use of the library, museums, and community and religious centers as sources of information; help-seeking from appropriate sources; and investments in reference and other education materials. In related but different domains are efforts directed at influencing children's choices of friends and peers, guiding and controlling use of their spare time, guiding and limiting their time spent watching television, and encouraging their participation in high-performance learning communities (Clark, 2002).

Parents of high-achieving students understand and emphasize academic achievement by supplementing their children's education with travel, dance lessons, scouting, tutoring, summer camp, and other activities. Indeed, informed parents, scholars, and educators have known for some time now that schools alone cannot enable or ensure high academic achievement (Coleman et al., 1966; Gordon, 2001; Wilkerson, 1985). James Comer (1997) asserts this position more forcefully in *Waiting for a Miracle: Why Our Schools Cannot Solve Our Problems—And How We Can*. Colloquial knowledge among many parents "in the know" reflects awareness that a number of experiences and activities occurring outside of school appear to enable schooling to work.

Exposure to Models of Academic Excellence and Exemplars of Scholarly Practice

We advocate the pairing of students with mentors who are professional role models in students' areas of interest. Mentors can be recruited from a variety of settings, including universities, private laboratories, government facilities, and corporations. Pairings or assignments of students and mentors should ideally be long term but can be targeted to the developmental phase or stage of the student. Mentors can consult with students on educational and career issues, as well as topics ranging from class scheduling, internship experiences, school placements, career choices, and personal concerns. Lectures, business meetings, laboratory visits, and social encounters with mentors can express mentor and mentoree relationships formally. The mentoring relationship also can be expressed informally through social outings, letter writing, and recreational activities. These facets of mentoring can facilitate educational and professional growth across the learning continuum.

ALL STUDENTS AT THE TOP: WHAT WILL IT TAKE?

The state of education for minority students is clearly multidimensional and complex. Arguably, the most critical problem in education faced by minority students is the gap in academic achievement known to exist between minority and nonminority students. This problem is manifested at all achievement and socioeconomic levels.

To remedy this situation, the National Study Group for the Affirmative Development of Academic Ability proposes that the education community embark upon a deliberate effort to develop academic abilities in a broad range of students who have a history of being resource deprived and who, as a consequence, are underrepresented in the pool of academically high-achieving students. The deliberate or affirmative development of academic ability should include more equitable access to a variety of capitals and educational interventions.

National Study Group members chose the title of the report to reflect our goal of enabling all students to reach the top, both academically and in their personal endeavors. Due to the urgency of the problem, there is a critical need for the education establishment to work together with the social and political institutions in this country to lead what we consider to be a charge to the nation. In describing this charge, we have attempted to marshal what we know from multiple research domains to address the achievement gaps. We recognize that our knowledge as researchers tends to be discrete and disconnected. What is most needed, then, is a bundling and systemic application of our best research, strategies, and practices to close the achievement gaps and to enhance learning opportunities for all students simultaneously in the home, classroom, school, and community.

CONCLUSION

Throughout this report, we emphasize a developmental approach to teaching and learning—the affirmative development of academic ability—that we believe will lead not only to higher academic achievement for all students and closing the academic achievement gaps between diverse student groups, but also to the development of intellective competence in segments of the population with whom schools have typically not been successful. We suggest that access to education-relevant forms of capital, combined with research-based educational interventions, may be necessary in closing the achievement gaps that exist between black, Hispanic, Native American, and low-income children and their European American, Asian American, and more economically advantaged peers. The conclusions and recommendations that follow provide a first step toward engaging education practitioners, policy makers, parents, and community members in leading the charge to ensure that all students receive the kinds of instruction and support necessary.

The National Study Group concludes that efforts at the affirmative development of academic ability should be guided by the following educational experiences in homes, classrooms, schools, and communities for all students:

- In local communities, attention should be given to socializing young people to the specific behavioral and dispositional requirements of high levels of academic work and to the explication of examples of what such efforts and products look like.

- Because academic success is associated with community and family environments that strongly support academic development, families and communities should be strengthened in their capacity to provide a wide variety of supplemental education supports for the academic and personal development of children.
- Schools and other educative institutions should give greater attention to the promotion of feelings of trust in our schools, trust in the people who staff these institutions, and trust in the processes by which teaching and learning transactions are managed.
- Schools can reinforce the belief that high levels of academic ability should be recognized as a universal civil right—a right that should not be compromised by fear of being stereotyped based on one's identity or the social division to which one is assigned.
- Attention should be given in schools and classrooms to reconciling the possible tensions between the several purposes of education—intellect development, skills development, and moral development (Wallace, 1966)—and the political agendas of diverse learners, to the end that academic learning can be seen as compatible with the purposes that inform those who must do the learning.
- Increased opportunities should be created for continuous exposure to high-performance learning environments in which children successfully experience high expectations and joyful but rigorous challenges that are at the growing edges of their zones of proximal development—the areas just beyond each student's learning comfort zone.
- Teaching and learning in the classroom should reflect a balanced focus between the content and processes that are expected to be mastered and the metacognitive understandings and strategies that are essential to making sense of one's experiences.
- For students, time and effort must be devoted to learning tasks that are relevant to the knowledge and skills to be mastered.

REFERENCES

Anderson, C. W. 1987. Strategic teaching in science. In B. F. Jones, A. S. Palincsar, D. S. Ogle, and E. G. Carr (Eds.), *Strategic teaching and learning: Cognitive instruction in the content areas* (pp. 73–91). Alexandria, VA: Association for Supervision and Curriculum Development.

Anderson, J., Reder, L., and Simon, H. 1996. Situated learning and education. *Education Researcher*, 25(4), 5–11.

Anderson, L., and Block, J. 1977. Mastery learning. In D. Treffinger, J. Davis, and R. Ripple (Eds.), *Handbook on teaching educational psychology*. New York: Academic Press.

Bandura, A. 1986. *Social foundations of thought and action: A social cognitive theory.* Englewood Cliffs, NJ: Prentice-Hall.

————. 2001. Social cognitive theory: An agentic perspective. *Annual Review of Psychology*, 52, 1–26.

Barnett, S. M., and Ceci, S. J. 2002. When and where do we apply what we learn? A taxonomy for far transfer. *Psychological Bulletin*, 128(4), 612–37.

Bassok, M., and Holyoak, K. J. 1989. Inter-domain transfer between isomorphic topics in algebra and physics. *Journal of Experimental Psychology: Learning, Memory, and Cognition*, 15(1), 153–66.

Bjorklund, D. F. 1995. Children's thinking: *Developmental function and individual differences* (2nd ed.). New York: Brooks/Cole.

Bloom, B. B. 1971. *Mastery learning*. New York: Holt, Rinehart, and Winston.

Bourdieu, P. 1986. The forms of capital. In J. Richardson (Ed.), *Handbook of theory and research for the sociology of education* (pp. 241–58). Westport, CT: Greenwood Press.

Bowen, W. G., and Bok, D. 1998. *The shape of the river: Long-term consequences of considering race in college and university admissions*. Princeton, NJ: Princeton University Press.

Bransford, J. D., Brown, A. L., and Cocking, R. R. (Eds.) 2000. *How people learn: Brain, mind, experience, and school* (expanded ed.). Washington, D.C.: National Academy Press.

Bransford, J. D., and Schwartz, D. L. 1999. Rethinking transfer: A simple proposal with multiple implications. In A. Iran-Nejad and P. D. Pearson (Eds.), *Review of research in education* (pp. 61–100). Washington, D.C.: American Educational Research Association.

Bransford, J. D., and Stein, B. S. 1993. *The IDEAL problem solver* (2nd ed.). New York: Freeman.

Braswell, J. S., Lutkus, A. D., Grigg, W. S., Santapau, S. L., Tay-Lim, B., and Johnson, M. 2001. *The nation's report card: Mathematics 2000*. Washington, D.C.: National Center for Education Statistics. Retrieved July 27, 2004, from nces.ed.gov/pubsearch/pubsinfo.asp?pubid=2001517

Bridglall, B. L., and Gordon, E. W. 2002. The idea of supplementary education. *Pedagogical Inquiry and Praxis*, 3, March. Retrieved July 27, 2004, from iume .tc.columbia.edu/reports/ip3.pdf

Brooks, J. G., and Brooks, M. G. 1999. *In search of understanding: The case for constructivist classrooms*. Alexandria, VA: Association for Supervision and Curriculum Development.

Brown, A. L. 1978. Knowing when, where, and how to remember: A problem of metacognition. In R. Glaser (Ed.), *Advances in instructional psychology* (vol. 1, pp. 77–165). Hillsdale, NJ: Erlbaum.

Brown, A. L., and Campione, J. C. 1994. Guided discovery in a community of learners. In K. McGilly (Ed.), *Classroom lessons: Integrating cognitive theory and classroom practice* (pp. 229–72). Cambridge, MA: MIT Press.

Brown, A. L., Campione, J. C., Webber, L. S., and McGilly K. 1992. Interactive learning environments: A new look at assessment and instruction. In B. R. Gifford and M. C. O'Connor (Eds.), *Alternative views of aptitude, achievement and instruction*. Boston: Kluwer.

Brown, J. S., Collins, A., and Duguid, P. 1989. Situated cognition and the culture of learning. *Educational Researcher*, 18(1), 32–42.

Bryk, A. S., and Schneider, B. 2002. Trust in schools: *A core resource for improvement.* New York: Russell Sage Foundation.

Camara, W. J., and Schmidt, A. E. 1999. *Group differences in standardized testing and social stratification* (College Board Report No. 99-5). New York: The College Board. Retrieved July 27, 2004, from www.collegeboard.com/repository/rr9905 3916. pdf

Cauce, A. M., Stewart, A., Rodriguez, M. D., Cochran, B., and Ginzler, J. 2003. Overcoming the odds? Adolescent development in the context of urban poverty. In S. S. Luthar (Ed.), *Resilience and vulnerability: Adaptation in the context of childhood adversities* (pp. 343–63). New York: Cambria University Press.

Cazden, C. 2001. *Classroom discourse: The language of teaching and learning.* Portsmouth, NH: Heinemann.

Cheng, P. W., and Holyoak, K. J. 1985. Pragmatic reasoning schemas. *Cognitive Psychology,* 17, 391–94.

Chi, M. T. H., Feltovich, P. J., and Glaser, R. 1981. Categorization and representation of physics problems by experts and novices. *Cognitive Science,* 5, 121–52.

Clark, R. 2002. *In-school and out-of-school factors that build student achievement: Research based implications for school instructional policy* (Policy Issues No. 13, December, pp. 11–18). Naperville, IL: North Central Regional Educational Laboratory. Retrieved July 27, 2004, from www. ncrel.org/gap/clark/

Cognition and Technology Group at Vanderbilt. 1997. *The Jasper Project: Lessons in curriculum, instruction, assessment, and professional development.* Mahwah, NJ: Erlbaum.

Cole, M., Gay, J., Glick, J., and Sharp, D. W. 1971. *The cultural context of learning and thinking.* New York: Basic Books.

Cole, M., and Scribner, S. 1974. *Culture and thought: A psychological introduction.* New York: Wiley.

Coleman, J. S., Campbell, E. Q., Hobson, C. J., McPartland, J., Mood, A. M., Weinfeld, F. D., et al. 1966. *Equality of educational opportunity.* Washington, D.C.: U.S. Government Printing Office.

College Board. 1999. *Reaching the top.* National Task Force on Minority High Achievement. New York: The College Board. Retrieved July 27, 2004, from www .collegeboard.com/repository/reachingthe 3952.pdf

College Entrance Examination Board. 2003. Graph 10: SAT scores vary by race/ethnicity. In *2003 College-bound seniors: Tables and related items.* Retrieved July 27, 2004, from www.collegeboard.con/prod-downloads/about/news_info/cbsenior/yr2003/pdf/graphil

Comer, J. 1997. *Waiting for a miracle: Why our schools can't solve our problems and how we can.* New York: Dutton.

Cremin, L. 1989. *Education and its discontents.* Cambridge, MA: Harvard University Press.

Crocker, J., and Major, B. 1989. Social stigma and self-esteem: The self-protective properties of stigma. *Psychological Review,* 96, 608–630.

Cull, W. 2000. Untangling the benefits of multiple study opportunities and repeated testing for cued recall. *Applied Cognitive Psychology,* 14, 215–35.

Dabady, M. 2003. Measuring racial disparities and discrimination in elementary and secondary education: An introduction. *Teachers College Record,* 105(6), 1048–51.

DeCorte, E. 2003. Transfer as the productive use of acquired knowledge, skills, and motivations. *Current Directions in Psychological Science*, 12(4), 142–46.

Dempster, F. N., and Perkins, P. G. 1993. Revitalizing classroom assessment: Using tests to promote learning. *Journal of Instructional Psychology*, 20, 197–203.

Detterman, D. K. 1993. The case for the prosecution: Transfer as epiphenomenon. In D. K. Detterman and R. J. Sternberg (Eds.), *Transfer on trial: Intelligence, cognition, and instruction*. Norwood, NJ: Ablex.

Detterman, D. K., and Sternberg, R. J. (Eds.) 1993. *Transfer on trial: Intelligence, cognition and instruction*. Norwood, NJ: Ablex.

Dewey, J. 1938. *Experience and Education*. New York: McMillan.

Di Sessa, A. A. 1988. Knowledge in pieces. In G. Forman and P. Pufall (Eds.), *Constructivism in the computer age* (pp. 49–70). Hillsdale, NJ: Erlbaum.

DuBois, W E. B. 1940. *Dusk of dawn: An essay toward an autobiography of a race concept*. New York: Harcourt, Brace, and Company.

Duckworth, E. 1987. *"The having of wonderful ideas" and other essays on teaching and learning*. New York: Teachers College Press.

Durán, R. 1983. Prediction of Hispanics' college achievements. In M. Olivas (Ed.), *Latino college students* (pp. 241–45). New York: Teachers College Press.

Dweck, C. S. 1989. Motivation. In A. Lesgold and R. Glaser (Eds.), *Foundation for a psychology of education* (pp. 87–13). Hillsdale, NJ: Erlbaum.

Dweck, C., and Legget, E. 1988. A social-cognitive approach to motivation and personality. *Psychological Review*, 95, 256–73.

Evans, J. St. B. T. 1989. *Bias in human reasoning: Causes and consequences*. Hillsdale, NJ: Erlbaum.

Everson, H. T. 2006. The problem of transfer and adaptability: Applying the learning sciences to the challenge of the achievement gap. In E. W Gordon and B. L. Bridglall (Eds.), *The affirmative development of academic ability*. Lanham, MD: Rowman & Littlefield.

Fine, M., Weis, L., and Powell, L. C. 1997. Communities of difference: A critical look at desegregated spaces created for and by youth. *Harvard Educational Review*, 67, 247–84.

Flavell, J. H. 1979. Metacognition and cognitive monitoring: A new area of psychological inquiry. *American Psychologist*, 34, 906–911.

Gentner, D., Ratterman, M. J., and Forbus, K. D. 1993. The roles of similarity in transfer: Separating retrievability from inferential soundness. *Cognitive Psychology*, 25, 524–75.

Gick, M. L., and Holyoak, K. J. 1983. Schema induction and analogical transfer. *Cognitive Psychology*, 15, 1–38.

Glasersfeld, E., von. 1989. Cognition, construction of knowledge, and teaching. *Syntheses*, 80, 121–40.

Glover, J. A. 1989. The "testing" phenomenon: Not gone but nearly forgotten. *Journal of Educational Psychology*, 81, 392–99.

Goldman, A. I. 1994. Argument and social epistemology. *Journal of Philosophy*, 91, 27–49.

Gordon, E. W. 1986. A descriptive analysis of programs and trends in engineering education for ethnic minority students: A report to the field. New Haven, CT: Yale University, Institute for Social and Policy Studies.

Gordon, E. W. 1999. *Education and justice: A view from the back of the bus.* New York: Teachers College Press.

———. 2001. The affirmative development of academic abilities. *Pedagogical Inquiry and Praxis*, 2, September. Retrieved July 27, 2004, from iume.tc.columbia.edu/reports/ip2.pdf

Gordon, E. W., with Meroe, A. S. 1999. Common destinies—Continuing dilemmas. In E. W. Gordon, *Education and justice: A view from the back of the bus* (pp. 52–66). New York: Teachers College Press.

Grigg, W. S., Daane, M. C., Jin, Y., and Campbell, J. R. 2003. *The nation's report card: Reading 2002.* Washington, D.C.: National Center for Education Statistics. Retrieved July 27, 2004, from nces.ed.gov/pubsearch/pubsinfo.asp?pubid=2003521

Habermas, J. 1990. *Moral consciousness and communicative action.* Cambridge, MA: MIT Press.

Halpern, D. F. 1998. Teaching critical thinking for transfer across domains: Dispositions, skills, structure training, and metacognitive monitoring. *American Psychologist*, 33(4), 449–55.

Halpern, D. F., and Hakel, M. D. (Eds.) 2002. *Applying the science of learning to university teaching and learning* (New Directions for Teaching and Learning, No. 89). San Francisco, CA: Jossey-Bass.

———. 2003. Applying the science of learning to the university and beyond: Teaching for long-term retention and transfer. *Change*, 35(4), 37–41.

Harvey, W. B. 2003. *Minorities in higher education, 2002–2003: Twentieth annual status report.* Washington, D.C.: American Council on Education.

Haskell, R. E. 2001. *Transfer of learning: Cognition, instruction and reasoning.* New York: Academic Press.

Herrnstein, R., and Murray, C. 1994. *The bell curve: Intelligence and class structure in American life.* New York: Free Press.

Hoffman, K., Llagas, C., and Snyder, T. D. 2003. *Status and trends in the education of blacks* (NCES 2003-034). Washington, D.C.: U.S. Department of Education. Retrieved July 27, 2004, from nces.ed.gov/pubsearch/pubsinfo.asp?pubid=2003034

Hook, P. E., and Jones, S. D. 2002. The importance of automaticity and fluency for efficient reading comprehension. *Perspectives*, 28(1) (winter), 9–14. Retrieved July 27, 2004, from www.resourceroom.net/readspell/2002 automaticity.asp

Hrabowski, F. A., III. 2002. Postsecondary minority student achievement: How to raise performance and close the achievement gap. *College Board Review*, 195, 40–48.

Huang, G., Reiser, M., Parker, A., Muniec, J., and Salvucci, S. 2003. *Institute of Education Sciences findings from interviews with education policy makers.* Arlington, VA: Synectics. Retrieved July 27, 2004, from www.ed.gov/rschstat/research/pubs/findingsreport.pdf

Hung, D. 2002. Situated cognition and problem-based learning: Implications for learning and instruction with technology. *Journal of Interactive Learning Research*, 13, 393–414.

Hunt, J. 1966. Toward a theory of guided learning in development. In R. J. Ojemann and K. Pritchett (Eds.), *Giving emphasis to guided learning.* Cleveland, OH: Educational Research Council.

Im, J., and Hannafin, M. 1999. Situated cognition and learning environments: Roles, structures, and implications for design. Retrieved July 27, 2004, from tecfa .unige.ch/staf/staf-e/ pellerin/stafl5/situacogn.htm

Jaynes, G. D., and Williams, R. M., Jr. 1989. *A common destiny: Black and American society*. Washington, D.C.: National Academy Press.

Jencks, C., and Phillips, M. 1998. *The black-white test score gap*. Washington, D.C.: Brookings Institution Press.

Judd, C. H. 1908. The relation of special training to general intelligence. *Educational Review*, 36, 28–42.

Klahr, D., and Carver, S. M. 1988. Cognitive objectives in a LOGO debugging curriculum: Instruction, learning, and transfer. *Cognitive Psychology*, 20, 362–404.

Kuhn, D. 1991. *The skills of argument*. Cambridge, England: Cambridge University Press.

Lave, J., and Wegner, E. 1991. *Situated learning: Legitimate peripheral participation*. New York: Cambridge University Press.

Lee, C. 2006. The educability of intellective competence. In E. W. Gordon and B. L. Bridglall (Eds.), *The affirmative development of academic ability*. Lanham, MD: Rowman & Littlefield.

Martinez, M. E. 2000. *Education as the cultivation of intelligence*. Mahwah, NJ: Erlbaum.

Maton, K., Hrabowski, F., and Schmitt, C. 2000. African American college students excelling in the sciences: College and postcollege outcomes in the Meyerhoff Scholars Program. *Journal of Research in Science Teaching*, 37(7), 629–54.

McKeough, A., Lupart, J., and Marini, A. 1995. *Teaching for transfer: Fostering generalization of learning*. Mahwah, NJ: Erlbaum.

Mendoza-Denton, R., and Aronson, J. 2006. Making the pinnacle possible: Psychological processes associated with minority students' achievement. In E. W. Gordon and B. L. Bridglall (Eds.), *The affirmative development of academic ability*. Lanham, MD: Rowman & Littlefield.

Mendoza-Denton, R., Purdie, V., Downey, G., and Davis, A. 2002. Sensitivity to race-based rejection: Implications for African-American students' college experience. *Journal of Personality and Social Psychology*, 83, 896–918.

Mercer, J. 1973. *Labeling the mentally retarded: Clinical and social system perspectives on mental retardation*. Berkeley: University of California Press.

Mickelson, R. A. 2003. When are racial disparities in education the result of racial discrimination? A social science perspective. *Teachers College Record*, 10(6), 1052–86.

Miller, L. S. 1995. *An American imperative: Accelerating minority educational advancement*. New Haven: Yale University Press.

Moll, L. C., Tapia, J., and Whitmore, K. F. 1993. Living knowledge: The social distribution of cultural sources for thinking. In G. Salomon (Ed.), *Distributed cognitions* (pp. 139–63). Cambridge, England: Cambridge University Press.

Mortenson, T. 2003. Earnings by educational attainment, 1958 to 2001. *Postsecondary Education Opportunity* (March), 129.

Moshman, D. 1995a. The construction of moral rationality. *Human Development*, 38, 265–81.

———. 1995b. Reasoning as self-constrained thinking. *Human Development*, 38, 53–64.

National Center for Education Statistics. 2001. Table 133. Scholastic Assessment Test (SAT) averages, by race/ethnicity: 1986–1987 to 1999–2000. In *Digest of education statistics, 2000*. Washington, D.C.: National Center for Education Statistics. Retrieved July 27, 2004, from nces.ed.gov/programs/digest/dO0/tables/PDF/table133.pdf

———. 2003. Table 133. Scholastic Assessment Test (SAT) averages, by race/ethnicity: 1986–87 to 2001–02. In *Digest of education statistics, 2002*. Washington, D.C.: National Center for Education Statistics. Retrieved July 27, 2004, from nces.ed.gov/programs/digest/dO2/tables/PDF/table133.pdf

National Commission on Excellence in Education. 1983. *A nation at risk: The imperative for educational reform*. Washington, D.C.: U.S. Government Printing Office.

Newstead, S. E., and Evans, J. St. B. T. (Eds.) 1995. *Perspectives on thinking and reasoning: Essays in honour of Peter Wason*. Hillsdale, NJ: Erlbaum.

No Child Left Behind Act of 2001, Pub. L. No. 107-110, 115 Stat. 1425 (2002). Retrieved July 27, 2004, from www.ed.gov/policy/elsec/leg/eseaO2/index.html

O'Sullivan, C. Y., Lauko, M. A., Grigg, W S., Qian, J., and Zhang, J. 2003. The nation's report card: Science 2000 (NCES 2003453). Washington, D.C.: National Center for Education Statistics. Retrieved July 27, 2004, from nces.ed.gov/pubsearch/pubsinfo.asp?pubid 2003453

Palincsar, A., and Brown, A. 1984. Reciprocal teaching of comprehension-fostering and comprehension-monitoring activities. *Cognition and Instruction*, 1(2), 117–75.

Pell Institute for the Study of Opportunity in Higher Education. 2003, June. College entrance rate by race/ethnicity and gender for recent high school graduates 1959 to 2002 [Spreadsheet]. *Opportunity*, 132. Retrieved July 27, 2004, from www.postsecondary.org/archives/Reports/Spreadsheets/EntranceRate.htm

Ramist, L., Lewis, C., and McCamley-Jenkins, L. 1994. Student group differences in predicting college grades: Sex, language, and ethnic groups (College Board Report No. 93-1). New York: The College Board.

Resnick, L. 1987. *Education and learning to think*. Washington, D.C.: National Academy Press.

———. 1988. Treating mathematics as an ill-structured discipline. In R. Charles and E. Silver (Eds.), *The teaching and assessing of mathematical problem solving* (pp. 32–60). Reston, VA: National Council of Teachers of Mathematics.

———. 1989. Problem solving in everyday practice. In R. J. Charles and E. A. Silver (Eds.), *The teaching and assessing of mathematical problem solving*. Hillsdale, NJ: Erlbaum.

Resnick, L., and Hall, M. W. 1998. Learning organizations for sustainable education reform. *Daedalus: The Journal of the American Academy of Arts and Sciences*, 127(4), 89–118.

Resnick, L. B., Saljo, R., Pontecorvo, C., and Burge, B. 1998. *Discourse, tools, and reasoning: Situated cognition and technologically supported environments*. Heidelberg, Germany: Springer-Verlag.

Salmon, M. H., and Zeitz, C. M. 1995. Analyzing conversational reasoning. *Informal Logic*, 17, 1–23.

Sanders, M. 2001. *Understanding dyslexia and the reading process: A guide for educators and parents*. Needham Heights, MA: Allyn and Bacon.

Scardamalia, M., Bereiter, C., and Steinbach, R. 1984. Teachability of the reflective processes in written composition. *Cognitive Science*, 8, 173–90.

Schauble, L. 1990. Belief revision in children: The role of prior knowledge and strategies for generating evidence. *Journal of Experimental Child Psychology*, 49, 31–57.

Sexton, P. C. 1961. *Education and income: Inequalities in our public schools.* New York: Viking Press.

Singley, M. K., and Anderson, J. R. 1989. *The transfer of cognitive skill.* Cambridge, MA: Harvard University Press.

Steele, C. M. 1992. Race and the schooling of black Americans. *The Atlantic Monthly*, April, 68–78.

Steele, C. M., and Aronson, J. 1995. Stereotype threat and the intellectual performance of African Americans. *Journal of Personality and Social Psychology*, 69, 797–811.

———. 2000. Stereotype threat and the intellectual test performance of African Americans. In C. Stangor (Ed.), *Stereotypes and prejudice: Essential readings (Key Readings in Social Psychology)*, pp. 369–89. Philadelphia: Taylor and Francis.

Steinberg, L. 1996. *Beyond the classroom. Why school reform has failed and what parents need to do.* New York: Simon and Schuster.

Sternberg, R. J. Ed. 1994. *Encyclopedia of human intelligence.* New York: Macmillan.

———. 2002. Raising the achievement of all students: Teaching for successful intelligence. *Educational Psychology Review*, 14(4), 383–93.

Thorndike, E. L., and Woodworth, R. S. 1901. The influence of improvement in one mental function upon the efficiency of other functions. *Psychological Review*, 8, 237–61.

Tobias, S., and Everson, H. T. 2002. Knowing what you know and what you don't: Further research on metacognitive knowledge monitoring (Research Report No. 2002-3). New York: The College Board. Retrieved July 27, 2004, from www .collegeboard.com/repository/cbreport20013 10769.pdf

Torgesen, J. K., Rashotte, C. A., and Alexander, A. W. 2001. Principles of fluency instruction in reading: Relationships with established empirical outcomes. In M. Wolf (Ed.), *Dyslexia, fluency, and the brain* (pp. 333–55). Timonium, MD: York Press.

Treisman, P. U. 1992. Studying students studying calculus: A look at the lives of minority mathematics students in college. *The College Mathematics Journal*, 23(5), 362–72.

Vosniadou, S., and Brewer, W. F. 1992. Mental models of the earth: A study of conceptual change in childhood. *Cognitive Psychology*, 24, 535–85.

Vygotsky, L. S. 1978. *Mind in society: The development of higher psychological processes.* Cambridge, MA: Harvard University Press.

Wallace, W. 1966. *Student culture: Social structure and continuity in a liberal arts college.* Chicago: Aldine.

Wheeler, M. A., and Roediger, H. L. 1992. Disparate effects of repeated testing: Reconciling Ballard's (1913) and Bartlett's (1932) results. *Psychological Science*, 3, 240–45.

Wilds, D. J. 2000. *Minorities in higher education, 1999–2000: Seventeenth annual status report.* Washington, D.C.: American Council on Education.

Wilkerson, D. A. 1985. *Educating all our children.* Westport, CT: Mediax.

Willingham, D. T. 2002. Inflexible knowledge. *American Educator*, 26(4), 31–33.

————. 2003. Students remember what they think about. *American Educator*, 27(2), 37–41.

Willingham, W. W. 1985. *Success in college: The role of personal qualities and academic ability*. New York: The College Board.

Wolf, R. M. 1966. The measurement of environments. In A. Anastasi (Ed.), *Testing problems in perspective* (pp. 491–503). Washington, D.C.: American Council on Education.

————. 1995. The measurement of environments: A follow-up study. *The Journal of Negro Education*, 64(3), 354–59.

Youniss, J., and Damon, W. 1992. Social construction in Piaget's theory. In H. Berlin and B. Pufal (Eds.), *Piaget's theory: Prospects and possibilities* (pp. 267–86). Hillsdale, NJ: Erlbaum.

Appendix:

Key Terms and Definitions

achievement gap. The statistical phenomenon of predictable lower performance on standardized tests by African-American, Hispanic, Native American, and low-income students as compared to their white, Asian, and more economically advantaged peers.

affirmative development of academic ability. The deliberate effort to equip students with strategies that build knowledge and develop techniques to solve both common and novel problems in pursuit of high academic achievement.

attributional ambiguity. The challenge that a student of color may face when receiving feedback about his or her performance and the difficulty of determining when feedback (particularly critical feedback) is accurate or is actually reflective of racial bias on the part of the one giving the feedback.

automaticity. The ability to perform a complex task without conscious awareness or effort. Through repeated practice, the task itself becomes an automatic process.

intellective competence. Systematic ways of reasoning, of inferring patterns from one's environments, and using them to maintain practices and to invent new ones; highly adaptive, rich habits of thinking; engagement in meaningful problem solving. Academic intellective competence is a highly specialized set of abilities that are a direct result of particular kinds of experiences over long periods of time in Western schooling.

stereotype threat. The awareness that others may judge one's performance in terms of one's racial background, rather than in terms of one's individual background.

supplementary education. The formal and informal learning and developmental enrichment opportunities provided for students outside of school and beyond the regular school day or year. Examples of supplementary education include reading with and to one's child on a daily basis, family trips to the museum or other learning environments, and community-based after-school tutoring programs, to name a few (Bridglall and Gordon, 2002).

transfer. The adaptation of what a person learns in one set of circumstances to other, novel situations.

Index

distributing responsibility, 174; epistemic games as, 172; evaluating goodness of fit, 174, 175; focusing attention on key features, 174; fostering positive collegial relationships, 175; as habits of mind, 172; instructional practices for, 174, 175; modeling problem-solving strategies, 174; narratives applied to, 175, 176; as result of long-term socialization, 172; selection of few general topics, 174; sequencing introduction of problems, 174; seven generic, 172; teaching, 176; in terms of subject area differences, 175

diversity and equality: enabling, 73; removal of barriers to achieving, 202

Dred Scott v. Sanford, 75

Drum, P. A., 4

DuBois, W. E. B., 90, 208, 240

Duguid, P., 248

Durkheim, E., 110

Dweck, Carol, 195

ecological models, 167

ecological orientation, 167; subject matter learning, 167

economic: inequality, 209; pursuit of universal justice, 92; scarcity, 11

education, 60; affirmative action in, 77; after-school care, 264; aims of, 41; alternative vision for, ix; benefits of extensive, 107; compensatory programs for, 109; context/process relationships of, 210; cultural currency as vehicle for, 134; development of craft unionism in, 207; development of intellect and, 117; effectiveness in, 13, 209; equality in, 216; equal opportunity policies in, 108; failure in, 13, 210, 216–19; history of, 133; honoring commitments to, 218; as human right/responsibility, 107; improving, 13, 136; individual v. collective, 110–13; intellective processes unique

to, 210; minorities state of, 265; minority of black students in higher, 83; national accountability in, 97; principle function of, 12; purpose of, xi, 110–13, 135, 211; reconciling tensions between several purposes of, 267; as social institution, 110; social justice and, 209–12; social purposes of, 112; status quo v. transformation, 110–13; studying, 151; substantive aims of, 110; supplementary, 264, 265, 267, 277; training and, distinction between, 117; underdevelopment in, 240; underrepresentation of black males in higher, 78

educational practice: discussions of, 41

Educational Testing Service, 97

Eisenhower, Dwight, 78

Eisner, Elliot, 152

Elements of a Post-Liberal Theory of Education (Bowers), 111

elite class, designation of, 96

Emancipation Proclamation, 74

enablement, 148

Engle, 32, 33

entity theorists, 195; performance orientation adopted by, 196

environment: academic, 262, 263; Alpha and Beta presses of, 121; community, 261, 262; consistencies in, 126; designing learning, 167; effects on genetic structure, 53; examination of, 122; existential, 121; family, 260, 261; genotype interactions with, 126; making sense of, 127; predicting adaptation to everyday, 58, 59; range of, 53; reality, 121; variation in, 55

environmental change, intellective behavior and, 11

environmentality: definition of, 52; heritability and, 52

equal access/equal justice: commitment to, 212

Equal Employment Opportunity Commission, 80; restriction of, 84

About the Editors and Contributors

EDITORS

Beatrice L. Bridglall holds a joint appointment as research scientist and editor in the National Center for Children & Families and the Institute for Urban and Minority Education at Teacher's College, Columbia University. She is also an adjunct assistant professor of health education in the Department of Health and Behavior Studies at Teachers College, Columbia University. Dr. Bridglall is conducting several programs of research, including one directed at investigating the correlates of minority high academic achievement. An emerging area of interest is early childhood education, particularly the role of parental practices/investment in mediating academic achievement. Dr. Bridglall coedited *Supplementary Education: The Hidden Curriculum of High Academic Achievement* (Rowman & Littlefield 2005). She received her doctorate in May 2004 from Teachers College, Columbia University, with specializations in health and human behavior, student academic development and educational program research and evaluation. She received her master's degree from New York University Wagner Graduate School of Public Service in New York with a specialization in health policy and management.

Edmund W. Gordon is the John M. Musser Professor of Psychology, Emeritus at Yale University; The Richard March Hoe Professor of Psychology and Education and director of the Institute for Urban and Minority Education at Teachers College, Columbia University; and senior scholar in residence at the College Board. Gordon's scholarship is documented in his authorship of more than two hundred articles in scholarly journals and book chapters, and in sixteen authored or edited books and monographs. He served for five years as editor of the *American Journal of Orthopsychiatry* and for three years as editor of the annual *Review of Research in Education*. Gordon is best known for his research on diverse human characteristics and pedagogy, and the education of the low status populations. His book, *Compensatory Education: Preschool Through College*, continues to be regarded as the classic work in its field. He coedited *Supplementary Education: The Hidden Curriculum of High Academic Achievement*. He is currently working on his latest text, *Defiers of Negative Prediction: Success Against the Odds*, which is concerned with the career development of Black men who have overcome enormous odds against success to become high achievers.

CONTRIBUTORS

Joshua A. Aronson is associate professor in the Department of Applied Psychology, New York University.

Ana Marie Cauce is chair of the Department of Psychology, Earl R. Carlson Professor of Psychology, and professor of American ethnic studies at the University of Washington, Seattle.

Howard T. Everson is executive director of NAEP-ESSI, American Institutes for Research, Washington, D.C.

James G. Greeno is visiting professor in the School of Education, University of Pittsburgh.

Elena L. Grigorenko is professor in the Department of Psychology, Yale Child Study Center, Yale University.

Carol D. Lee is professor of learning sciences, associate professor of African American studies, and co-coordinator of the SESP Spencer Research Training Program, School of Education and Social Policy, Northwestern University, Evanston, Illinois.

Rodolfo Mendoza-Denton is assistant professor in the psychology department at the University of California, Berkeley.

Joseph Renzulli is Raymond and Lynn Neag Chair for Gifted Education and Talent Development, Neag School of Education, University of Connecticut.

Robert J. Sternberg is dean of the School of Arts and Sciences, Tufts University.